ecpr PRESS

Matching Voters with Parties and Candidates

Voting Advice Applications in a Comparative Perspective

Edited by
Diego Garzia and Stefan Marschall

ecprPRESS

First published by the ECPR Press in 2014

The ECPR Press is the publishing imprint of the European Consortium for Political Research (ECPR), a scholarly association, which supports and encourages the training, research and cross-national cooperation of political scientists in institutions throughout Europe and beyond.

ECPR Press
University of Essex
Wivenhoe Park
Colchester
CO4 3SQ
UK

Typeset by ECPR Press

Printed and bound by Lightning Source

British Library Cataloguing in Publication Data

A catalogue record for this book is available from the British Library

Hardback ISBN: 978-1-907301-73-5
Paperback ISBN: 978-1-785521-41-6
PDF ISBN: 978-1-907301-87-2
Kindle ISBN: 978-1-910259-24-5
ePub ISBN: 978-1-910259-25-2

www.ecpr.eu/ecprpress

Political Participation in France and Germany
ISBN: 9781907301315
Oscar Gabriel, Silke Keil, and Eric Kerrouche

Political Trust: Why Context Matters
ISBN: 9781907301230
Edited by Sonja Zmerli and Marc Hooghe

Practices of Interparliamentary Coordination in International Politics: The European Union and Beyond
ISBN: 9781907301308
Edited by Ben Crum and John Erik Fossum

The Political Ecology of the Metropolis
ISBN: 9781907301377
Edited by Jefferey M Sellers, Daniel Kübler, R. Alan Walks and Melanie Walter-Rogg

Please visit www.ecpr.eu/ecprpress for up-to-date information about new publications.

Contents

List of Figures and Tables

See http://press.ecpr.eu/resources.asp for full colour figures.

Tables

Contributors

JOEL ANDERSON is a research lecturer in Philosophy at Utrecht University. His research focus lies at the intersection of social philosophy, moral psychology, ethics, and political theory, examining how social institutions can enable autonomous agency while avoiding paternalism. He directed the NWO-funded research project 'VAAs and the Politics of Citizen Competence'.

IOANNIS ANDREADIS is an assistant professor at Aristotle University of Thessaloniki. His research areas include VAAs, web survey methodology, voting behaviour, political elites and ecological inference. He is active in many research actions including the True European Voter, the Comparative Candidate Survey, the Comparative Study of Electoral Systems, and Webdatanet.

PATRICK DUMONT is researcher at the University of Luxembourg. He is co-founder of the 'Selection and Deselection of Political Elites' (SEDEPE) network and co-editor of the Routledge 'Research in Social and Political Elites' book series. He has published on coalition theory, political elites, parties and party systems, Europeanization processes and is member of the Luxembourg National (and European) Election Study.

ANDREA DE ANGELIS is a researcher in political science at the European University Institute, Florence. His research is on media, economic information and political behaviour in Western democracies. His interests also include VAAs, Italian Politics and Quantitative Methods. He received a M.Sc. in 'Economics and Social Science' from Bocconi University, Milan.

JAN FIVAZ is a researcher at the University of Bern and a PhD candidate in political science at the University of Lausanne. In 2009 he obtained an MA in 'History, Political Science and Economics' from the University of Bern. Since 2003 he has been involved in the development of the Swiss VAA *smartvote*.

THOMAS FOSSEN is postdoctoral fellow in political philosophy at Leiden University. His research focuses on political legitimacy and democratic theory. He presently participates in the NWO-funded project 'Between Deliberation and Agonism', and previously participated in 'VAAs and the Politics of Citizen Competence' at Utrecht University, also funded by NWO.

DIEGO GARZIA is Jean Monnet Fellow at the Robert Schuman Centre for Advanced Studies, European University Institute, Florence. He authored several articles and book chapters on VAAs. Together with Lorella Cedroni, he co-edited *Voting Advice Applications in Europe: The State of the Art* (Civis, 2010) the first comparative volume ever devoted to the topic.

KOSTAS GEMENIS is assistant professor of research methods at the University of Twente. He has published articles, among others, in *Acta Politica, Electoral Studies, Party Politics, Political Studies*, and the *European Political Science Review*. He is founding member of the consortium behind *EUvox*, a VAA across all EU member-states for the 2014 elections to European Parliament.

CAROLIEN VAN HAM is a post-doctoral researcher at the University of Twente and a research fellow at the Electoral Integrity Project, University of Sydney. She has published on election integrity, representation and turnout in *Democratization, West European Politics,* and *Electoral Studies*, as well as book chapters in various edited volumes.

RAPHAËL KIES is researcher at the University of Luxembourg. He is co-responsible for the Luxemburg National and European Electoral Studies. His publications include articles as well as books on e-democracy, local and deliberative democracy. He is author of 'Promises and Limits of Web-Deliberation' (Palgrave, 2010).

ANDRÉ KROUWEL teaches political science and communication at the Vrije Universiteit Amsterdam. His research focuses on political parties and elections. He is also Academic Director of *Kieskompas*, through which he developed online party profiling applications in over 40 countries and a founding member of the consortium that developed *EUvox*, a VAA for the 2014 elections to the European Parliament across all EU member-states.

ANDREAS LADNER is professor for political institutions and public administration at the Swiss Graduate Institute of Public Administration (IDHEAP) at the University of Lausanne. His areas of research include political parties, local government, institutional change and e-democracy. He has conducted several major research projects of the Swiss National Science Foundation, among others on the Swiss VAA *smartvote*.

JONAS LEFEVERE is an assistant professor of political communication at the University of Amsterdam. His research centers on the effect of political communication on public opinion. His current work focuses on priming, issue ownership, exemplification, VAAs and the development of political knowledge.

TOM LOUWERSE is assistant professor of political science at the Department of Political Science, Trinity College Dublin. His research interests include political representation, parliamentary politics, VAAs and political parties.

STEFAN MARSCHALL is professor of political science and chair of German Politics at the University of Düsseldorf. He is a specialist on political (online) communication and comparative as well as transnational parliamentarism. He is in charge of the research on the German VAA *Wahl-O-Mat* since 2003.

FERNANDO MENDEZ is director of the eDemocracy Centre and senior researcher at the Centre for Research on Direct Democracy, University of Zurich. He is one of the founders of the *PreferenceMatcher* research consortium, which has developed numerous VAAs, and co-developer of the *EUvox* VAA platform.

JOËLLE PIANZOLA holds a PhD from the University of Lausanne and has worked as a research assistant at the Swiss Graduate School of Public Administration (IDHEAP). She has published on political behaviour, experimental research and VAAs. Currently she is working in Public Sector Consulting.

DANIEL SCHWARZ holds a PhD in political science from the University of Bern. He was visiting fellow at the London School of Economics and Political Science. He was co-founder of the Swiss VAA *smartvote* and the legislative monitoring platform *smartmonitor*.

LAURA SUDULICH is a research fellow at the Centre d'étude de la vie politique (Cevipol) at the Université Libre de Bruxelles. She holds a PhD from Trinity College Dublin and she previously worked as a postdoctoral research fellow at the University of Amsterdam and the European University Institute, Florence.

ALEXANDER H. TRECHSEL is professor of political science and head of the SPS Department at the European University Institute, Florence (EUI). He is a faculty fellow at Harvard's Berkman Center and directs the EUI's European Union Democracy Observatory (EUDO). His research interests include e-democracy, European integration and political behaviour.

VASILIKI TRIGA is lecturer at the Department of Communication and Internet Studies, Cyprus University of Technology. Her research interests lie in the field of ICT/internet based applications and political processes. She has designed and coordinated several VAAs (through *PreferenceMatcher*) and was involved in the *EUvox* team, the pan-EU VAA for the 2014 elections to the European Parliament.

KIRSTEN VAN CAMP is a PhD candidate at the University of Antwerp. Her main research interests include media coverage of political elites and issue ownership.

KRISTJAN VASSIL is a Marie-Curie post-doctoral research fellow in the Institute of Government and Politics at the University of Tartu. He graduated from the European University Institute, Florence. His PhD thesis focused on the impact of information and communication technologies on political behaviour. His research interests cover internet voting, VAAs, political behaviour and econometric modelling.

THOMAS VITIELLO is a PhD candidate at Sabanci University, Istanbul, and at Sciences Po, Paris. His dissertation focuses on VAAs and political campaigns. He has published research articles in *Party Politics* and the *International Journal* *of Electronic Governance*. He was involved as member of the French team in the development of *EUvox*, a VAA for the 2014 elections to the European Parliament.

STEFAAN WALGRAVE is professor of political science at the University of Antwerp. His research deals with media and politics, protest and political participation, and public opinion and elections. With colleagues, since 2003, he has built five different VAAs in Belgium. He published several research papers on VAA effects and VAA functioning.

MATT WALL is a lecturer in politics at Swansea University. His research interests include vote advice application websites; online politics; electoral campaigns; and electoral system effects. He has published research articles in journals including *Electoral Studies, Party Politics*, and the *British Journal of Political Science.*

JONATHAN WHEATLEY is a senior researcher at c2d (Centre for Democracy, Aarau). He has written extensively on democratic transition and state-building in post-communist countries and has carried out research into how VAA response data can be used to investigate party systems in modern democracies.

Acknowledgements

The Editors would like to acknowledge the professional support of the editorial team of ECPR Press in the production process of this book. We would like to thank in particular Peter Kennealy, Laura Pugh and Kate Hawkins. We are grateful for the feedback to the book proposal we received by an anonymous reviewer of ECPR Press. It helped us and the authors to recalibrate our common book endeavour. Melissa Schiefer and Greta Tumbrink, both student assistants at the University of Düsseldorf, did a great job in supporting the formatting and editing of the manuscript.

A special thanks goes to Andreas Ladner who organized the book workshop in Lausanne where we discussed draft versions of the chapters. The workshop took place at the Swiss Graduate Institute of Public Administration (IDHEAP, University of Lausanne) and was funded by the NCCR Democracy of the Swiss National Science Foundation. Finally, we owe a debt of gratitude to the ECPR who accepted and financed a VAA workshop at the ECPR Research Sessions held at the European University Institute (Florence) in June 2012 where the idea for this book was born.

Diego Garzia is especially grateful to Brigid Laffan and the Robert Schuman Centre for Advanced Studies at the EUI for contributing to the fantastic conditions surrounding the development of this book during his Jean Monnet post-doctoral fellowship. He wishes to dedicate this book to the loving memory of our colleague and friend Lorella Cedroni.

Diego Garzia and Stefan Marschall
San Domenico di Fiesole and Düsseldorf
May 2014

Chapter One

Voting Advice Applications in a Comparative Perspective: An Introduction

Stefan Marschall and Diego Garzia

The success story of VAAs

At the verge of the new millennium, the internet has emerged as a new player in political communication, supplementing and partly substituting traditional media such as television, radio and newspapers. Nowadays, the internet represents a major source of political information, communication and participation for a growing number of citizens (Zittel and Fuchs 2007; Norris and Curtice 2008). Not only parties and candidates but also non-party organizations offer online political platforms (Farrell and Schmitt-Beck 2008). This book will focus on one type of non-party online tool that has mushroomed within the last years in European countries and beyond: Voting Advice Applications (hereafter: VAAs). These applications assist voters in the electoral decision by comparing their policy preferences with the programmatic stances of political parties and/or candidates. VAA users are prompted to fill in a web-questionnaire marking their positions on an ample range of policy 'statements' (e.g. 'social programmes should be maintained even at the cost of higher taxes' or 'abortion should be forbidden'). After comparing the user's answers with the position of each party and/or candidate on the various statements, the application produces a result in the form of a rank-ordered list or a graph displaying which party or candidate stands closest to the user's policy preferences.

Voting Advice Applications have turned into a widespread online feature of electoral campaigns in Europe, attracting a growing interest from citizens (Garzia and Marschall 2012) as well as within the political science community (Cedroni and Garzia, 2010; Triga *et al.* 2012; Garzia *et al.* 2014). In some countries, VAAs like the *Stemwijzer* (Netherlands) or the *Wahl-O-Mat* (Germany) have developed into outstandingly popular political web applications used by millions of voters at election time. VAAs have not only been deployed on the national level. Before the EU elections of 2009, a supranational VAA was launched under the auspices of the Florence-based European University Institute. In only six weeks, the *EU Profiler* was able to attract more than 2.5 million users from all around the continent. A second transnational tool – *VoteMatch Europe* – was offered for the same elections by a consortium of national VAA makers. Also for the European Elections of 2014, several initiatives have been launched offering national as well transnational Voting Advice Applications throughout Europe.

The (offline) history of VAAs started in the late 1980s. What can be considered the 'ancestor' of all VAAs, the *StemWijzer*, was developed in 1989 by the Dutch Stichting Burgerschapskunde in collaboration with the Documentatiecentrum Nederlanse Politieke Partijen and the faculty of Political Management at the University of Twente. The *StemWijzer* package consisted of a small booklet with 60 statements taken from political party manifestos and a diskette. An internet-based *StemWijzer* was released a few years later, on the occasion of the 1998 parliamentary elections. In the following years, *StemWijzer* grew into the most used political application on the internet by Dutch voters at election time. From 50 sold brochures in 1989 to 6.500 given advices in 1998, the number of users rose to more than 2 million in both 2002 and 2003, then up to about 5 million in the elections that followed (de Graaf 2010). Throughout the years, the *Stemwijzer* kept its distinctive simplicity intact through a limited number of response categories (i.e. 'yes' and 'no', plus a neutral option), an intuitive matching algorithm and visualization of results through a 'match-list' (*see* Figure 1.1).

At the beginning of the new century, the highly successful experience of *StemWijzer* was exported to several other countries, such as Germany, where *Wahl-O-Mat* was fielded for the first time in 2002 and quickly became the most used VAA in the world in absolute numbers (Marschall and Schmidt 2010). Its most recent version, launched before the German federal election of 2013, accounted for over 13 million user sessions. Further versions of the Dutch pioneering VAA also appeared in Bulgaria (*Glasovoditel*) and Switzerland (*Politarena*). Besides Switzerland and Germany, Belgium has also been inspired by the Dutch example. In 2004, the Flemish public broadcaster VRT launched *Doe de Stem Test!* – a VAA for the regional elections of that year. The Flemish VAA was able to issue over 840,000 voting advices during that campaign (Walgrave *et al.* 2008). A similar media-driven development can be observed in the case of Finland. The public broadcasting company developed the first VAA already in 1996. Following this example, *Helsingin Sanomat* (the largest daily newspaper in Finland) built its own application in occasion of the 1999 EP election. In 2007, as many as twenty different VAAs were available to Finnish voters, with the most popular among these applications attracting over a million users (Ruusuvirta 2010).

Apart from the expansion of the *Stemwijzer* model, a second VAA type contributed to the success story of Voting Advice Applications: the Dutch *Kieskompas*. This VAA was explicitly designed as an alternative to the *Stemwijzer* by implementing different methods for the positioning of the parties/candidates and for calculating and displaying the issue congruence between the users and the political supply (*see* Figure 1.2). In the Netherlands, *Kieskompas* has become a strong rival of *Stemwijzer* attracting 1.5 million users in 2010. The *Kieskompas* prototype was transferred to many other countries (e.g. Belgium, France, Israel, Portugal, Sweden, Turkey as well as several Arabian and Southern American countries) and also served as a prototype for the *EU Profiler* at the European elections of 2009 (Breuer 2010; Trechsel and Mair 2011).

Some of the most innovative features of the *EU Profiler* (especially in terms of visualizations, *see* Figure 1.3) were indeed inspired by the forerunner of a third family of VAAs: the Swiss *smartvote*. Launched in 2003 as a competitor

Figure 1.1: A Stemwijzer statement (left), the match-list (right)

Figure 1.2: A EU Profiler statement (left), the two-dimensional matching (right)

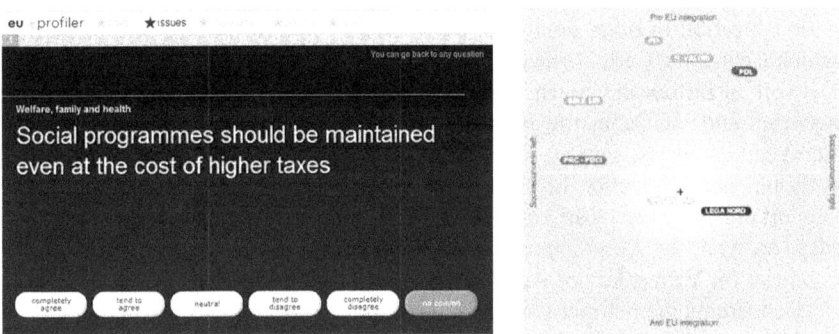

Figure 1.3: The smartvote questionnaire (left), the 'smartspider' matching (right)

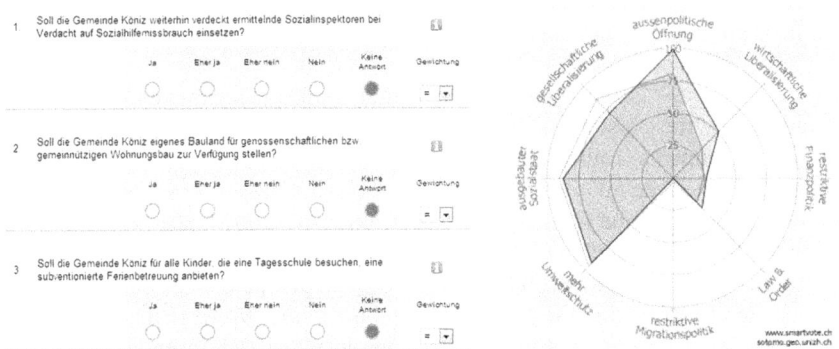

See http://press.ecpr.eu/resources.asp for full colour figures.

of *Politarena*, this VAA experienced an astonishing career. The first version of *smartvote* in 2003 provided over 255,000 voting advices. In only four years, the use of *smartvote* had increased almost fourfold, with about a million voting advices issued in 2007 (Ladner *et al.* 2010). Apart from contributing to the development of the *EU Profiler*, the *smartvote* team successfully exported their model to other European democracies (e.g. Bulgaria, Luxembourg, Scotland).

Due to these developments, practically all European countries – but also many other democracies and transformation countries – have VAA experiences. Focusing on VAA versions that have been developed on the national level, over 40 online tools of this kind have been implemented in Europe within the last few years. Apart from very few exceptions, all European countries can be considered familiar with VAAs (for an extensive discussion, *see* Garzia and Marschall 2012).

How could such a success story be explained? Why have these tools spread over the world and why are they so attractive to many voters? Regarding their expansion in and beyond the European countries, a snow-balling effect can be observed. Once a VAA has become successful in a country and this phenomenon is then observed by or communicated to actors such as media or organisations of civic education in other countries, these actors 'import' the idea into their own national contexts. Certain channels served to promote the spread of VAAs, e.g. the Network of European Citizenship Education (NECE) – a group that encompasses agencies and NGOs in the field of citizenship education from more than 25 European countries, serving as a forum on which VAA projects were presented early on. The production of the *EU Profiler* for all EU countries relying on the support of local expert teams also served as a channel of dissemination of the VAA idea. As well, the *Kieskompas* initiative has been very active in recruiting new countries for Voting Advice Applications.

Concerning their attractiveness for users, the spread of Internet communication could be seen as a main driving force for the success of Voting Advice Applications, since the popularity of these tools is related to their online existence, as is illustrated by the offline/online history of *Stemwijzer*. The unique and intriguing functionality of VAAs completely unfolds once the questionnaires have been implemented as user-friendly online tools (Alvarez *et al.* 2014). The general spread of the internet in recent years has supported the rise of VAAs. The more people have used the net for their political communication and for collection of information, the larger the potential VAA user-group has become.

Referring to general tendencies within political behaviour in modern democracies, the erosion of cleavage-based voting (Franklin *et al.* 1992) and partisan alignments (Dalton and Wattenberg 2000) in Western democracies might have augmented the number of floating, undecided voters who resort to VAAs in order to find orientation for their voting decision (Garzia 2010; 2012). A number of additional, context-specific conditions can also account for the success of VAAs. For example, the way in which traditional mass media promote these applications is a key to understanding the popularity of (some of the) VAAs (Ruusuvirta 2010; Carkoglu *et al.* 2012). Indeed, the countries in which VAAs enjoy the widest popularity are also those in which VAAs are the protagonist of a national TV show (Walgrave *et al.* 2008).

VAA research – state of the art

VAAs have long been seen as an interesting epiphenomenon. It is only in the past few years that political and social scientists have begun investigating VAAs and their potential effects on users from a quantitatively oriented as well as a normative point of view (Lander and Fivaz 2012). In the early phase, involved scientists attempted by and large to establish a common language for future studies (Fivaz and Nadig 2010). Indeed, a common agreement that these tools constitute a coherent group of applications and what this group should be called was reached only at the end of the 2000s (for a review, *see* Garzia 2010).

Early studies have primarily concentrated on the characteristics of the users (Edwards 1998; Boogers and Voerman 2003; Hooghe and Teepe 2007; Trechsel 2007; Wall *et al.* 2009; De Rosa 2010; Dziewulska 2010). With the growing number of voters using these tools during election times, interest has arisen concerning the consistency, validity and reliability of the 'voting advice' provided by such applications. This stream of research on VAA-quality focused on the formulation of transparency requirements (Ladner *et al.* 2010; Mayer and Wassermair 2010; Cedroni 2010; Ladner and Fivaz 2012); the quality of the questionnaire and the selection of the statements (Walgrave *et al.* 2009; Nuytemans *et al.* 2010); the way in which parties' positions on the statements are – or should be – established (Trechsel and Mair 2011; Gemenis 2013; Krouwel and van Elfrinkhof 2013); and the effect of different calculation methods on the final advice provided to users (Louwerse and Otjes 2012; Lowerse and Rosema 2013; Krouwel *et al.* 2012; Mendez 2012; Wagner and Ruusuvirta 2012). This body of methodological research can be boiled down to one crucial observation: namely, that the design of the tool matters. For example, Walgrave *et al.* (2009) show by means of experimental simulation that the respective composition of theses has an impact on the advice that is provided to users. Such research on VAA methodology raises awareness of how much responsibility is given to the developers of VAAs, as their decisions for a specific design and methods could exert a heavy influence on the quality of the tool and on its possible effects on users/voters.

VAAs can be thought to have an effect on users in at least three ways. At first, they can affect individuals' information-seeking behaviour: that is to say, motivating users to gather further information about politics and political parties (Marschall 2005; Mykkänen *et al.* 2007; De Rosa 2010; Ladner *et al.* 2010; Marschall and Schmidt 2010). Obviously, cognitive effects would be of little relevance if we could not detect any reflection in the actual behaviour of users. Indeed, a growing body of research shows that VAAs can also affect vote choice, both quantitatively (turnout) and qualitatively (vote intention).

Questions about VAAs' ability to affect the behaviour of their users have commonly been framed within issue voting theories. Issue voting refers to the assumption that vote choice is determined by the individual voter's proximity/distance to/from the position of the parties on salient issues (Downs 1957). In order to link their policy preferences to party positions, voters need not only to have preferences, but also a sufficient amount of information available regarding the policy stances of the parties contesting the election (Carmines and Huckfeldt 1996). By comparing the user's position on the various issues with that of the parties, VAAs provide users with readily accessible information about the parties' stances and the extent to which these match their own political preferences. In turn, additional information may mobilise users to the polls and, eventually, affect their propensity to vote for a certain party on the basis of issue proximity.

Consistent with low-information rationality theories, the individual-level probability of casting a vote is inversely proportional to the effort required to gather enough information (Delli Carpini and Keeter 1996). Voters are expected to cut the cost of voting by relying on whatever 'free' or inexpensive information can be picked up (Popkin 1994). In this respect, the usage of VAAs potentially reduces the cost of getting informed about politics and political parties, thereby increasing the chances of voting *vis-à-vis* abstention. VAA-providers have great confidence in the mobilising capacity of these tools. Indeed, many VAAs are actually developed as an attempt to mobilise voters and increase turnout (Marschall 2005). Previous research on the impact of VAAs confirms the hypothesized relationship between VAA-usage and electoral participation (Ruusuvirta and Rosema 2009; Fivaz and Nadig 2010; Ladner and Pianzola 2010; Marschall and Schmidt 2010; Hirzalla *et al.* 2011; Marschall and Schultze 2012a; Vassil 2012; Dinas *et al.* 2014).

VAAs have also been found to affect the actual vote-choice of users. By measuring the degree of match between users' and parties' issue positions, VAAs may lead users to a learning process that can, under certain conditions, affect their partisan preferences accordingly. Indeed, previous research has found that a proportion of VAA users declare themselves willing to 'move' their vote in line with the advice obtained (Aarts and van der Kolk 2007; Mykkänen *et al.* 2007; Walgrave *et al.* 2008; De Rosa 2010; Ladner *et al.* 2010; Nuytemans *et al.* 2010; Dumont and Kies 2012; Ladner *et al.* 2012; Pianzola *et al.* 2012; Vassil 2012; Wall *et al.* 2012; Pianzola 2013; Alvarez *et al.* 2014).

Eventually, the spread of VAAs among voters and across political systems has opened up novel possibilities for social and political science research. At the present stage, VAAs' most relevant contribution to the discipline probably rests with the huge number of parties' issue positions coded across time and space by VAA developers. In several instances, a closer correspondence between coder placement and party self-placement has been noted than was found between expert judgments and manifesto scores in previous comparative analyses (Trechsel and Mair 2011). Such multitude of party positions can easily contribute to our understanding of new cleavage lines that structure the party room, overcoming or supporting the left–right dichotomy (Lobo *et al.* 2010). VAA-generated data can also provide insights on the extent to which parties translate their pre-electoral positions into policy-making once in power (Ramonaite 2010; Skop 2010). By comparing what parties stand for and what government actually produces, we can more easily assess how representatives are responsive to the demands and preferences of the electorate (Bressanelli 2013). Furthermore, in countries where candidate-based voting systems are in place, VAA data can be employed in the study of intra-party cohesion during the legislature (Schwarz *et al.* 2010;

Hansen and Rasmussen 2013). Finally, VAA data can be fruitfully employed in analyses of elite-mass congruence (Rose 2013; Wheatley 2012; Wheatley *et al.* 2012). Traditional analyses of the ideological positions of the general population commonly resort to traditional surveys. Again, VAAs would seem to feature a number of advantages *vis-a-vis* more-traditional research tools. For one thing, VAAs are able to attract a much wider number of respondents as compared to the typical *n* of mass election surveys. Even more importantly, they allow comparisons of the issue positions of parties and voters using the same data source. In turn, this can help in understanding the working and effectiveness of representative government by means of a straightforward measurement of the extent to which parties and voters are mutually congruent (Trechsel and Mair 2011; Garzia *et al.* 2014).

So far, VAAs have chiefly been addressed from the perspective of empirical research. However, first initiatives have started to understand VAAs from the angle of political and democratic theory, too. As a matter of fact, the development and implementation of VAAs carry normative implications and reflect theoretical assumptions which deserve scrutiny and discussion (Cedroni 2010; Garzia and Marschall 2012; Fossen and Anderson 2014).

Structure of the book

Despite the valuable contribution of previous works to an understanding of these applications and their role in representative democracies, no systematic and reliable comparative assessment of these tools has been provided yet. At the present stage, research on VAAs has resulted almost exclusively in national case studies. Clearly, the lack of an integrated framework for analysis has made research on VAAs so far unable to serve the scientific goal of systematic knowledge accumulation. Moreover, the potential of the data and findings of VAA research for other fields of political science has not been exploited appropriately yet. Against this background, this volume aims first at a comprehensive overview of the VAA phenomena in a truly comparative perspective. Featuring the largest number of European experts on the topic ever assembled, *Matching Voters with Parties and Candidates* provides answers to a wide number of open questions and debates within VAA research. As well, it tries to bridge VAA research to other fields of political science.

The first three chapters are devoted to VAA-making, to the design and the methods VAAs employ as well as to the implications that the operational choices in the development of VAAs could have. It falls into the strand of methodological literature and provides for a comparative overview of different aspects of VAA design and methods, such as the process of item selection and question formulation (van Camp, Lefevere and Walgrave), the ways party positions are estimated (Gemenis and van Ham) and the algorithms used to calculate the distance or proximity between the users' and the parties' position (Mendez).

The chapter by Krouwel, Vitiello and Wall bridges the perspective of VAA makers with that of users through a detailed discussion of their reciprocal interaction, and paves the way for the following chapters dedicated to VAA usage and impact. Andreadis' chapter provides a valuable discussion and a few empirical criteria to 'count' users, while in Marschall's, data on the numbers of users are surveyed and critically analysed; additionally, this chapter comparatively takes stock of findings concerning the 'typical' characteristics of a VAA user. The following two chapters deal with a topic that has been the subject of several national research projects – i.e., the consequences of using VAAs on electoral participation and electoral preferences. The point of departure of these chapters is the hesitant state of the available empirical literature. A lack of standardisation in the field to date means that the specific questions used to elicit estimates of VAAs' influence vary substantially across national case studies. Moreover, these analyses are often based on opt-in surveys administrated to users right after having performed the VAA test. Apart from being subject to a heavy self-selection bias, this kind of data tends to overestimate to a substantial extent the actual effect exerted by VAA-usage on the voting decision. The chapters by Garzia, De Angelis and Pianzola (turnout) and Andreadis and Wall (vote choice) reassess the impact of VAAs in a truly comparative perspective, making use of representative national election studies from a number of selected European countries.

Triga's chapter focuses on the expectations connected to VAAs and whether these are fulfilled by applying a methodically innovative 'bottom-up' focus-group analysis. While this chapter looks at users' evaluation of VAAs, the following one by Dumont, Kies and Fivaz deals with candidates' perception and usage of VAAs.

The final group of chapters deals with the relationship between VAAs, parties and candidates by especially focussing on the potential contribution of VAA research to the general study of party politics, campaigning and representation in contemporary European democracies. The chapter by Wheatley and Mendez addresses how the VAA data could be used to map parties within the ideological space in national/local elections. Sudulich, Garzia, Trechsel and Vassil expand on this by looking at the ideological space at the supranational (i.e. European) level, making use of the unique *EU Profiler* 2009 dataset. The effect of different electoral rules on party and candidate positioning in different VAAs is investigated in the chapter by Ladner. Fivaz, Louwerse and Schwarz's analyzes the extent to which parties'/candidates' post-electoral policy position in parliament is similar to their pre-electoral policy position, as documented in their answers to the VAA items. Finally, a so-far neglected yet fundamental perspective will be addressed in the final chapter by Anderson and Fossen: How are VAAs and their making implicitly or explicitly connected to democratic theories and normative models of citizenship?

This book is a truly collective endeavor; it represents the result of a process of discussions and cooperative work among a large international group of VAA researchers. The roots of this process are marked by the first meetings and conferences, at which formerly disconnected national VAA research teams started to exchange experiences and findings from different countries. The 2008 Antwerp conference *Voting Advice Applications: Between Charlatanism and Political Science* organized by University of Antwerp and *Kieskompas* could be viewed as a starting point for an academic discussion among international experts on VAAs. In later years, VAAs became a topic on several political science conferences, at the outset as panels. In April 2011, the Francophonian Benelux political science dedicated a panel to VAAs (title: *Les systèmes d'aide au vote: nouveaux instruments de l'analyse politologique? Défis et potentialities*). And in June 2011, a VAA research meeting took place at the national Dutch political science conference in Amsterdam (panel title: *Voting Advice Applications and Citizen Competence*). On the ECPR General Conference in Reykjavik (August 2011), a panel on *Voting Advice Applications (VAAs) under Scrutiny – Assessing their Impact on Elections* again discusses studies on these tools. In July 2012, on the IPSA Conference in Madrid, a panel with the title *Dangerous Toys? Assessing the Electoral Integrity of Voter Engagement Application Websites* was dedicated exclusively to VAA research.

A structured form of cooperation and networking had already been initiated by a research workshop in March 2012 at the University of Düsseldorf. The explicit goal of this Düsseldorf workshop had been to reflect on the state(s) of the art in VAA research and to ponder common international research perspectives. Shortly afterwards, a small group of VAA researchers developed within the frame of the ECPR Research Sessions in Florence the plan for a collective volume on VAA research (June 2012). The idea was to set up international author groups and apply a consequently comparative perspective. After an agreement was reached with potential contributors to the book as well as with ECPR Press, the actual work for the book was started. Preliminary drafts of some of the chapters had been discussed in the context of a mini-section on VAAs at the Italian Political Science Association, in September 2012 (Rome), as well as on the ECPR General Conference in Bordeaux in September 2013. In Bordeaux, for the first time a full Section with four panels featuring about 20 papers was dedicated solely to VAA research (the ECPR General Conference in Glasgow in September 2014 will serve as the second time a complete Section on VAAs is organized).

As an important milestone for finalizing and revising the chapters of the volume, a book conference in Lausanne/IDHEAP took place in May 2013, where contributors attended and presented their chapters. The authors commented on each other's work and made the book possible the way it is.

In Lausanne we also began reflecting upon the normative implications of VAAs as well as on the ethical and methodological standards VAAs should comply with in order to serve their purpose within liberal democracies. Under the heading 'Lausanne Declaration', the editors of this volume compiled major points stemming from our repeated discussions with all the researchers in the group. The outcome, for which the editors are solely responsible, but for which we nonetheless thank all for input and debates (especially Andreas Ladner and Stefaan Walgrave), is presented at the end of the volume.

This declaration aims to provide a first ethical guideline for the makers and researchers of this tool. It takes into account the growing relevance of VAAs within modern election campaigns and that VAAs have an impact on voting behavior and thereby in the end could change the results of elections; it acknowledges the effects methodological choices could have on those using the tool. This declaration is supposed to serve as a basis for a so-far neglected discussion of the ethical aspects of making VAAs, and represents – possibly – a helpful contribution of our research group to the further developments of VAAs in contemporary democracies.

Chapter Two

The Content and Formulation of Statements in Voting Advice Applications: A Comparative Analysis of 26 VAAs

Kirsten Van Camp, Jonas Lefevere and Stefaan Walgrave

Voting Advice Applications (VAAs) have become increasingly popular throughout Europe during the last decade(s). Slowly but surely, these online tools are gaining ground in other parts of the world, such as North America (e.g. *Vote Compass in Canada*) and Latin America (e.g. *Questatildeo Puacuteblica* in Brazil). The two most cited determinants for this steep rise of VAAs are the expansion of the internet and the decline in party alignment and the corresponding increase in party volatility (e.g. Walgrave, Nuytemans and Pepermans 2009; Walgrave, Van Aelst and Nuytemans 2008). Dealignment increases voters' need for substantive information on where parties stand on the issues that are important to them. The purpose of most VAAs lies in this information-providing task: by matching the responses of voters to policy-related statements with the responses of parties or candidates to the same statements, they provide information to voters about which parties correspond 'best' to their preferred policy.

In this chapter, we analyse statements from twenty-six VAAs in nine countries to assess whether VAAs fulfil their information purpose, meet VAA builders' own criteria, and adhere to basic survey methodology. Statement selection is one of the first steps when developing a VAA. The methodology section of the European VAA *EU Profiler* in 2009 stated that 'The most critical aspect of preparing a party profiler is the selection of the statements used in the questionnaire'. In this chapter, we scrutinise the content and the formulation of these statements, in order to answer two research questions:

RQ1: To what extent do VAA builders produce VAAs that meet their own statement selection and formulation criteria?

RQ2: Do the statements conform to widely accepted standards for survey question formulation?

The questions we deal with are important. Firstly, VAAs are widely used tools, with millions of users. The Dutch VAA *StemWijzer*, for example, reached 4.9 million voters during the 2012 national election campaign in the Netherlands, representing 40 per cent of the Dutch electorate. VAAs are based on the proximity-voting model, assuming that voters vote for the party that is closest to their own political preferences. Recent research shows that 43 per cent of all voters in Europe cast their vote based on the aforementioned proximity model (Singh 2010), making the group of voters that can potentially be influenced by VAAs substantial. Previous research has shown that VAAs can influence both electoral participation (Ladner and Pianzola 2010) and voting decisions (Wall, Krouwel and Vitiello 2012). Secondly, our study deals with the core of every VAA: the statements. As with any survey technique, statement selection and phrasing have the potential to significantly alter the result – in this case, the advice the Voting Advice Application provides to a given user (Walgrave *et al.* 2009). Notwithstanding the importance of statement selection, previous research scrutinising whether statements used in VAAs are methodologically sound is very rare. This chapter adopts a comparative perspective and compares different VAAs and their statements over time in different countries. As far as we know, this is the first time such a comparative approach has been used to examine VAA statements.

The information-providing task of Voting Advice Applications

Our first aim is to investigate whether VAAs achieve the goals of their builders. To formulate concrete expectations, we build on VAA builders' own guidelines. Quite a few VAA builders have published such guidelines (*see* e.g. Deschouwer *et al.* 2007; Louwerse and Rosema 2013; Walgrave *et al.* 2009). These internal rules of statement selection and formulation boil down to a number of core criteria, which we summarise in Table 2.1.

First, based on what VAA builders claim, we expect that VAA statements will typically be dispersed across a large amount of issues. VAA creators have to decide whether they incorporate a wide variety of issues or limit the tool to a few hot topics of the day. Judging from Table 2.1 (first column), builders that address the distribution of statements in their guidelines invariably indicate that they aim for a 'wide' or 'balanced' selection of issues.

Second, we expect the amount of statements to be larger for issues that are salient in the political debate. One of the most important rules of thumb used by VAA builders is that statements should handle 'relevant political and social issues' (*Kieskompas*) that 'play an important role in the campaign and will dominate the political debate during the next legislation' (*StemWijzer*). There seems to be a general agreement that the chosen issues should be relevant, that they should cover current affairs, and that they should receive a fair amount of attention in the political debate. To test this we compare the issues that are covered by VAA statements with the issues that are mentioned in the party manifestos of the same election. We expect that the more salient an issue is in the party manifestos, the more statements in the VAA cover the issue. Table 2.1 also suggests a potential point of disagreement between VAA builders concerning the issues to cover: should VAAs follow the debate and choose issues accordingly, or should they take a more proactive role and put neglected issues on the agenda? Most builders seem inclined to follow the debate – issues should already be important or relevant.

However, because VAA builders also want a wide array of issues in their tool, less-important issues might receive comparatively great attention.

Related to this, our third expectation is that there are more statements on an issue that is connected to an important political cleavage in the country at stake than on other issues. VAAs are developed to inform voters about which political party is closest to their own political preferences. Ever since the influential essay by Lipset and Rokkan (1967), political cleavages have been one of the most important concepts to differentiate between political preferences. The socio-economic left–right opposition has been considered as the most important cleavage in Western European politics (Enyedi, 2008). In recent decennia a new cultural divide between conservatives and progressives has also become relevant (e.g. Kriesi 1998; Hooghe *et al.* 2010). This second fault line focuses on equal rights between different groups, on environmental issues and on religious themes. The salience of the socio-economic left–right and conservative–progressive dimensions in the national political sphere varies: in some countries these cleavages dominate the debate, whereas they have less bearing upon politics in other countries. Since VAA builders want to focus on 'important' issues and debates (*see* Table 2.1) we expect that the more salient the left–right and conservative–progressive cleavages are in a country, the more statements in the VAAs in that country cover the left–right and conservative–progressive cleavage.

Fourth, we expect that VAA builders focus their statements on issues that will be important 'in the upcoming campaign and in the next legislation' (*StemWijzer*). A number of VAAs are based on the campaign manifestos of political parties. This indicates that VAAs essentially deal with future policy, since programs are policy proposals for the next term. Also, while not all VAAs explicitly reference future policy, their focus on current affairs suggests an intention to look forward rather than backward. Thus, statements, we anticipate, are formulated prospectively, i.e. looking to future policy, rather than retrospectively. In short, we expect that VAAs contain more prospective than retrospective statements.

Finally, statements will discriminate between parties – not all parties will adopt the same position on a statement. This discrimination criterion is frequently mentioned by VAA builders (*see* Table 2.1, column 4). If a VAA only included statements on which all parties agree, there would be little information to gather from it: the reason why people would need a VAA to help them make a choice is that it is hard for them to get information about the differences between the parties. Therefore, a pragmatic need for any VAA statement is that it discriminates between parties: some parties must have a positive and others a negative stand on it.

Voting Advice Applications and survey methodology

Our second aim in this study is to examine to what extent VAAs match voters with political actors based on methodologically sound measures. VAAs calculate the closeness of their users to the various political parties by presenting the user with what is essentially a small questionnaire, consisting of various statements. Because there is ample research on what constitutes a 'good' survey measure, it seems natural that VAAs would follow these rules (Presser and Krosnick 2010).

Table 2.1: Overview of rules-of-thumb for statement selection put forward by VAA builders

	Distribution of statements across issues	Which issues/political cleavages	Prospective – Retrospective	Discriminant
StemWijzer		– Issues that play an important role *in the campaign*. – Issues that will dominate the *political debate* during the next legislation. – Issues that receive a *fair amount of attention* both within the political world as in the election campaigns. – Issues that *follow the political agenda and public opinion*. – *StemWijzer* is an instrument to test political preference. – *StemWijzer* has as a primary goal to highlight the differences in the *political content* put forward by each of the political parties.	– The statements are developed on the basis of the election programs. – Issues that play an important role in the campaign and will dominate the political debate during the *next four years*.	– An important selection criterion is the degree to which the statements *discriminate between parties*. If parties hold a similar opinion regarding an issue, then a statement concerning this issue becomes less interesting and useful.
Kieskompas		– *Relevant* political and social issues. – *Important* issues. – *Kieskompas* positions users in the *political landscape*. It shows you which parties are close to your views and which parties least represents *your political profile and preferences*.	– The answers given by parties to our statements are calculated based on *election programs*.	

	Distribution of statements across issues	Which issues/political cleavages	Prospective – Retrospective	Discriminant
Wahl-O-Mat		– The *most important issues of the elections*. – The core policy statements. – Topics that are of particular interest to *young people*. – Found out which party best represents *your opinion*.	– Statements are developed based on the core policy statements, platforms and *election manifestos* of the different parties and voters' associations.	– Show *differences* between parties. – The statements which best serve to *differentiate the parties* were selected. – We focused primarily on topics where the different parties *differ in their opinions*.
smartvote	– Based on a *wide range* of political topics.	– Compare own political viewpoints with those of *political parties* and candidates.		
Doe de Stemtest	– *Balanced selection* with regard to the different policy domains.	– *Important or relevant* policy choices. – Important issues should get *more statements* than less important issues. – Statements are based on *current* affairs, party programs and on party opinion. – Investigate how large the *ideological distance* is between your own opinions and those of different political parties. – The statements should as much as possible be *linked to the big classical fault lines* in Belgian politics.	– Statements should in general be about *future policy*, although they can also question past policy. – Statements are based on current affairs, *party programs* and on party opinion.	– A statement on which *all parties agree or disagree is useless* since it doesn't help to link users to parties. – Statements should be *discriminant*: if parties all agree on the statement, the statement is out.

	Distribution of statements across issues	Which issues/political cleavages	Prospective – Retrospective	Discriminant
Vote Compass	– Based on their _breadth of coverage_ across multiple policy fields.	– Policy issues that figure _most prominently_ in the platforms and public statements of the candidates/parties and in media discourse about national politics. – Based on their salience in the upcoming election. – The purpose is to provide information on _party platforms_.	– The purpose is to provide information on _party platforms_.	– Based on the questions' ability to _differentiate_ between candidates and amongst voters.
Vote Match		– Inform people about the policy differences between candidates.	– We are sceptical that a VAA could ever adequately take issues such as personality, competence or record of the candidates into account.	– Inform people about the policy differences between candidates. – We filter out statements where there was uniform agreement or which did not otherwise provide us with discriminating information.
Wahlkabine	– Questions from _diverse fields_ are selected to be included.	– _Political issues_ and _current issues_. – _Wahlkabine_ helps to compare your _political views_ with those of the parties. It is an online tool for _political education_.	– Party policies on _current_ issues.	

Note: No information was available for the Finnish VAA YLE.
Source: For *StemWijzer:* http://www.stemwijzer.nl/Veelgestelde-vragen-over-de-StemWijzer; for *Kieskompas:* http://home.kieskompas.nl/page/Home/1/en/content.html# and http://www.kieskompas.be/faq/; for *Wahl-O-Mat:* http://www.bpb.de/politik/wahlen/wahl-o-mat/45270/wie-funktioniert-der-wahl-o-mat, http://www.bpb.de/politik/wahlen/wahl-o-mat/45292/fakten-zum-wahl-o-mat and http://www.wahl-o-mat.de/europa2009/popup_faq.php?womeuropa2009=04ab7b6040b501fc62eafeab45591 313&servername=www.wahl-o-mat.de; for *smartvote:* http://www.smartvote.ch/about/idea; for *Doe de Stemtest:* Deschouwer, Hooghe, Devos and Walgrave 2007; for *Vote Compass:* http://usa2012.votecompass.com/assets/media/site/pdfs/US2012AlgorithmTechnicalDocumentEN.Pdf and http://usa2012.votecompass.com/faq; for *Vote Match:* http://www.votematch.org.uk/faq.php; for *Wahlkabine:* http://wahlkabine.at/ueber/Infofolder_wahlkabine_ENGL.pdf.

Especially, because most VAAs are built by political scientists it is reasonable to assume that these guidelines will be adhered to. Specifically, we scrutinise four features of VAA statements that relate to survey methodology: concreteness, double-barrelledness, quantifications and qualifications.

Statements should concern concrete policy choices instead of general ideological values. The need for concreteness and specificity are common truisms in survey research (Billiet 2006; Presser and Krosnick 2010). Survey items and statements that are too vague can lead to biased answers due to misinterpretation. Vague statements also do not yield useful information for voters. Voters may have a general sense of where parties stand but what they lack is knowledge on parties' specific positions on concrete policies. For example, knowing whether a party agrees that 'All nuclear power plants should be closed by the end of 2015' is more informative than 'Environmental pollution should be tackled'. While for the first statement it is clear which policy measure is suggested, the second statement leaves plenty of room for interpretation. If voters and parties agree that environmental pollution should be tackled but have diverging ideas about how this should be done, the agreement is superfluous. Thus, statements should be concrete, not vague.

Statements should not be double-barrelled either: they can only measure one thing at a time. Statements that do not follow these rules can be interpreted differently by each voter and party filling in the VAA, leading to incomparable results (Presser and Krosnick 2010). Double-barrelled questions combine multiple elements in a single measure: statements in which two questions are asked or in which an argument is given fall under this category (e.g. 'Should Switzerland legalise the consumption of hard and soft drugs as well as the possession of such drugs for personal consumption?' – *smartvote* 2011). They are unsuitable because they do not allow voters and parties to give a straightforward answer, creating problems regarding what constitutes 'agreement' between voters and parties (Kumar 2011). In a VAA context, they also allow parties to avoid taking a certain (unpopular) position by playing on the conditionality of the statement.

Third, statements should not include quantifications. Gemenis (2013) indicates that statements used in online voting tools should not be quantitative (e.g. 'Criminals who are repeat offenders should be punished *more* heavily' – *StemWijzer* 2002). The use of words like more, less or other comparative forms of adjectives or adverbs, indicate that the statement is trying to measure a sort of quantity. As with double-barrelled and vague statements, they could lead to biased and unreliable answers due to misinterpretation. When voters do not agree with the aforementioned statement, it is unclear what their attitude towards the issues is: do they agree with the present policy or do they think that the current punishments are too strict? Thus, it is impossible to ascertain that voters and parties actually match when they have the same answer on the statement.

Fourth, qualifications should be avoided as well. Qualifications occur when additional, but not crucial, information is provided in the statement. This also introduces bias because the qualification may bring other attitudes to attention that would not have played a role otherwise. The policy position that is chosen may then differ from the one that would have been picked if the qualification was absent. For example, *Wahl-O-Mat* in 2002 used the statement 'Gay marriages should have the same rights as heterosexual marriages, e.g. adopt children'. The attitude voters have regarding the statement in general (i.e. the rights of gay marriage) will be coloured by the attitudes voters have concerning the adoption of children by married gay people. Since VAAs are essentially about policy positions, such contaminated positions should be avoided (Gemenis 2013).

Data and methods

We analyse data from twenty-six national election VAAs from nine countries: Austria, Belgium (Flanders), Finland, Germany, Switzerland, the Netherlands, the UK, Canada and the USA. Some countries have a long-standing tradition of VAAs (e.g. the Netherlands). Other countries such as Canada have only recently witnessed the appearance of such online tools. To make data as comparable as possible, we only include VAAs that were developed for national elections. In total, twenty-six VAAs from nine different VAA builders were scrutinised: *StemWijzer, Kieskompas, Wahl-O-Mat, smartvote, Doe de Stemtest, YLE, Vote Compass, Vote Match* and *Wahlkabine*. The VAAs and their statements were mainly retrieved through websites. If VAAs were no longer available online, VAA builders were contacted and asked to send the data (*see* Appendix 2.3). The 26 VAAs made up a total of 954 statements. Table 2.2 provides an overview of our sample of VAAs per VAA builder. One-fifth of the examined VAAs were tools made by *StemWijzer*, while *Vote Match* delivered only one VAA. All voting advice tools were implemented between 2002 and 2012. Appendix 2 provides more information about the VAAs in the sample.

Table 2.2: Overview of VAAs in the sample

	Country	Year
StemWijzer	Netherlands	2002, 2003, 2006, 2010, 2012
Kieskompas	Netherlands	2006, 2010, 2012
	Belgium	2007
Wahl-O-Mat	Germany	2002, 2005, 2009
smartvote	Switzerland	2007, 2011
Doe de Stemtest	Belgium	2003, 2007
YLE	Finland	2003, 2007, 2011
Vote Compass	Canada	2011
	USA	2012
Vote Match	UK	2010
Wahlkabine	Austria	2002, 2006, 2008, 2012

All statements were manually coded by human coders, which resulted in eight indicators, described below. The full codebook is available in Appendix 2.2. Using eighteen issue dummies, statements were coded as covering (1) or not covering (0) a given issue (e.g. Foreign Policy, Economy and Society, Ethical Themes and Religion). Next, two dummy variables were used to indicate whether or not the statement was related to the socio-economic or conservative–progressive cleavage. Two variables track whether a statement was retrospective/prospective (1) or not (0). An additional dummy variable was used to track double-barrelledness. To calculate whether statements were discriminant, party stances on each of the statements were coded. They were then reduced to a simple agree–disagree opposition. For this purpose, 'skip' and 'neutral' categories (if present) were discarded and the categories that 'totally agree' (resp. 'totally disagree') and 'tend to agree' (resp. 'tend to disagree') were collapsed into one category. Finally, a calculation was made of how many parties were in each of the two categories. The level of concreteness was coded through a three-point scale ranging from 1 (vague) to 3 (very concrete). Finally, two dummy variables track the presence (1) or absence (0) of quantitative statements and of qualifications. A small percentage of the statements were coded by two coders, in order to calculate intercoder reliability. An average Krippendorff's alpha of 0.8 was achieved.

Analysis and results

We first assess whether VAA statements are dispersed over a wide range of issues. Table 2.3 presents the proportion of statements covering each of the 18 issues. We calculate the normed Herfindahl index to provide a measure of dispersion of the statements across issues. This index can take a value between 0 (there are a large number of issues present that all take an equal proportion) and 1 (all statements cover the same issue). By and large, there is a strong tendency amongst VAA builders to cover a wide range of issues: the Herfindahl index is extremely low (between 0.01 and 0.06), indicating a very high dispersion of statements across the various issues. As expected, all VAA builders seem eager to include a wide range of topics in their calculations rather than concentrating the statements just on the hot issues of the day.

Looking at statement content, we see that 10 per cent of statements cover the topic of Government Finances, Taxes and Budget (*see* Table 2.3) (e.g. 'The highest rate of income taxes should be reduced', *StemWijzer* 2002). A reason that might explain the high score of this issue is the fact that many policy measures can easily be translated into what we would call a 'financial formulation' of a policy measure in terms of spending more or less money on a given need. The second issue category often covered in VAA statements is Society, Ethical Themes and Religion. This can be explained by the almost continuous attention of VAAs to themes such as rights of the BTGL community (e.g. 'Gay couples should have fully equal rights to adopt children' – *Wahl-O-Mat* 2009) or societal discussions with a religious foundation (e.g. 'Euthanasia should once again become fully punishable' – *StemWijzer* 2002). Statements of YLE refer to this topic significantly less than

Table 2.3: Issue salience in VAA statements (mean)

	SW	KK	WOM	SV	DST	YLE	VC	VM	WK	Total
Government Finances, Taxes and Budget	.14	.13	.11	.10	.08	.10	.16	.19	.05	.11
Society, Ethical Themes and Religion	.10	.10	.12	.07	.10	**.03**	.14	.06	.08	.09
Foreign Policy, Defence and Development Aid	.08	.06	.10	.09	.05	.07	.13	.03	.10	.08
Social Security	.08	.08	.05	.08	.10	.06	.07	.14	.12	.08
Public Order and Safety, Justice and Police	.07	.07	.05	.08	.09	.06	.09	.11	.12	.08
Internal Affairs	.04	**.02**	.06	.06	.04	**.15**	.03	.11	.11	.07
Work	.05	.08	.08	.06	.08	.10	.01	.06	.04	.06
Education and Research	.05	.04	**.13**	.06	.02	.06	.04	.08	.09	.06
Welfare, Family and Health	.08	.08	.04	.07	.05	.04	.06	.00	.04	.06
Mobility, Traffic and Transport	.05	.04	.02	.05	**.11**	**.09**	**.00**	.00	.04	.05
Immigration and Integration	.04	.06	.02	.06	.06	.05	.04	.08	.07	.05
Environment and Energy	.04	.02	.04	.05	.05	.06	.10	.06	.00	.04
Other	.04	.03	.04	.07	.04	.05	.00	.00	.03	.04
Economy	.04	.04	.04	.03	.01	.02	.06	.03	.02	.03
Europe	.03	.05	.04	.03	.04	.01	.00	.06	.04	.03
Culture and Recreation	.04	.03	.01	.02	.02	.02	.03	.00	.06	.03
State Reform	.01	.03	.02	**.00**	**.05**	.04	.03	.00	.00	.02
Housing	**.03**	**.03**	.01	.01	.00	.01	.00	.00	.00	.01
Herfindahl Index (normed)	0.02	0.02	0.03	0.01	0.02	0.02	0.05	0.06	0.03	---

Note: Indicated in bold are the averages that are higher or lower than the other values in the same row as derived from adjusted standardised residuals in crosstabs for which χ^2 had a significant value.

Abbreviations: SW = StemWijzer; KK = Kieskompas; WOM = Wahl-O-Mat; SV = smartvote; DST = Doe de Stemtest; VC = Vote Compass; VM = Vote Match; WK = Wahlkabine.

other VAAs ($\chi^2(8)=18.24$, $p<.05$). This could be due to the fact that Scandinavian countries are in general more progressive, with the aforementioned topics perhaps leading to less debate.

Some issues are hardly addressed in VAAs. The issue of Housing, for example, is present in only 1 per cent of the statements; State Reform, Culture and Recreation, and Europe are not very popular either. With percentages from 2 to 3 per cent, and an average of 33 statements per VAA, this means that on average less than 1 statement covering these issues is present in each VAA.

To scrutinise whether issues that are salient in the political debate in a country at a given point in time are also covered by more statements, we compare the issue attention in VAA statements with the issue attention in the party manifestos of the same year. In order to do so, we make use of the data collected by the Comparative Manifesto Project (CMP). For 19 of the 26 VAAs under scrutiny, CMP has data available for almost all of the political parties. For 13 of our 17 issue categories – we disregard the issue category 'Other' in this exercise – a match could be made. We recalculate the proportion of each issue in both the CMP and the VAA data so that in each dataset they sum up to 1. Table 2.4 has the results. Overall, no significant correlation ($r=-.18$, $p=.55$) can be found between our VAA data and the CMP data, indicating that issues receive a different amount of attention in both platforms. While Economy covers roughly 20 per cent of the manifestos, it is highly underrepresented in the VAA statements. On the other hand, Government Finances, Taxes and Budget, and Society, Ethical Themes and Religion, the two issues that are overall most present in VAA statements (*see* Table 2.3), are not very salient in the manifestos. All other issues are more or less equally represented in both manifestos and VAAs. Indeed, this suggests that the high dispersion of issues conflicts with the correlation between issue salience in the political debate and in VAAs: hugely salient issues, such as the economy, get less attention since VAA builders aim at including a wide array of issues. Conversely, what may be a small issue in the current political debate may get more than its share of VAA statements.

Regarding political cleavages, we expected that the more salient the cleavages in a country are, the greater the amount of statements related to those cleavages in VAAs from that country. The two major cleavages are covered by a substantial batch of statements in almost all analysed VAAs (*see* Table 2.5). One out of four statements can be attributed to the classic divide between the socio-economic left and right (e.g. 'A nationwide minimum wage should be introduced' – *Wahl-O-Mat* 2009). To test whether the proportion of left–right statements corresponds with the prevalence of the classical left–right cleavage in the political systems under study, we compare our results with the Chapel Hill Expert Survey data (CHES) (Hooghe *et al.* 2010). Taken as research units are the countries that are present in both our study and the CHES (i.e. the Netherlands, Belgium, Germany, Finland, the UK and Austria). Based on party positions on a left–right scale, as determined by experts in the CHES, each country is given a score for how extreme political parties in that country are on average. The higher this score, and thus the more political parties are labelled as being extreme on the left–right axis, the more polarised the political landscape should be and the more important the socio-

Table 2.4: Comparison of issue salience in party manifesto phrases and VAA statements

	CMP	VAA
Government Finances, Taxes and Budget	.05	.14
Society, Ethical Themes and Religion	.04	.11
Public Order and Safety, Justice and Police	.08	.11
Foreign Policy, Defence and Development Aid	.08	.10
Social Security	.13	.10
Work	.05	.09
Internal Affairs	.07	.09
Education and Research	.07	.08
Environment and Energy	.09	.05
Culture and Recreation	.03	.04
Economy	.23	.04
Europe	.04	.04
State Reform	.04	.03
Total	1	1

Table 2.5: Statement content (mean)

	SW	KK	WOM	SV	DST	YLE	VC	VM	WK	Total
Socio-economic Left–Right	.31	**.38**	.33	.20	.26	**.12**	**.40**	.20	**.13**	.25
Conservative–Progressive	**.35**	.35	.23	.28	**.40**	.25	.37	.17	**.13**	.28
Retrospective	**.24**	.09	.09	**.16**	.04	**.03**	.05	.00	.10	.11
Prospective	**.98**	.89	.98	**.68**	.89	**.75**	**1.00**	.97	**.79**	.86
Discriminant	**1.00**	.99	.91	.89	.96	**.78**	.93	.97	**.98**	.93

Note: Indicated in bold are the averages that are significantly higher or lower than the other values in the same row.

Abbreviations: SW = *StemWijzer*; KK = *KiesKompas*; WOM = *Wahl-O-Mat*; SV = *smartvote*; DST = *Doe de Stemtest*; VC = *Vote Compass*; VM = *Vote Match*; WK = *Wahlkabine*.

economic left–right cleavage becomes. Consequently, in countries with a higher score, VAAs should make more references to this dimension. Our results confirm this expectation. A strong correlation (r=.87, p<.05) exists between the salience of the left–right cleavage in a country and the amount of statements covering that cleavage in the VAA in that country.

Statements that deal with the conservative–progressive cleavage account for about one-fourth of all statements. However, when we again compare our data with the expert positioning of the CHES dataset, there is no correlation between the salience of the conservative–progressive divide in a country and the presence of statements related to this fault line in VAA statements (r=-.176, p=.74). Although it seems to be the case that VAAs reflect the prevalence of the socio-economic left–right divide, this does not seem to hold true for the conservative–progressive divide.

Are statements[1] formulated in a prospective way? Table 2.5 confirms that this is the case. Nine out of ten statements used in VAAs look at future policy measures. This is to be expected, since VAAs all emulate the proximity model of voting, which is mostly concerned with prospective policy considerations. Despite the primary task of providing voters with information regarding future policy, we also found a number of retrospective statements. This runs counter to our expectations, and also against the claims made by VAA builders themselves (*see* Table 2.1). Significant differences can be found between VAA builders ($\chi^2(8)=$ 56.46, p<.001). Remarkably, *StemWijzer* has the highest proportion of retrospective statements (x =.24), despite the fact that they have an additional online tool named *Stemmentracker* that is especially designed to offer voters a retrospective tool.

Our final expectation was that VAA statements would be discriminant. As expected, a large majority of statements are discriminant, meaning that they at least separate one party from all others. A small percentage however lacks this discriminating power. For the Finnish YLE this proportion increases significantly ($\chi^2(8)=73.64$, p<.001) to about one-fifth of all statements. These results merit some additional methodological information, since one would intuitively expect all statements to be discriminant. Firstly, some of the smaller political parties (representing less than one per cent of the electorate) were not incorporated in this study. By consequence, statements that are labelled as non-discriminant in this study may in fact have been discriminant in the real VAA. Nonetheless, these statements do not discriminate between the most important political parties. Secondly, in order to contrast parties that were pro and anti a certain policy, the answering categories 'neutral' and 'skip' were disregarded and the categories 'tend to agree' and 'agree' (resp. 'tend to disagree' and 'disagree') were collapsed into one. This means that statements were labelled non-discriminant when for

---

1. It should be noticed that statements can be prospective and retrospective at the same time. The phrase 'Euthanasia should once again become fully punishable', for example, refers to a past policy (euthanasia was not allowed in the past) and asks whether voters would like to see this policy reinstated once again in the future. That is why the total for retrospective and prospective sometimes exceeds 100%.

example three parties answered 'tend to agree', four parties answered 'agree' and two parties answered 'neutral'. When scrutinising statements that were labelled discriminant, 31 per cent of them cut the political landscape in the middle and 20 per cent separate one party from all others. About one-fourth of such 'single-party' statements separate a party that represents 5 per cent or less of the electorate. Thus, these statements are mainly included to be able to separate an electorally marginal party. Consequently, their informative value is quite low. On the other hand, 54 per cent of the 'single-party' statements discriminate a party that represents more than 10 per cent of the electorate.

Our second aim was to assess to what extent VAA statement formulation adheres to mainstream survey methodology. We test the concreteness, double-barrelledness, and the presence of qualifications and quantifications in the statements. Table 2.6 lists the average presence of these methodological problems in each of the VAAs. Regarding concreteness, on a scale from 1 (vague statements) to 3 (precise statements), an overall average of 2.51 is reached. While some differences between VAAs exist, the results suggest that all VAA builders largely adhere to their claim of using concrete policy statements. This is decidedly a good thing since survey methodologists have long suggested that the more specific questions are, the better.

More troubling is that Table 2.6 shows that every VAA includes at least one double-barrelled statement and that, overall, almost 20 per cent of the statements are double-barrelled. There exist large differences between VAAs: one out of three statements of *Wahlkabine* is double-barrelled compared to only one out of ten statements of *Vote Compass*. We should however indicate that the guidelines used were fairly strict, whereby double-barrelled statements that are incorporated to clarify the situational context of a given policy measure were nevertheless coded as double-barrelled. After all, regardless of good intentions, double-barrelled statements leave room for interpretation, which is problematic. To test whether VAA builders have learned from experience, we compared the amount of double-barrelled questions throughout the years under study. However, the average proportion of double-barrelled statements seems to fluctuate through the years, reaching its peak as recently as 2010. Thus, the matter of double-barrelled questions seems to be an ongoing problem in VAAs.

Table 2.6: Statement formulation (mean)

	SW	KK	WOM	SV	DST	YLE	VC	VM	WK	Total
Concrete	2.48	**2.39**	**2.31**	2.57	2.58	2.53	2.48	2.67	**2.65**	2.51
Double-barrelled	.23	.20	.10	.16	.10	.12	.07	.17	.32	.17
Quantitative	.27	.25	.15	.11	.22	.15	.23	.10	.20	.19
Qualification	.03	.00	.02	.07	.00	.00	.00	.00	.10	.03

Note: Indicated in bold are the averages that are significantly higher or lower than the other values in the same row.
Abbreviations: SW = *StemWijzer*; KK = *KiesKompas*; WOM = *Wahl-O-Mat*; SV = *smartvote*; DST = *Doe de Stemtest*; VC = *Vote Compass*; VM = *Vote Match*; WK = *Wahlkabine*.

Finally, one in five statements is quantitative (e.g. 'Should the state provide more funding for the integration of foreigners?' – *smartvote* 2011). The issue seems pretty evenly present in most VAAs. There clearly is room for improvement here, across the board. Concerning qualifications, there is a general tendency, throughout all VAAs, not to include examples in VAA statements. Only *Wahlkabine* and *smartvote* incorporate exemplifications significantly more ($\chi^2(8)$=41.86, p<.001), but five of the nine VAA builders never use examples to illustrate the meaning of their statements.

Conclusion and discussion

In this contribution we conducted a large-scale comparison of the content and the formulation of twenty-six Voting Advice Applications in nine countries. We focused on two crucial aspects of VAAs: To what extent do VAAs stay true to the selection and formulation criteria put forward by their builders? And to what extent do they adhere to the rules of survey methodology? Regarding the first research question, the results suggest that all VAA builders tend to include a wide variety of issues in their tools, which made even minor issues receive attention. This is a not-unimportant decision VAA builders make: by including such minor issues instead of merely the hot topics of the day, VAAs put new issues on the agenda, or at least force political actors to pay attention to them. The stated aim of the 'wideness' of the issues covered conflicts with the oft-mentioned aim to include 'relevant' statements, because wideness implies that less-relevant issues get into the VAA.

VAA builders tend to include more socio-economic left–right statements if this dimension is more salient in their country, which is a good thing. However, for the conservative–progressive dimension, this connection was not found. Finally, VAAs feature predominantly prospective issue statements that have a very discriminant nature. Overall, VAA builders do achieve their aims for the most part but definitely not always.

Our analysis of the survey methodology criteria yielded striking results: in particular, the high amount of double-barrelled questions and quantifications in the statements is troubling. The first type of question is universally considered as inadequate, so it is worrisome that they are present in all VAAs under scrutiny. Nevertheless, the practical requirements and specific political context may push VAA builders to include them regardless. However, it should be clear that they should be avoided at all costs. Added to that, numerous statements were coded as being quantitative, making it hard to interpret, and match, the results of parties and voters in a uniform manner. Conversely, the statements included in VAAs seem to be quite specific for the most part, which is undoubtedly a good thing. Besides the fact that too general statements can be misinterpreted, they leave room for manipulation on the side of the political parties. When statements are concrete, it becomes harder for parties to distort their position on the issue.

However, survey methodologists' push for concreteness may actually cause the aforementioned problems of double-barrelledness and quantitative statements:

specific policy positions, for example, include specifics – years by which a policy should be in place, a specific increase in a policy that should be achieved. VAA builders then include all these aspects in one (very concrete) statement, resulting in a double-barrelled and/or quantitative and/or qualified statement. Methodologists might counter-argue that using multiple statements solves this problem; however, the amount of statements is limited. If the VAA takes too long to complete, the public will not use it and it cannot achieve its aim of informing the public about parties' policy positions. There is no doubt that the aim of specificity is crucial, since this is where the main informative potential of VAAs lies; however, there is a fine line between being specific enough and being so specific so that the answer to the statement becomes unclear.

In response to methodological criticisms, some VAA builders (e.g. *StemWijzer*) have indicated that their Voting Advice Application is not designed scientifically and does not serve any scientific goal. The tools are primarily developed to serve educational goals and therefore should not be scrutinised scientifically. Nevertheless, their timing – usually right before an election – their reach – sometimes with millions of users – and their potential effects necessitate rigorous methods. Making sure the statements meet important criteria – especially those of common survey methodology – will only benefit the tool. Good statement-selection and formulation forms the base for any further methodological development when building a VAA, such as the placement of the parties on the selected statements. This aspect of the VAA methodology is discussed in the next chapter.

Appendix 2.1 Overview of sample of VAAs

Design characteristics on the VAA level (per VAA)

	VAA	Country	Year	# statements	# participants	Output	Answer categories	Weighting	# parties
1	*StemWijzer*	Netherlands	2002	30	2,025,284	matchlist	3 point Likert	Thematic	10
2	*StemWijzer*	Netherlands	2003	30	2,227,686	matchlist	3 point Likert	Thematic	10
3	*StemWijzer*	Netherlands	2006	30	4,767,611	matchlist	3 point Likert	Statement	10
4	*StemWijzer*	Netherlands	2010	30	/	matchlist	3 point Likert + skip	Statement	10
5	*StemWijzer*	Netherlands	2012	30	4,850,000	matchlist	3 point Likert + skip	Statement	10
6	*Kieskompas*	Netherlands	2006	36	3,400,000	matchlist + coordinate system	5 point Likert + skip	Thematic	9
7	*Kieskompas*	Netherlands	2010	30	1,500,000	matchlist + coordinate system	5 point Likert + skip	Thematic	10
8	*Kieskompas*	Netherlands	2012	30	1,200,000	matchlist + coordinate system	5 point Likert + skip	Thematic	10
9	*Kieskompas*	Belgium	2007	36	900,000	matchlist + coordinate system	5 point Likert + skip	Thematic	8
10	*Wahl-O-Mat*	Germany	2002	27	>1,000,000	matchlist	3 point Likert + skip	Thematic	6
11	*Wahl-O-Mat*	Germany	2005	30	5,200,000	matchlist	3 point Likert + skip	Statement	7
12	*Wahl-O-Mat*	Germany	2009	38	6,739,667	matchlist	3 point Likert + skip	Statement	6
13	*Smartvote*	Swiss	2007	73	350,000	/	5 point Likert + skip	/	7
14	*Smartvote*	Swiss	2011	75	437,000	matchlist + smartspider	5 point Likert + skip	Statement	8
15	*Doe de Stemtest*	Belgium	2003	36	/	matchlist	3 point Likert + skip	No	7
16	*Doe de Stemtest*	Belgium	2007	36	760,203	matchlist	3 point Likert + skip	Thematic	8

	VAA	Country	Year	# statements	# participants	Output	Answer categories	Weighting	# parties
17	YLE	Finland	2003	18	/	/	4 point Likert + skip	/	12
18	YLE	Finland	2007	29	/	/	4 point Likert + skip	/	12
19	YLE	Finland	2011	33	/	/	4 point Likert + skip	/	10
20	Vote Compass	Canada	2011	30	1,940,000	matchlist + coordinate system	5 point Likert + skip	Thematic	5
21	Vote Compass	USA	2012	30	27,000	matchlist + coordinate system	5 point Likert + skip	Thematic	5
22	Vote Match	UK	2010	30	1,200,000	matchlist	3 point Likert + skip	Thematic	6
23	Wahlkabine	Austria	2002	26	/	/	2 point Likert	/	4
24	Wahlkabine	Austria	2006	26	/	/	2 point Likert	/	6
25	Wahlkabine	Austria	2008	26	850,000	/	2 point Likert	/	7
26	Wahlkabine	Austria	2010	25	/	matchlist	2 point Likert + skip	Statement	9

Appendix 2.2: Codebook

Issues. A list of eighteen possible issues was composed, based on the topics used by the VAA builders themselves. Each of the statements was coded as to whether or not each of the items was present.

Socio-economic left–right divide. Divide based on socio-economic differences between parties, such as divided opinions regarding social security and the role government should play in society. Each statement was coded as to whether or not a reference to this cleavage was present.

Conservative–progressive divide. Divide based on the new cultural left–right divide between conservatives and progressives, focusing on themes such as equal rights, environmental issues, religious themes and the trend towards more globalisation. Each statement was coded as to whether or not a reference to this cleavage was present.

Prospective statements. Statements that look forward to future policy. In order to create a reliable and reproducible measurement of whether or not a statement was labelled prospective, special attention was given to the verbs used in the statements. Four different types of verbs were distinguished: (1) verbs conjugated in the present tense, (2) verbs conjugated in future tenses, (3) the use of the normative tense, and (4) alternative phrases such as 'are you in favour of [...]?' or 'is it alright that [...]?'. Statements from groups 2 and 3 were coded as prospective, and statements from groups 1 and 4 as non-prospective.

Retrospective statements. A statement was considered retrospective when at least one of the following criteria applied: (1) the statement dealt with reintroducing a policy measure that was employed once before in the past, or (2) an evaluation was made concerning present or past policy measures (for example, whether you wish to continue or discontinue the current policy or even want to replace it with an alternative measure).

Concrete versus vague statements. To determine the extent to which statements could be labelled concrete, a classification was designed to categorise statements into 'not at all concrete', 'concrete' or 'very concrete'. Statements that were rather abstract or vague were coded into the first category (e.g. 'the tax system should be reformed'). When the statements described a concrete policy but with few details, it was coded into the second category (e.g. 'a property tax needs to be introduced'). When the statements described a concrete policy measure with an eye for detail, the statement was assigned to the third category (e.g. 'a property tax of 6% needs to be introduced by 2014').

Double-barrelled statements. Statements containing two questions in one, or a policy measure and an argument. Such statements can often be recognised by the word 'and', however this is not a necessary precondition. Each statement was coded as to whether or not it was double-barrelled. A statement was labelled as such if it was formulated in such a way that a respondent was not able to give a straight yes-or-no answer (e.g. he/she agrees with what is said in one part of the sentence, but not with the other part).

Discriminant statements. For each statement, all party positions were collected. They were then reduced to a simple agree–disagree opposition. For this purpose 'skip' and 'neutral' categories (if present) were discarded and the categories 'totally agree' (resp. 'totally disagree') and 'tend to agree' (resp. 'tend to disagree') were collapsed into one category. Finally, a calculation was made of how many parties were in each of the two categories.

Qualifications. Dummy variable that turns one when there is a qualification or example present in the statement. These are indicated by one of the following phrases: 'such as', 'for example', etc.

Quantitative statements. Dummy variable that turns one when a quantitative cue is present in the statement (e.g. 'criminals should be punished more severely').

Appendix 2.3: Origin of data on VAAs and statements

Bundeszentrale für Politische Bildung (2012) *Wahl-O-Mat* Archiv. Online. Available http://www.bpb.de/politik/wahlen/wahl-o-mat/45484/archiv (accessed 23 October 2012).

de Grafaf, J. (12.11.2012) Statements *StemWijzer* 2002 and 2004. Database. Den Haag: Prodemos.

EU Profiler (2009) *EU Profiler*. Online. Available http://www.euprofiler.eu (accessed 22 October 2012).

Finnish Broadcasting Company (YLE) (02.11.2006) Parliamentary Elections 2003. Candidate Responses to YLE Candidate Selector (FSD 1295). In Finnish Social Science Data Archive (FSD). Tampere: FSD.

Finnish Broadcasting Company (YLE) (11.02.2008) Parliamentary Elections 2007. Candidate Responses to YLE Candidate Selector (FSD 2286). In Finnish Social Science Data Archive (FSD). Tampere: FSD.

Finnish Broadcasting Company (YLE) (16.11.2012) Parliamentary Elections 2011. Candidate Responses to YLE Candidate Selector (FSD 2702). In Finnish Social Science Data Archive (FSD). Tampere: FSD.

Finnish Broadcasting Company (YLE) (24.06.2009) European Parliamentary Elections 2009. Candidate Responses to YLE Candidate Selector (FSD 2427). In Finnish Social Science Data Archive (FSD). Tampere: FSD.

Kieskompas (2007) *Kieskompas*. Online. Available http://www.*kieskompas*.be (accessed 22 October 2012).

Kieskompas (2012) *Kieskompas*. Online. Available http://www.*kieskompas*.nl (accessed 22 October 2012).

Politools (2011) *smartvote*. Online. Available http://www.smartvote.ch (accessed 23 October 2012).

Prodemos (2012) Archive StemWijzers. Online. Available http://www.stemwijzer.nl/Archief-StemWijzers (accessed 22 October 2012).

Spiegel.de (2002) *Wahl-O-Mat* 2002. Online. Available http://www.spiegel.de/static/wahlomat (accessed 8 November 2012).

Vote Compass (2012) *Vote Compass* U.S. Presidential Election. Online. Available http://www.votecompass.ca (accessed 8 March 2013).

Vote Match (2012) Votematch. Online. Available http://www.votematch.org.uk/2010 (accessed 6 May 2013).

Wahlkabine (2012) *Wahlkabine*. Online. Available http://www.wahlkabine.at/archiv (accessed 6 May 2013).

Chapter Three

Comparing Methods for Estimating Parties' Positions in Voting Advice Applications

Kostas Gemenis and Carolien van Ham[1]

Introduction

Despite the proliferation of Voting Advice Applications (VAAs), there has been limited interest in researching how the positions of parties (and/or candidates) are estimated in VAAs. This is quite surprising, considering that there are many competing methods for doing so (Laver 2001; Volkens 2007) and that the quest for identifying the most appropriate one in terms of validity and reliability has sparked extensive debates in political science. With some notable exceptions (*see* Gemenis 2013; Krouwel and van Elfrinkhof 2013), this debate has not permeated the VAA research community. This is unfortunate for two reasons. First of all, VAAs have potential consequences for voting behaviour (Ladner *et al.* 2012; Walgrave *et al.* 2008; Wall *et al.* 2012), and hence considering the reliability and validity of party-position estimates used in VAAs is of vital importance to evaluate their quality as voter information tools. Secondly, VAAs generate a wealth of party-position estimates on a variety of policy issues that could be potentially useful in answering questions of interest to political science outside the domain of VAAs (Gemenis 2013; Hansen and Rasmussen 2013; Krouwel *et al.* 2012; Wagner and Ruusuvirta 2012; Wheatley *et al.* 2012).

With this chapter we aim to contribute to the emerging debate by performing a direct comparison of four popular methods used to estimate party positions in VAAs. Specifically, we compare party self-placement, the conventional expert survey, the iterative method between party self-placement and expert coding proposed by *Kieskompas*, and the Delphi method as applied to the use of experts. Using data from the 2012 Dutch parliamentary election, we compare the competing methods in terms of their ease of use, the degree to which they provide estimates that have face validity, and, where appropriate, in terms of inter-coder agreement. Our conclusions have implications for both VAA designers and third-party users of VAA party-position data.

1. We would like to thank Martin Rosema for his invaluable help in designing the empirical study, André Krouwel for providing the party self-placement data, as well as all the colleagues who participated in the expert survey and the Delphi estimation. For the latter, we acknowledge the financial support of the Institute for Innovation and Governance Studies, University of Twente. The usual disclaimer applies.

An overview of the methods compared

Party self-placement

Without a doubt, the most obvious thing to do if one wants to estimate the position of a particular party is to ask the party itself. This is what *StemWijzer* (the Netherlands), *VoteMatch* (UK), and *Wahl-O-Mat* (Germany) do, along with many other candidate-based VAAs such as *smartvote* (Switzerland), *Vaalikone* (Finland), *Manobalsas* (Lithuania) and the VAAs designed by Danish newspapers and internet media. In its simplest form, this method consists of sending a questionnaire to each party (or its candidates) asking them to place themselves on a number of statements and provide a brief justification of this placement. Despite its intuitive appeal, this method has been proven as difficult to replicate in many electoral settings. This is because, while political parties are often willing to reveal their positions on issues that they 'own', they are less likely to reveal their positions on controversial issues which they consider to be non-salient or electorally damaging. Parties have long been resisting attempts by political scientists to survey the attitudes of their cadres and MPs, and continue to do so when confronted with questionnaires sent by VAA designers. It is therefore telling that only 103 out of the 274 (37.6 per cent) parties in the *EU Profiler* agreed to provide their placements on the 30 issue statements provided by the VAA designers (Trechsel and Mair 2011: 15).

Since VAA designers who adopt this method do not necessarily verify, let alone challenge, the positions and justifications provided by parties, we should also consider the possibility that parties may provide strategic responses intended to manipulate the direction of advice given to VAA users. Indeed, there are several instances where parties attempted to manipulate the process of self-placement in order to place themselves in positions that are perceived to be more popular among voters (*see* Krouwel *et al.* 2012: 233; Ramonaitė 2010: 134–137; Wagner and Ruusuvirta 2012: 406). Most often, centrist positions are more popular as VAA users tend to cluster in the middle of distributions in scales consisting of multiple items (as in the case of the two-dimensional political space of *Kieskompas* and the VAAs in this family), or in the middle of response scales in questions which have been framed so as to present a dilemma between two different policies (Baka *et al.* 2012).

Conventional expert surveys

Ever since Castles and Mair (1984) popularised this method in political science, expert surveys have been regularly used to estimate parties' positions, including VAAs such as *Pick-Your-Party* (Ireland), *HelpMeVote* (Greece), and *VoteMatch* (Italy). In its simplest form, an expert survey consists of a questionnaire sent to political scientists asking them to place certain political parties using the provided scales. Conventional expert surveys do not ask experts to justify the given placements. It is assumed that their expertise is enough to produce valid estimates. Budge (2000) argued that expert surveys are problematic inasmuch as different experts might evaluate different aspects of the party, may use different criteria, and different time frames. Steenbergen and Marks (2007) countered this by arguing that errors emanating from such problems tend to 'cancel each other out'. This cancelling out, however, may not necessarily lead to better estimates. As Tilley and Wlezien (2008) have shown, the 'cancelling' of errors by simple mathematical aggregation via some measure of central tendency (mean/median) may lead to implausible party placements near the centre of the scales. Experts are not as sophisticated as expert survey designers usually assume, and should not necessarily know how to place small parties on very specific statements such as the ones typically asked in VAAs. Instead of mathematical aggregation one needs to select and use the responses of the most sophisticated experts for each question posed in the expert survey, something that is impossible to do in conventional expert surveys since we have no means to evaluate experts' expertise.

Even though we cannot evaluate their expertise, we know that experts estimate party positions with much uncertainty, as evident by their disagreement. Steenbergen and Marks (2007: 353–355) and Hooghe *et al.* (2010: 693) showed that expert disagreement seems to be a function of party differentiation, issue salience, internal dissent, party size, and party extremism. Experts are least in agreement when placing smaller parties on very specific issues, especially if the parties in question are not 'owners' of the issues. These findings imply that experts' estimates are reliable in some cases but not in others. Unfortunately, the latter are exactly the cases VAAs often attempt to estimate: very specific issue positions for very small parties. This is why VAAs often use expert surveys intended to capture party positions on more general policy scales (environment, social policy, immigration) than the more specific questions used by the same VAAs to capture voter preferences (Wall *et al.* 2009). If such general scales are used at the party level, it follows that similar scales need to be used to measure users' preferences since the general logic of VAAs is to match voters to parties by using common questions and scales. Asking users to self-place on such general scales, however, might compromise the measurement of their attitudes, as the perception of their content varies considerably among respondents (Evans *et al.* 1996).

Finally, we should note that expert survey estimates of party positions might be biased since a considerable majority of political scientists are known to be leftist or liberal in their own preferences (Mariani and Hewitt 2008). Curini (2010) investigated this hypothesis and found that experts who are unsympathetic towards extreme right and conservative parties would sometimes place such parties (statistically) significantly more to the right compared to experts that are indifferent in terms of sympathy. Therefore, the switch from party self-placement to an expert survey does not necessarily imply an absence of bias. The parties' strategic manipulation of self-placement may be replaced by implicit bias coming from political scientists' own partisan sympathies and levels of expertise.

The Kieskompas method

The pitfalls of party self-placement and expert survey methods have prompted VAA designers to opt for a hybrid method (Krouwel *et al.* 2012). This hybrid method has been used by *Kieskompas* (the Netherlands), and its variants, like *La Boussole Présidentielle* (France), *Aftonbladets Valkompass* (Sweden), *Bússola Eleitoral* (Portugal), as well as the *EU Profiler*. This method can be best described as iteration between party self-placement and party placement by a small team of experts. The VAA questionnaire is sent to parties, who are asked to position themselves on the given statements and provide some factual evidence of their placement, while a small team works concurrently but independently to place parties based on their manifestos and public statements. The two placements are compared to one another and, in cases of disagreement, parties are asked to reconsider their initial placement. After several rounds of iteration between the team and the parties, the percentage of statements in which parties and the coding team agree with regard to the placement rises from 70–80 per cent to around 95 per cent (Krouwel and van Elfrinkhof 2013: 14). In the remaining statements where disagreement between parties and the team persists, despite the iteration over several rounds, the team makes the final decision about how party positions should be coded.

Krouwel and van Elfrinkhof (2013) argue that the *Kieskompas* method is an improvement over previously used methods such as party self-placement and expert surveys, as it combines their strengths in order to counter their weaknesses. The positions provided by parties aim to help the team (of experts) in cases where policy positions are not clearly stated in the publicly available documents, while the positions provided by the team aim to counter-balance the possibility of strategic manipulation by parties. The development of this hybrid method has been particularly welcome in the VAA literature, but it is not entirely unproblematic. For one, the *Kieskompas* method still requires the cooperation of parties. As already noted, however, the majority of parties in Europe are not willing to respond to questionnaires, and some even turn hostile when they realise that the placements they provided can be challenged by VAA designers (*see* Trechsel and Mair 2011: 13–15). Without the full and unfettered cooperation of political parties the *Kieskompas* method cannot work as originally intended.

Secondly, while it has been shown that the iteration between parties and teams of experts leads to a consensus position for the vast majority of the cases, we know little if anything about how the team reaches consensus for their own part of the estimation process. The *Kieskompas* method tries to ensure that the members of the team will be on the same 'page' and minimise inter-coder disagreement, by establishing a 'hierarchy of (document) sources' (Krouwel *et al.* 2012: 227–228). Yet disagreements can emerge as coders might be using the same piece of information but interpret or weight it differently (Bolger and Wright 1992: 61–63). Gemenis (2013: 278–279), for instance, found extensive disagreement among student coders when they were asked to code parties on selected *EU Profiler* statements using their Euromanifestos as the sole piece of information. Trechsel and Mair (2011: 13) mention that such inter-coder disagreements were resolved through discussions among team members and the team leader. This implies that consensus in the team was reached through a process which can be characterised as 'unstructured behavioural aggregation' (Ferrell 1985: 135). Nevertheless, methodologists often advise against the use of such discussions as a mean to achieve consensus (Armstrong 2006), as such processes are known to be affected by the personalities and prestige of those involved in the discussion (Ferrell 1985: 136; Krippendorff 2004: 217).

The Delphi method

The problems with inter-expert/coder agreement in conventional expert surveys and the *Kieskompas* method have prompted VAA researchers to use an alternative method of eliciting and aggregating expert opinion. This approach uses the so-called 'Delphi method', originally developed to forecast technological change (Dalkey and Helmer 1963). This Delphi method has been used to estimate parties' and candidates' positions in VAAs developed by the 'Preference Matcher' consortium starting with *Choose4Greece* (Greece), and continuing with *Xmamkvlevi* (Georgia), *VotulMeu* (Romania) and *Choose4Cyprus* (Cyprus). The Delphi method is an interactive forecasting technique that relies on the judgmental input of a panel of experts through a process of 'structured behavioural aggregation' (Ferrell 1985: 140) characterised by anonymity and controlled feedback. In its simplest form, a 'moderator' selects a panel of experts who work independently of each other, and asks them to provide estimates on parties' policy positions, and justify them by providing a piece of information. Subsequently, the moderator collects the individual estimates and associated pieces of information and feeds them anonymously back to the panel for a new round of estimation. The panellists are then asked to update their initial estimates based on the new information. Once sufficient consensus is reached, the responses are aggregated mathematically (by taking a measure of central tendency) for establishing final estimates.

A considerable body of evidence (for a comprehensive meta-analysis, *see* Rowe and Wright 1999) has shown that the Delphi method gives more accurate estimates compared to mere mathematical aggregation via conventional expert surveys or unstructured behavioural aggregation via unstructured group discussions. Anonymity plays a crucial role as it guarantees that consensus is reached due to the quality of information associated with the estimates and is not affected by the personalities (and biases) of individual panellists. The mechanism is simple: knowledgeable panellists will stick to their original estimates, whereas those with little information will revise their estimates towards the group average (Parenté and Anderson-Parenté 1987). Gemenis (2012a) argues that the Delphi method performed well in eliciting consensus among panellists in *Choose4Greece*, including many 'difficult' cases, after two rounds of iteration. An additional advantage of using the Delphi method is that VAA designers need not rely on the cooperation of political parties, although party self-placement may be solicited and incorporated in the estimation process as an additional piece of feedback information between rounds. The main disadvantage of this method regards its cost. As the panel of experts cannot consist in its entirety of the VAA design team members, external expertise must be solicited. Panellists need to be remunerated for their involvement in the estimation process since the Delphi method is considerably cognitively and time-taking compared to a conventional expert survey.

Data

In order to conduct a fair 'shoot-out' among the four methods, we sought to compare their efficiency using a common set of VAA statements. For practical reasons, we drew six statements from the 2012 Dutch parliamentary election *Kieskompas* as we would be unable to replicate the exact process of estimation (discussions within the *Kieskompas* team and iteration with political parties) should we have chosen statements from another VAA. Our choice of statements (*see* Table 3.2) attempted to reflect the typical differences in policy areas, complexity, and framing strategies found in VAAs. For all statements the response was a five-point scale ranging from 'completely disagree' (1) to 'completely agree' (5) with a 'no response' option. Choosing the Netherlands as the country for comparison ensured the fairness of the shoot-out as the country is known for having high response rates in both conventional expert surveys and requests for party self-placement. For practical reasons associated with time constraints and cost, we chose to survey the eight largest parties from the eleven that are currently represented in *Tweede Kamer*.

The party self-placement data consist of the initial party responses to the request for self-placement made by *Kieskompas*. For the expert survey data we conducted a conventional expert survey by contacting 42 Dutch political scientists specialising in party politics and electoral research through the online Lime Survey platform. In addition to placing the eight parties on the six statements, we asked experts to place the same parties on a ten-point left–right scale. To gauge experts' sympathy towards the parties, we asked them to indicate the degree to which each parties' policies corresponded to their own, using ten-point scales. We received twenty-five valid responses (a 59.2 per cent response rate), more than those received by the Chapel Hill team (Bakker *et al.* 2012) and Benoit and Laver (2006) expert surveys. For the *Kieskompas* method data, we extracted the final estimates from the 2012 Dutch parliamentary election *Kieskompas* website. Finally, for the Delphi method data we solicited the help of a panel of fourteen experts. Since the Delphi method has been designed for use with disparate experts, our panel included four faculty members holding doctorates, four PhD researchers, and six Masters students. The panellists were assigned through a block haphazard procedure to estimate the positions of four parties each, so as to have seven panellists for each party (*see* Appendix 3.1). Estimation took place over two rounds with controlled feedback from one round to another through the use of J. Scott Armstrong's online Delphi platform. The panellists received instructions regarding the Delphi method and the online platform. More specifically, they were asked to refer to the 2012 election manifestos of the parties as much as possible when they were justifying their estimates, although they were also told that they could use other pieces of information or provide a personal justification in case the election manifesto was not helpful enough. After the second round of estimation, the panellists were remunerated for their participation.

Analysis

We begin the analysis with an evaluation of agreement among experts/coders. Since the party self-placement method provides only a single estimate, and since we were unable to fully replicate the unstructured group discussions in a way that would be fair to the *Kieskompas* method, we limit our examination of inter-expert/coder agreement to the expert survey and Delphi methods. To measure agreement, we use van der Eijk's (2001) coefficient A. As van der Eijk (2001: 328) demonstrated, in ordinal rating scales such as the five-, seven- and ten-point response scales used in VAAs and expert surveys, the standard deviation (which is typically used to evaluate expert surveys, e.g. Benoit and Laver 2006: 162–164; Steenbergen and Marks 2007: 353–355; Hooghe *et al.* 2010: 693) is inappropriate as a measure of agreement or consensus because it reflects the skewedness of a distribution in addition to dispersion. Conversely, coefficient A mitigates this problem as it conceptualises agreement as a function of dispersion and deviation from unimodality. Table 3.1 presents the A coefficients for each of the six statements. As can be seen from the figures in the table, agreement among the experts is quite high for both the expert survey and the Delphi method estimation.

The level of perceptual agreement in the first Delphi round is similar to that of the expert survey, although the figures are higher in the Delphi in four out of six statements. The comparison to the second Delphi round, however, is unequivocal. The anonymous iteration with feedback of the Delphi method leads to an even higher agreement among the panellists, higher than any figure observed in the expert survey. The examination of the figures for individual parties confirms this pattern although it also shows that the average figures mask considerable cross-party variation, especially for the expert survey where 17 out of the 48 A coefficients were under 0.7, indicating a high degree of disagreement. For the Delphi, only two A were under 0.7 after the second-round estimation. Both of these were about the placement of the Democraten 66 (D66) party on the two statements about the economy. Most likely, this difficulty in agreeing about the position in these statements, even after the iteration with feedback, can be attributed to the well-established centrist position of D66 in economic issues that can be a source of conflicting messages in its manifesto. In general, the results point to the efficiency of the Delphi method in terms of achieving consensus among experts in comparison to the conventional expert survey.

Of course, reliability, measured in terms of perceptual agreement among experts, may not necessarily lead to valid estimates, as reliability is generally considered to be a necessary but not sufficient condition for validity (Krippendorff 2004: 212–213). Unfortunately, when party positions are concerned, we lack the 'gold standard' benchmark against which estimates from various methods

Table 3.1: Perceptual agreement among experts

Statement	PvdA 1st	PvdA 2nd	VVD 1st	VVD 2nd	CDA 1st	CDA 2nd	PVV 1st	PVV 2nd	CU 1st	CU 2nd	D66 1st	D66 2nd	GL 1st	GL 2nd	SP 1st	SP 2nd	Mean 1st	Mean 2nd
1. Taxes	0.93	1	1	1	0.4	0.79	0.55	0.86	0.22	0.71	0.55	0.48	1	1	1	1	0.71	0.86
2. State/economy	0.86	1	0.86	1	0.71	0.93	0.71	0.93	0.55	0.86	0.57	0.71	0.38	0.93	1	1	0.71	0.92
3. Gay couples	1	1	0.93	1	0.86	0.79	0.93	1	1	1	1	1	0.93	1	0.45	1	0.89	0.97
4. Organ donors	0.53	1	0.93	1	0.31	0.57	0.79	0.79	0.86	1	0.86	0.93	0.93	1	0.92	1	0.77	0.91
5. Euro	1	1	0.93	0.93	1	1	1	1	0.64	0.79	1	1	0.86	1	0.75	0.86	0.9	0.95
6. Burqa	0.75	0.79	0.93	1	0.63	0.7	1	1	0.29	0.86	0.83	1	0.86	0.93	0.42	0.79	0.71	0.88
Mean	0.85	0.97	0.93	0.99	0.65	0.80	0.83	0.93	0.59	0.87	0.80	0.85	0.83	0.98	0.76	0.94	0.78	0.92
1. Taxes	0.84		0.98		0.76		0.48		0.73		0.66		0.86		1		0.79	
2. State/economy	0.86		0.92		0.82		0.5		0.52		0.66		0.78		0.96		0.75	
3. Gay couples	0.79		0.68		0.68		0.65		0.92		0.98		0.94		0.54		0.77	
4. Organ donors	0.71		0.48		0.82		0.63		0.89		0.93		0.75		0.44		0.71	
5. Euro	0.86		0.8		0.76		0.85		0.6		0.96		0.82		0.52		0.77	
6. Burqa	0.73		0.51		0.61		0.98		0.68		0.72		0.72		0.5		0.68	
Mean	0.8		0.73		0.74		0.68		0.72		0.82		0.81		0.66		0.75	
Left-right	0.79		0.74		0.79		0.53		0.73		0.86		0.75		0.72		0.72	

can be compared. This is why the attempts to validate party positions usually involve comparisons among different, yet imperfect, methods, and discussions as to which method positions parties according to well-established intuitions (e.g. Dinas and Gemenis 2010; Krouwel *et al.* 2012; Marks *et al.* 2007). We follow a similar approach. We refrain from summarising the relationship between different methods using statistical measures of association because the nature of the party placements in VAAs cannot be represented accurately through non-parametric measures of association based on rank order.[2] In Table 3.2 we compare the placements of the eight parties on each of the six issues across the four methods. As evident from this table, the four methods generally agree on most placements but there are many disagreements as well. We discuss some of these below with reference to what parties argue in their 2012 election manifestos.

First of all, in line with previous research, agreement appears to be highest for issues that were salient in the campaign, and disagreement appears to be highest for centrist parties, and for parties that do not 'own' an issue, while party size seems to matter less. For example, while the economic crisis was the major issue in the 2012 election campaign, two issues that received quite some media attention were the proposal by the radical right Party for Freedom (PVV) to pull out of the euro and return to the guilder (statement 5) and the discussion about whether or not registrars should be allowed to refuse to marry same-sex couples if they had moral objections to doing so (statement 3). On these two issues, all methods differentiate clearly between parties for and against: in the case of the euro, only the PVV was against remaining in the eurozone, all other parties were in favour; and in the case of gay marriage, only the Christian-democratic (CDA and CU) parties were in favour of allowing registrars to refuse to marry same-sex couples, with all other parties against. In the case of the PVV, the consensus among all the methods can be attributed to its ownership of the euro issue. Another example of the effect of issue ownership on the clarity of party positioning is the position of D66 on automatic organ donation, a proposal put forward by D66 (statement 4).

---

2. More specifically, Spearman's ρ and Kendall's τ_a cannot handle the ties in the dataset (two parties placed in the same position). Kendall's τ_b can handle ties by using a divisor term, but like the aforementioned measures assumes rank ordered data. VAA party-position data are not rankings but continuous variables that are observed as ordinal measures through a process of discretisation (e.g. experts assigning parties to the 'agree', 'disagree', etc. categories). Pearson's polychoric correlation coefficient ρ is not based on rank order and has attractive properties for VAA data as it assumes a continuous latent variable behind the ordered ratings. Its estimation, however, assumes bivariate normality that is clearly not satisfied by the skewed nature of the VAA party-position data. Moreover, the use of correlation coefficients overestimates the degree of concordance between methods of party positioning in the presence of systematic error (Gemenis 2012b: 600--601). Consider the following example: 'Method A' places parties A=1, B=2, C=3, and 'Method B' A=3, B=4, C=5 respectively. In this case, Spearman's ρ, Kendall's τ_b and Pearson's ρ all equal 1 indicating a perfect correlation, as the rank ordering of the parties remains the same. However, the correlations disregard the systematic difference between the two methods. While 'Method A' places party B as 'disagree', 'Method B' places it as 'agree'. Lin's concordance correlation coefficient ρ_c accounts for the presence of systematic error by using a bias correction factor, but assumes continuous data.

Moreover, disagreement between methods appears to be higher for the CU and CDA, and to a lesser extent the radical left Socialist Party (SP) and D66, on issues on which these parties have either a centrist or unclear position. For example, on the issues of increasing tax rates for high incomes, and state involvement in the economy (statements 1 and 2), the CU gets positioned by the different methods on 'disagree', 'agree' as well as 'neither agree nor disagree'. Closer scrutiny of the manifesto shows that the CU takes a rather centrist position on these issues, stating for example that taxes should be proportional to incomes, without directly proposing that taxes for higher incomes should be increased.[3] As another example, on the issue of organ donation the CDA gets four different positions from the different methods, being positioned from 'completely disagree' to 'agree'. In fact, the manifesto states that the CDA wishes to further stimulate organ donation, however there is no mention of an automatic registration system.[4] Moreover, in the run up to the election this was one of the issues of contention at the party members' congress, and hence it is not surprising that there was disagreement among the different methods, given the party's unclear position.

Now, while there is generally rather high agreement between the different methods, some differences do appear. As regards the self-placement of parties, parties appear to position themselves generally in accordance with other methods. However, there are several occasions where parties place themselves as slightly less extreme than the other methods, which might indicate strategic behaviour to appeal more easily to the median voter. There is only one case in which a party places itself opposite to other codings, i.e. the CDA in the case of organ donation. Turning to *Kieskompas*, this method appears to use more dispersed party placements, and, more importantly, never uses the middle category of 'neither agree nor disagree'. Arguably, however, in some cases parties do take a centrist position, such as the position of the CU on the issues mentioned above. The expert surveys seem to have the reverse tendency to *Kieskompas*, i.e. to position parties more often on a centrist position or on less extreme positions. Also, on some issue positions, experts may have been using ideological dimensions of party competition as a heuristic short-cut to position parties, rather than using information from the party manifesto. A clear example of the latter is the issue of the CDA organ donation, where the position of the party was at best unclear, while experts nevertheless placed the party on 'completely disagree'. It seems likely that experts did not actually know the party's position on this issue, but used its conservative position on the liberal–conservative dimension as a cue. Finally, the Delphi method appears to be placing parties in more dispersed positions than party self-placements or the expert survey, and yet uses the middle position more often than *Kieskompas*. Contrary to the other three methods, the Delphi method allows us to check why parties were positioned in a centrist position, or other positions.

---

3. CU election manifesto, *Voor de verandering: 7, Christelijk-sociale hervormingen. Verkiezingsprogramma* 2013–2017, 57.

4. CDA election manifesto, *Iedereen, verkiezingsprogramma* 2012–2017, 55.

Table 3.2: Party positions in the selected statements

	Completely disagree	Disagree	Neither agree nor disagree	Agree	Completely agree
1. Tax rates for the highest incomes should be increased.					
Self-placement	VVD	CDA, PVV, CU, D66		PvdA	SP, GL
Kieskompas	VVD, PVV	CDA, CU, D66			SP, PvdA, GL
Expert survey	VVD	CDA, D66	PVV, CU	PvdA, GL	SP
Delphi method	VVD	CDA, PVV, D66		CU	SP, PvdA, GL
2. The government should intervene more in the economy.					
Self-placement	VVD	PVV, CU, D66	CDA	PvdA, GL, SP	
Kieskompas	VVD, PVV	CDA, CU, D66		PvdA, GL	SP
Expert survey		VVD, PVV, CDA, D66	CU	PvdA, GL	SP
Delphi method	VVD	PVV	CDA, D66	PvdA, GL, CU	SP
3. Registrars should be allowed to refuse to marry gay couples.					
Self-placement	VVD, PvdA, D66, GL	PVV, SP		CDA, CU	
Kieskompas	VVD, PVV, PvdA, D66, GL, SP			CDA	CU
Expert survey	PVV, D66, GL	VVD, PvdA, SP		CDA	CU
Delphi method	VVD, PVV, PvdA, D66, GL, SP				CU, CDA
4. All adults are automatically registered as organ donors, unless they have explicitly declared otherwise.					
Self-placement		VVD, PVV, CU		CDA, SP, GL	PvdA, D66
Kieskompas	PVV	VVD, CDA, CU			PvdA, D66, GL, SP
Expert survey	CDA, CU	VVD, PVV	SP	PvdA, GL	D66
Delphi method	VVD, CU	PVV	CDA		PvdA, D66, GL, SP

	Completely disagree	Disagree	Neither agree nor disagree	Agree	Completely agree
5. The Netherlands should stay part of the Euro.					
Self-placement	PVV			VVD, CU, SP	CDA, PvdA, D66, GL
Kieskompas	PVV	CU		VVD, SP	CDA, PvdA, D66, GL
Expert survey	PVV			VVD, CU, SP	CDA, PvdA, D66, GL
Delphi method	PVV		CU	SP	CDA, PvdA, D66, GL, VVD
6. Wearing a burqa should be prohibited.					
Self-placement		PvdA, D66, GL, CU, SP			VVD, PVV, CDA
Kieskompas		PvdA, D66, GL, CU, SP			VVD, PVV, CDA
Expert survey	D66, GL	PvdA, SP	CDA, CU	VVD	PVV
Delphi method	D66, GL	PvdA	SP	CDA, CU	VVD, PVV

Table 3.3: Polarisation in party positions

	Self-placement	*Kieskompas*	Expert survey	Delphi method
1. Taxes	0.46	0.66	0.41	0.64
2. State/economy	0.4	0.45	0.29	0.35
3. Gay couples	0.34	0.24	0.35	0.5
4. Organ donors	0.44	0.6	0.48	0.51
5. Euro	0.3	0.32	0.3	0.26
6. Burqa	0.53	0.53	0.41	0.55
Mean	0.41	0.46	0.37	0.47

Moreover, experts can use more sources than just the party manifesto, which greatly helps to clarify potential party shifts in position during an electoral campaign.

For instance, in the case of the CDA's position on automatic organ donation the CDA manifesto was unclear about the party's position while its former position as stated on the party website had been removed during the campaign. The panellists indicated (always referring to verifiable sources) that there had been a debate at the party members' congress, as a result of which the party eventually adopted the position to accept a system of automatic donor registration that would, however, give citizens many more chances to opt out than the system originally proposed by D66. This example hints at the efficacy of the Delphi method in estimating parties' positions under uncertainty.

As discussed, a general pattern that emerges from Table 3.2 is that some methods tend to give a more polarised picture of party placements. Since looking directly at 192 (6x8x4) placements makes it difficult to assess this pattern, we summarise the degree of polarisation by using the (1-A)/2 formula, where A is van der Eijk's (2001) coefficient of agreement calculated among the placements of the eight parties on each of the statements. As evident in Table 3.3, the expert survey (followed by party self-placement) is the method that gives a more centripetal picture of Dutch party positions on every statement, with the exception of the statement about the euro where the Delphi method gives a slightly more centripetal picture due to the centrist placement of CU. The *Kieskompas* and the Delphi methods clearly give the most polarised picture compared to the other two methods. Although we have no benchmark to assess which scenario is the more plausible, we nevertheless contend that, for the expert survey, the observed centripetal tendency is related to the uncertainty associated with the estimates. When faced with uncertainty, respondents tend to pick the middle responses as a 'safe' value or as a proxy for 'I don't know' (*see* Baka *et al.* 2012). Alternatively, respondents might pick a less centrist response, but under uncertainty these will cancel each other out and bring the median estimate to the centre of the scale (*see* Tilley and Wlezien 2008). In the case of self-placement by parties, polarisation is somewhat more pronounced. Here, centrist placements are less likely to be associated with uncertainty and either the result of a true centrist position or the product of a strategy intended to give a position that would look appealing to the median voter. For these reasons we contend that the polarised picture presented by the *Kieskompas* and Delphi methods is likely to be more plausible.

Conclusions

We draw several conclusions from the comparison of the four methods in estimating party positions in VAAs. Firstly, we consider that the party self-placement method is impractical in many contexts since party response rates tend to be low. Nevertheless, even when parties do respond to VAA questionnaires, as is the case for the Dutch parties, strategic manipulation remains as a possibility.

Our empirical analysis noted the tendency of this method to portray parties as centrist, at least more so than alternatives such as the *Kieskompas* method. The degree to which these centrist positions can be attributed to strategic placement is not directly verifiable, yet we note that parties have been shown to be able to manipulate the direction of voting recommendations in VAAs by taking carefully calculated combinations of extreme positions (*see* Ramonaitė 2010). Our conclusion is that VAAs should not uncritically rely on party self-placements. Expert surveys transfer the responsibility of party positioning from parties to political scientists. Nevertheless, expert survey estimates of party positions exhibit much uncertainty.

Although the average picture is one of modest to considerable agreement among the experts, prompting researchers to unequivocally label expert surveys as 'reliable' (Hooghe *et al.* 2010; Steenbergen and Marks 2007), a closer examination reveals that agreement varies considerably from issue to issue. Disagreement often leads to centrist estimates, and our comparison with the remaining three methods showed that such estimates may be invalid. Our conclusion is that expert surveys cannot reliably estimate the positions of all parties on all statements in a VAA. The *Kieskompas* method promises to counter the weaknesses of the aforementioned methods by combining their strengths. Our comparison showed that this promise is generally satisfied although two concerns remain. To begin with, the method still requires parties' full cooperation. If parties respond, the aggregation of responses can be structured on the party/team interaction. In cases where parties do not co-operate, however, the estimation on the team side becomes something of a black box. Although there is evidence that team members often disagree with each other as to how parties should be placed, the process of fostering consensus via unstructured team discussions cannot be validated empirically through replication (*see* Krippendorff 2004: 217–219), so claims that 'inter-coder reliability was maximized' (Trechsel and Mair 2011: 13) should be viewed with much caution.

The Delphi method aims to overcome these concerns associated with the *Kieskompas* method. Consistent with previous research (Gemenis 2012a), our application of the Delphi method to the case of the Dutch parties showed that the anonymous iteration with feedback over two rounds increased the consensus among experts to levels considerably higher than those observed in a conventional expert survey. Moreover, our comparison showed that this consensus gave rather plausible estimates of party positions even in several 'difficult' cases. The problems in applying this approach in the VAA context are largely practical (e.g. costs for recruiting panellists, technical problems with the available platforms for Delphi estimation). With these issues practically solved, the next goal is to test the accuracy of the Delphi method in randomised experiments for determining: *a*) the optimal type of feedback (median position and/or justifications versus simple iteration), and *b*) the optimal composition of the panel in terms of size and expertise. Although such questions have been rigorously tested in other contexts (*see* Rowe and Wright 1999; Rowe *et al.* 2005), it is necessary to examine them in the VAA/party positions context. With such issues addressed, we will be in possession of a method that is practical, as well as capable of producing reliable and valid estimates of parties' policy positions.

Appendix 3.1

Panellists: Loes Aaldering, Klaas Derks, Mark Hessels, Rens Hogeling, Elmar Jansen, Joyce Kuipers, Paul Lucardie, Jannine van de Maat, Daphne Van der Pas, Martin Rosema, Mariken Van der Velden, Cynthia Van Vonno, Annemarie Walter, Marc Van der Wardt

Assignment of Delphi panellists to parties

Panellist	PVV	CDA	D66	VVD	GL	PvdA	SP	CU
Faculty member 1	X	X			X	X		
Faculty member 2		X	X			X	X	
Faculty member 3			X	X			X	X
Faculty member 4	X			X	X			X
PhD researcher 1	X			X	X			X
PhD researcher 2	X	X			X	X		
PhD researcher 3		X	X			X	X	
PhD researcher 4		X	X				X	X
Master student/graduate 1	X		X		X		X	
Master student/graduate 2		X		X		X		X
Master student/graduate 3	X		X		X		X	
Master student/graduate 4		X		X		X		X
Master student/graduate 5	X		X		X		X	
Master student/graduate 6		X		X		X		X

Chapter Four

What's Behind a Matching Algorithm? A Critical Assessment of How Voting Advice Applications Produce Voting Recommendations

Fernando Mendez

Voting Advice Applications (VAAs) have enjoyed a growing popularity in recent years, especially in Europe, and are increasingly attracting the attention of political scientists and researchers investigating the impact of new technologies on society and politics. Reflecting this interest, an emergent literature has begun to critically evaluate the promises and possible problems with VAAs (for recent reviews *see* Cedroni and Garzia 2010; Triga *et al.* 2012). This chapter follows this line of inquiry by taking up a core methodological aspect related to the design of VAAs: how are policy preferences aggregated to match respondents with candidates/parties? In other words, this chapter deals with a core function of a VAA – its explicit (or implicit) recommendation. Given the centrality of this VAA function, it is paradoxical how little attention has been paid to matching algorithms by the political science community.

I begin by outlining the two main preference-matching techniques used in VAAs, which are based on low-dimensional and high-dimensional modelling. The aim is to describe some of the theoretical assumptions that underpin this type of matching. The following section then describes the datasets generated by a number of VAA experiences and the methodology I will deploy for testing the performance of various matching algorithms. The next section presents the results of various empirical tests of high-dimensional and low-dimensional models on real-world data. The discussion in the concluding section then relates the analysis back to questions of further VAA design and development.

Theoretical models and assumptions

The idea behind VAAs is to allow citizens to better define their own subjective, political preferences and to match these with the stated (or academically coded) preferences of candidates or political parties that are stored in the online application. To this end, the core output of most VAAs is usually a similarity score between the respondent and the parties/candidates across the 30-odd policy statements typically included in a VAA. In such cases, the VAA's algorithm is performing a match in a high-dimensional policy space – the exact dimensionality being determined by the number of policy items included in the VAA. This is not the only preference match used in VAAs, however. In most VAAs a low-dimensional match based on the spatial positioning of the respondent *vis-à-vis* the parties/candidates is also provided. Although the number of dimensions may vary, the theory underling both types of matches is essentially the same.

Currently, VAAs draw on a social choice theory of democracy (Downs 1957).[1] The respondent is assumed to be an 'issue voter' whose vote choice is based on the range of policy options dominating the campaign, rather than a voter motivated by other considerations, such as their emotional attachment to a party (known as party identification), their subjective evaluation of leaders (i.e. valence considerations), their personal economic gain (sometimes known as economic voting). We know that all these other factors can influence vote choice, however, these are not factored into present VAA design. VAAs are predicated on a rational, programmatic logic of voting, referred to as 'issue-voting'. Furthermore, within the issue-voting model VAAs are mostly based on a proximity model. Such a model draws on a spatial theory of electoral choice whereby a voter chooses the party/candidate whose policy position is most proximate to theirs (Westholm 1997; Tomz and Houweling 2008). Proximity models form the theoretical basis of a VAA and determine the choice of metric for matching VAA respondents to candidates/parties.

High-dimensional models

Most VAA designers adopt a City Block metric in their proximity model for matching in high-dimensional space (e.g. *smartvote* and the *EU Profiler*). There are other metrics even within the proximity model, such as a Euclidean metric. Furthermore, there is also a well-known competing theory of issue-voting: the 'directional model' (which is based on Rabinowitz and Macdonald 1989). In such models the policy dimension is conceptualised rather differently (Westholm 1997; Tomz and Houweling 2008; Lacy and Paolino 2010). Whereas in a proximity model what matters most is the distance between the policy alternatives, in the directional model what matters most is for the voter and candidate/party to be on the 'correct side' of the argument. Indeed, according to directional theories, not only do citizens not tend to distinguish between fine policy gradations but, within certain bounds of acceptability, they also prefer more extreme candidates/parties. It is possible to represent the differences in the metrics or algorithm used in a VAA in matrix form (this builds on Mendez 2012). In principle, at least two different metrics, Euclidean and City Block, can be used for proximity models. For the directional model of issue-voting the Scalar Product metric has been proposed by Rabinowitz and Macdonald (1989).

---

1. It is worth pointing out that alternative high-dimensional matching algorithms have been used based on the logic of recommendation systems. These applications draw on the field of computer science.

Let us begin with a typical matching matrix for a VAA based on City Block logic:

	CA	A	N	D	CD
CA	1	0.5	0	-0.5	-1
A	0.5	1	0.5	0	-0.5
N	0	0.5	1	0.5	0
D	-0.5	0	0.5	1	0.5
CD	-1	-0.5	0	0.5	1

The headings in the columns and rows are based on a five-point Likert scale with the following answer categories: Completely Agree (CA); Agree (A); Neither Agree nor Disagree (N); Disagree (D); Completely Disagree (CD). The numbers in the cells of the matrix represent the points assigned for a 'hit' by the VAA algorithm when a voter (rows) and a candidate (columns) lands in one of the possible cells for each policy statement. The scale ranges from -1 to +1. Excluding the 'no opinion' answer category from the matrix, this results in 25 possible 'matches' between a respondent and candidate. The distances are scaled so that the maximum distance, e.g. a 'completely agree' by a voter and a 'completely disagree' by a candidate, equals -1. A perfect match, e.g. 'completely agree' by both voter and candidate, equals 1. The overall similarity coefficient is calculated by summing the total number of points and dividing by the total number of items. Having presented the City Block matrix and its underlying logic we can now take a look at alternative algorithms for calculating similarity scores.

A Euclidean square model:

	CA	A	N	D	CD
CA	1	0.875	0.5	-0.125	-1
A	0.875	1	0.875	0.5	-0.125
N	0.5	0.875	1	0.875	0.5
D	-0.125	0.5	0.875	1	0.875
CD	-1	-0.125	0.5	0.875	1

A directional model based on a Scalar Product metric:

	CA	A	N	D	CD
CA	1	0.5	0	-0.5	-1
A	0.5	0.25	0	-0.25	-0.5
N	0	0	0	0	0
D	-0.5	-0.25	0	0.25	0.5
CD	-1	-0.5	0	0.5	1

A fourth, Hybrid model is introduced, inspired by directional logic:

	CA	A	N	D	CD
CA	1	0.5	0	-0.5	-1
A	0.5	0.625	0.25	-0.125	-0.5
N	0	0.25	0.5	0.25	0
D	-0.5	-0.125	0.25	0.625	0.5
CD	-1	-0.5	0	0.5	1

The Hybrid model simply splits the difference in the matching scores between the City Block proximity model and the directional model based on the Scalar Product matrices above. A key difference can be seen from the respective scores attached to a match on 'neither agree nor disagree' by a voter (row) and a candidate (column). In the Hybrid model the score of 0.5 is half-way between the Scalar Product score (0 points) and the proximity model (1 point). Indeed, the 0.5 score for a match in the 'neither agree nor disagree' cell captures the intuition that prospective voters/candidates can see both sides of the argument on a given policy issue. A further difference in the Hybrid model is that it aims to capture the intensity of a preference. In short, the Hybrid model conceives the middle category differently whilst also taking intensity of preferences into account.

Low-dimensional models

Low-dimensional modelling can be seen as analogous to a proximity match in high-dimensional space. The logic is the same: a respondent should prefer the closest-matched party/candidate depicted in the spatial maps. The difference relates to the number of dimensions used to calculate a respondent's position in the spatial maps provided by the VAA, which is not determined by the number of VAA policy items but rather by ex-ante assumptions of the dimensionality of the political space. Typically, low-dimensional matching is based on the two dimensions that are widely held to define the issue space in most Western democracies – a cultural dimension involving social liberalism versus social conservativism on the one hand, and an economic dimension related to economic left versus economic right on the other (on political dimensionality, *see* e.g. Kriesi *et al.* 2006; Hooghe *et al.* 2002). Indeed, for some VAA designers, such as the *Kieskompass* team, the low-dimensional map is the core VAA output.

Low-dimensional modelling raises a number of issues in the context of a VAA. The actual calculation of the coordinates is rather straightforward. The policy items of a VAA questionnaire are assigned to a particular scale, say the economic dimension represented by an x axis on a scatter plot, and the item scores are summed. In many cases it will be necessary to reverse the item scores for particular policy statements so that, to use our economic dimension example, higher values always indicate an economic-right orientation. The sum of the item scores is then typically normalised to vary from 0 (for an economic-left orientation) to 1 (indicating an economic-right orientation). The same procedure is followed for the 'cultural dimension' (to use the Kriesi *et al.* terminology). The resulting coordinates are then used to position the respondent and candidates/parties in the spatial maps.

At this point it may be necessary to briefly mention how dimensionality is studied by political scientists and how this relates to VAAs. The matrix in Figure 4.1 depicts the main approaches (De Vries and Marks 2012). In terms of the broader conceptualisation of dimensionality it is possible to focus on the political supply side (i.e. strategic party competition) or the demand side (i.e. mass public opinion). Furthermore, methodologically speaking, dimensions can be deductively identified on the basis of theory and in advance of measurement, or inductively generated from empirical analysis of datasets. The various combinations are represented in the matrix. A type 1 approach can be said to go back to the seminal work by Rokkan and Lipset (1967) on cleavage structures, whereas a type 2 approach also parts from a sociological perspective but would typically be based on extracting dimensions from mass opinion survey data (examples include Sani and Sartori 1983). Alternatively, the focus could be on the political supply side. Type 3 approaches are typically inspired by rational choice theory (Tsebelis and Garrett 2000) and focus on strategic competition among parties, whereas type 4 parts from a similar understanding of strategic competition but would be based on the analysis of, say, roll-call voting data in legislatures or expert surveys of party positions, to extract dimensions of political conflict (e.g. Hix and Crombez 2005; Marks *et al.* 2007).

So, where do VAA designers stand in relation to the matrix? To begin with they are firmly in the type 1 box. That is, they have a-priori theoretical knowledge of the political system and some intuitions as to its dimensionality. Unfortunately, there is typically no consensus on how many dimensions best characterise the political space – a topic of heated debate among political scientists (Benoit and Laver 2012). They do, however, have some type 4 data from the positioning of parties or candidates included in the VAA. The latter can be useful as a check on how the assignment of specific policy items to a scale affects the spatial positioning of parties. The problem here is that there are typically too few parties in a VAA – a

Figure 4.1: The study of dimensionality in political science: A typology

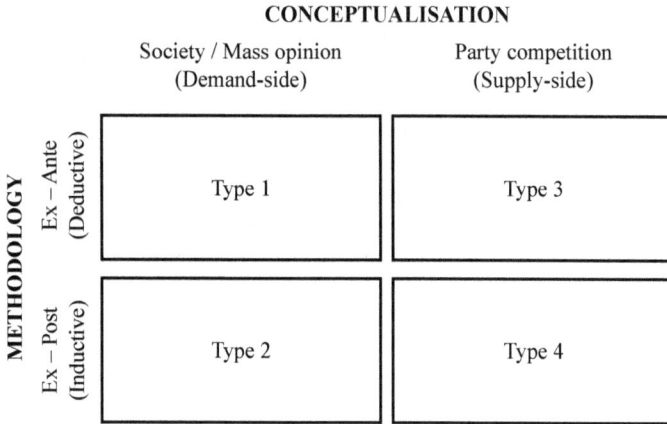

CONCEPTUALISATION

	Society / Mass opinion (Demand-side)	Party competition (Supply-side)
Ex – Ante (Deductive)	Type 1	Type 3
Ex – Post (Inductive)	Type 2	Type 4

METHODOLOGY

dozen at most – to perform rigorous scalability analyses, and most importantly the dimensionality of the supply side, i.e. strategic party competition, need not be identical to that of society at large. Indeed, dimensionality analyses on the supply side typically identify uni-dimensional structures whereas the sociological variants are more likely to uncover two or more dimensions of political conflict (De Vries and Marks 2012).

Ultimately, VAA designers are engaged in a type 1 exercise, which consists of ex-ante (1) identifying the number of dimensions that best capture the political space and (2) assigning policy items from a VAA questionnaire to the respective scale(s). In other words, VAA designers are making a series of conjectures from the vantage point of the type 1 box about what is likely to emerge in the type 2 box. As we shall see in the subsequent sections, it is possible to test such conjectures.

Description of the data and empirical tests

The datasets on which this chapter's analysis is based have all been generated by the Preference Matcher research consortium.[2] Six cases of VAA deployment during the period between October 2010 and February 2013 have been selected. Three of the VAAs were for presidential elections that took place in Brazil (October 2010), Peru (April 2011) and Cyprus (February 2013). The three other cases were for parliamentary elections held in Europe: Scotland (May 2011), Cyprus (May 2011) and Greece (May 2012).

---

2.   For further information on the datasets, *see* http://www.preferencematcher.org/?page_id=18.

My primary empirical goal is to evaluate the relative performance of various high-dimensional models and the validity of low-dimensional modelling. Furthermore, since the theories informing the models are all based on issue-voting, I will base the analysis on issue voters. Specifically, I want to test the performance of various matching techniques in terms of assigning issue voters to their preferred candidates/parties. Creating the dataset of respondents involved three steps. First, cleaning the datasets of rogue entries (*see* Chapter Six by Andreadis in this volume for steps involved). Second, based on pragmatic grounds I only consider candidates/parties that crossed the 5 per cent vote-share threshold.[3] A third, and crucial, step was to identify issue voters with a clearly stated vote intention. This could be done quite easily since all the VAAs included a set of questions on vote intention that were asked before the results were produced. Another question that was asked before the VAA results were displayed was the reason why a respondent would vote for a particular candidate/party. In addition to issue-voting, a range of answer options was included such as party identification, charismatic leadership, perceptions of competence and clientelism. It was thus straightforward to create a binary variable, issue voter or non-issue voter, for each respondent in the dataset. By filtering out 'floating voters' and identifying 'issue voters' it was possible to create a reduced dataset for testing the various matching techniques. In total we are left with a dataset of 79,449 respondents fulfilling these criteria (*see* Appendix 4.1).

High-dimensional matching

We identified four VAA models based on different theories and metrics – two proximity models based on a Euclidean metric and a City Block metric, respectively, and two directional-inspired models based on the Scalar Product metric and a Hybrid metric, respectively. My aim here is to evaluate the predictive performance of each model in terms of matching respondents with their preferred candidate/party. All algorithms assign a coefficient of similarity between the respondent and every candidate/party. It is therefore possible to generate a rank order of candidates/parties for each respondent based on their vote intention. A rank of 1 is assigned if the highest coefficient is for the respondent's chosen candidate/party, a rank of 2 if it is the second-highest coefficient, and so on. Also, if two candidates/parties, including the respondent's preferred one, rank equal-first, we assign a rank of 1.5. If they rank equal-second, we assign a rank of 2.5, and so on.

The empirical test is to see how well the four VAA models can 'correctly' rank respondents' chosen candidate/party. The closer to 1 the mean rank, the better the performance of the VAA algorithm since a score of 1 would mean that the VAA model 'correctly' ranked in first place the candidate/party of all respondents that had the same vote intention. Conversely, the lowest possible score will depend on

---

3.   Marginal parties were not always included in every VAA, given the difficulties involved in coding them on all the policy issues and, furthermore, using a different threshold, say, 4 or 3 per cent, would have resulted in only one extra party being included: the Scottish Green Party – a party which did not compete in the constituency vote for the Scottish elections.

the number of candidates/parties above the 5 per cent threshold in a given electoral contest. Where there are seven parties (as in Greece) the lowest possible score is 7, which would occur if the VAA model ranked a respondent's party choice last, i.e. seventh in the Greek case. A series of additional tests are conducted in order to check whether the results hold under different conditions, including a further test of a more limited number of items derived from a scalability analysis.

Low-dimensional mapping

For testing the validity of low-dimensional modelling I shall draw on the results of the analysis in Wheatley *et al.* (2012) conducted on four of the cases (Brazil 2010, Peru 2011, Scotland 2011 and Cyprus 2011) and the results of Chapter Twelve in this same volume for the two remaining cases (Greece 2012, and Cyprus 2013). The techniques used for identifying latent policy dimensions are the same for all six cases. Essentially, the procedure involves two steps: (1) performing an exploratory factor analysis of the polychoric correlations of the user dataset, and (2) testing the reliability and homogeneity of the scales uncovered through Mokken scale analysis (packages for performing these types of analyses are available in standard statistics programme such as Stata and R). However, what concerns us in this chapter is less the technique used for uncovering scales (the interested reader can consult Chapter Twelve in this volume) than the validity and reliability of ex-ante low-dimensional modelling.

Analysis and results

High-dimensional matching

Let us begin by examining whether the data reveal differences between issue voters and non-issue voters by comparing the rank scores of the two types of respondents when they have expressed the same candidate/party vote intention. Given that a core part of the argument being advanced rests on issue voters it is expected that the overall scores of non-issue voters, i.e. those respondents who base their vote choice on matters of non-programmatic factors, will be less consistent than issue voters. At the party level, much as expected, the average rank generated by the four algorithms for the twenty-six candidates/parties was higher for issue voters than for non-issue voters. *See* Appendix 4.2, where the closer to 1 the average rank was for respondents whose vote intention was for a party/candidate in the rows, the better the score. There were two cases (with the Cypriot party, Diko, and with the Peruvian presidential candidate, Castañeda) where this was not the case. Except for these outlier cases, issue voters were more consistent than non-issue voters in terms of the correspondence between their policy positions and those of their preferred candidate/party. We have reasonable support for the argument that issue voters using VAAs appear to be more consistent. But our main interest here is to compare how well the various algorithms (theories) perform in terms of predicting the vote intention of issue voters.

Table 4.1 reports the average performance of the four models for each of the elections. As with the table in Appendix 4.2, the closer to 1 the final score, the better the predictive performance of the respective algorithm. The table shows that the directional-inspired models (based on the Scalar Product or the Hybrid algorithm) outperformed the proximity models (based on Euclidean or City Block algorithms) in ranking issue voters' preferred candidate/party across all six electoral settings. The Hybrid model came first in three electoral settings and equal-first alongside the Scalar Product algorithm in the remaining elections. In Table 4.2 we report the average rank performance of the four algorithms for non-issue voters. Not surprisingly, the overall scores are worse and in the hypothesised direction (i.e. higher) across all models.

Tables 4.3 and 4.4 present the results of a slightly different test. The aim is to see whether the same results hold if the focus is only on the first ranked party/candidate. Note that we are here concentrating solely on the proportion of first-placed parties/candidates and not assigning further points to other ranks. Thus, the higher the percentage, the better the predictive power of the algorithm. The table presents the average for each of the four models across the six country settings. Again, we find that the Hybrid model performed best across all settings.

In Tables 4.5 and 4.6 the results are based on a reduced set of times derived from Mokken scaling analysis (*see* Chapter Twelve in this volume and Wheatley 2012) that, in effect, reduces the dimensionality of the political space. The dimensionality thus changes from the original 3 vector space to one defined by the total number of items extracted from the Mokken scale analysis. This varies from 9 items for Peru; 12 items for Brazil; 14 items for Scotland; 15 items for the Cyprus presidential elections; 17 items for the Cyprus parliamentary elections; and 20 items for Greece. Using this reduced set of policy items and thereby excluding non-scalable items, we find the results to be largely consistent with those reported based on the broader 30 policy items. Table 4.5 focuses on the average of the rank order performance where we find that the Hybrid model performs best in four out of the six elections, and second to the Scalar Product in the two remaining settings. A similar picture emerges with regard to issue voters correctly assigning first place to their preferred party/candidate in Table 4.6. Again, we find that the Hybrid algorithm outperforms the other models.

One objection that could be made relates to the sensitivity of any high-dimensional match to the accurate coding of parties/candidates on each policy item. It is possible, of course, that the placement of parties may not reflect their 'real' position. This is certainly not the case for two of the presidential election cases (Cyprus and Peru) where the coding reflected the stated positions of the candidates. We also find that for these two cases the directional-inspired models perform better. Indeed, across the range of tests the directional-inspired algorithms (especially the Hybrid) appear to perform better in terms of their accuracy in assigning respondents to their preferred party/candidate. Crucially, this is the case for the important subset of respondents that are at the core of our analysis: issue voters.

Table 4.1: Issue voters' overall scores for each election

Country	Euclid	City Block	Scalar	Hybrid	Best performer
Brazil	1.63	1.64	1.61	1.61	Scalar/Hybrid
Cyprus 2011	1.74	1.75	1.76	1.69	Hybrid
Greece	2.03	2.03	2.03	1.99	Hybrid
Peru	2.39	2.39	2.31	2.31	Scalar/Hybrid
Scotland	1.64	1.64	1.63	1.59	Hybrid
Cyprus 2013	1.33	1.32	1.27	1.29	Scalar

Table 4.2: Non-issue voters' overall scores for each election

Country	Euclid	City Block	Scalar	Hybrid	Best performer
Brazil	1.72	1.72	1.68	1.69	Scalar
Cyprus 2011	2.04	2.03	1.94	1.93	Hybrid
Greece	2.48	2.48	2.39	2.42	Scalar
Peru	2.5	2.5	2.4	2.44	Scalar
Scotland	1.86	1.87	1.83	1.79	Hybrid
Cyprus 2013	1.48	1.47	1.42	1.44	Scalar

Table 4.3: Issue voters correctly ranking first place for each election

Country	Euclid	City Block	Scalar	Hybrid	Best performer
Brazil	53.1	50	49.6	53.8	Hybrid
Cyprus 2011	50.6	49.6	50.8	53.3	Hybrid
Greece	47.2	46.6	47.2	49.5	Hybrid
Peru	37.2	37.1	35.8	39.2	Hybrid
Scotland	58.4	57.4	59.9	62	Hybrid
Cyprus 2013	74.7	74.7	78.8	77.4	Scalar

Table 4.4: Non-issue voters correctly ranking first place for each election

Country	Euclid	City Block	Scalar	Hybrid	Best performer
Brazil	48.6	44.6	46.2	49.1	Hybrid
Cyprus 2011	36.9	37	44.5	43	Scalar
Greece	36.2	35.1	37.4	38.2	Hybrid
Peru	34.5	33.9	33.9	35.2	Hybrid
Scotland	47.3	47.1	47.1	52.1	Hybrid
Cyprus 2013	63.1	62.9	62.9	66	Scalar

Table 4.5: Issue voters' overall scores for each election (Mokken items)

Country	Euclid	City Block	Scalar	Hybrid	Best performer
Brazil	1.743	1.716	1.694	1.691	Hybrid
Cyprus 2011	1.707	1.711	1.789	1.678	Hybrid
Greece	2.023	2.02	2.032	1.995	Hybrid
Peru	2.596	2.575	2.489	2.544	Scalar
Scotland	1.623	1.631	1.643	1.595	Hybrid
Cyprus 2013	1.42	1.4	1.34	1.37	Scalar

Table 4.6: Non-issue voters' overall scores for each election (Mokken items)

Country	Euclid	City Block	Scalar	Hybrid	Best performer
Brazil	45.5	46.7	44.6	49.3	Hybrid
Cyprus 2011	50.5	47.2	48.8	54	Hybrid
Greece	47.6	46.5	47	49.8	Hybrid
Peru	31.5	29.7	30.6	32.8	Hybrid
Scotland	58.8	57.5	59.2	62.1	Hybrid
Cyprus 2013	66.7	66.4	71.2	69.2	Scalar

Low-dimensional mapping

For our low-dimensional modelling let us recall the distinction between a deductive method whereby policy items are assigned to dimensions ex-ante (type 1 in Figure 4.1) and an inductive method which involves analysing VAA-generated datasets (type 2). My focus in this section is whether the ex-ante conjectures about dimensionality and item scalability are corroborated by the empirical analysis of the datasets generated.

At least three common problems could arise when evaluating the performance of ex-ante derived scales against the results of an empirical analysis of the datasets generated: 1) including a scale that is not revealed by the data, or missing a scale altogether; 2) including ambiguous policy items that load on more than one scale; 3) the assignment of non-scaleable policy items to a particular scale. I would submit that, in the absence of a rigorous pretest, problems 2 and 3 are unavoidable. Since most VAAs are deployed in this way, most VAAs will suffer from problems regarding the scalability of policy items used in low-dimensional mapping. The dangers of problem 1 can be mitigated given that VAA designers are typically aware of the dimensionality of the political space – though this must be countered by the fact that there is no consensus on this point. Word constraints do not allow us to go into all the details, but it can be confirmed that all these problems afflicted low-dimensional matching in the six VAAs considered in this chapter.

Possibly the most serious violation is the ex-ante inclusion of a scale not confirmed by subsequent data analysis. This occurred in the case of the landmark

Greek elections of May 2012, which took place at the height of the eurozone financial crisis. The VAA designers, myself included, decided to incorporate a scale related to the financial crisis, specifically a pro-EU bailout versus anti-EU bailout scale on the y axis as well as the traditional left versus right on the x axis. There were compelling reasons for doing this such as the fact that this was the issue dominating the elections and, crucially, the fact that it was possible to scale the parties on these two dimensions. Furthermore, since our scale could be thought of as pro- versus anti-EU sentiment we could – theoretically speaking – draw on a Hix/Lord model of the dimensionality of the European political space, which is predicated on precisely these two dimensions. Our intuitions were not confirmed by the user data, however. The bailout and EU issues all loaded onto a left–right scale while we missed the cultural dimension (social conservative versus social liberal), which did emerge from the analysis (*see* Table 12.3 in Chapter Twelve). Another example where this occurred was in the Scottish VAA. Here, rather than misspecifying a dimension we omitted one altogether. Our ex-ante assignment was based on a two-dimensional understanding: an economic left–right and a cultural dimension. However, data analysis revealed a third rather obvious (with the benefit of hindsight) dimension: a regional autonomy dimension (*see* Table 12.2 in Chapter Twelve).

Another common problem relates to ambiguous items. An example is the issue of scrapping the Trident missile system, which was a policy statement used in the Scottish parliamentary VAA. This item loaded both on the economic dimension (i.e. cost-cutting in the financial crisis) as well as the regional autonomy dimension (i.e. Trident could be perceived as an imposition from Westminster). Where an item taps two distinct latent traits it should be excluded from a scale. The most common problem, however, is the inclusion of unscalable items in a scale. Even the most deductively compelling and carefully worded statement can fail to load on the prescribed dimension. Again, this can only be known a posteriori. Furthermore, both problems are not exclusive to the cases used for illustration purposes in this chapter. Scalability problems are known to have afflicted the *EU Profiler* (Louwerse and Otjes 2012; Gemenis 2013).

To illustrate the effects of validating the dimensionality of the political space I shall use the most recently deployed VAA of the six cases: the presidential elections of Cyprus in 2013. There is nothing particularly special about the case, indeed it could be considered as one of the most accurate ex-ante conjectures among the six. Our preassigned dimensions – an economic dimension (left versus right) on the x axis and a cultural dimension (liberal versus conservative) on the y axis – were confirmed in the empirical analysis of the user-generated datasets. Where we found differences between our deductive item assignment and the results of our scaling analysis was in relation to the inclusion of seven items on the economic dimension and three items on the cultural dimension which were not scalable. What is quite striking here is the effect of the omission of the three unscalable items on the cultural dimension rather than the seven items related to the economic dimension. This effect can be seen in Figure 4.2. The dots represent the scores

Figure 4.2: Ex-ante positioning of candidates vs. ex-post validated scales

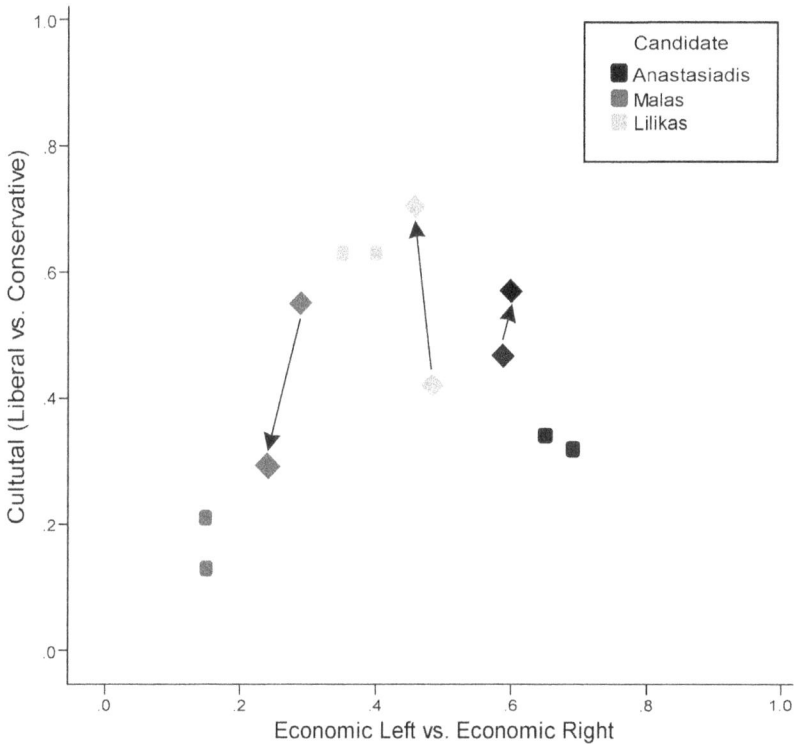

See http://press.ecpr.eu/resources.asp for full colour figures.

of the candidates based on their expressed policy preferences. As one can see, there is little movement between the ex-ante positioning of candidates and their position resulting from the ex-post validated scales based on Mokken analysis. The candidate Malas acquires a more socially liberal position whereas Lilikas is slightly more economically right, and there is little change in the position of Anastasiadis.

A very different picture emerges with regard to the respondents, however. The rhomboids represent the mean position of respondents whose vote intention is for one of the three candidates and who claim to be voting for their preferred candidate based on the latter's policy positions (i.e. for programmatic reasons). What can be clearly seen is the effect of applying a more rigorous scaling analysis. In particular, those intending to vote for Malas and Lilikas are significantly repositioned closer to their preferred candidate. The direction of the arrow represents the change from ex-ante assigned scales to Mokken-based scales (with the arrow head pointing to the Mokken-scaled position). What this illustrates is that inclusion of even a few unscalable items can have quite a significant effect on a respondent's placement in low-dimensional space.

Conclusion

This chapter has reviewed the two main techniques for matching the policy preferences of respondents with candidates or parties typically used in VAAs. I have referred to these as high-dimensional models (matching based on all VAA policy items) and those following as low-dimensional modelling (based on ex-ante assumptions about political dimensionality). We set out the theoretical assumptions guiding these various matching techniques, which in the main draw on the proximity logic of voting models.

Firstly, in terms of high-dimensional matching we examined the theoretical basis of various issue-voting models and the competing metrics that they give rise to: a proximity model based on a City Block metric (the most common method) or a Euclidean distance, and a directional model based on a Scalar Product metric. We also introduced a so-called Hybrid model that takes into account both the 'side of the argument' and the 'intensity' of preferences on a given policy statement. The basic claim made is that the directional-inspired models performed better than proximity-based algorithms. Directional theory points to two factors: being on the 'correct side of the argument' and the intensity of preferences; that could be important for a VAA design, especially when based on a five-point Likert scale that includes a middle category. Secondly, in relation to low-dimensional models, it was shown how ex-ante assignments of political dimensionality are susceptible to a number of problems such as: the misspecification of dimensions, the inclusion of ambiguous items in a scale and the inclusion of non-scalable items in a scale. The last two are almost by definition impossible to avoid for VAA designers in the absence of a pretest. Furthermore, in the example I used for illustration, the improvement in spatial placement after scale validation was non-trivial.

Evidently, these results are based on but one of a variety of tests that could be used to potentially adjudicate between competing matching techniques. Many other tests will no doubt be performed on the datasets produced by VAAs. What is likely to emerge from the resulting research is that there is no single best way to aggregate policy preferences to produce a voting recommendation. Much will depend on institutional factors, such as the type of electoral system, the structure of political competition, the number of effective parties included in a VAA, and the coding of parties, as well as design issues concerning the type of answer scales used and how middle categories and 'no opinions' are treated. Many of these issues have been beyond the scope of this chapter but further research by the scholarly community is likely to be conducted in this direction. The choice of algorithm is not a neutral affair and low-dimensional modelling, in the absence of real-time validation (say, on a group of early users), is especially prone to error. At a minimum, greater efforts to 'qualify' VAA results to the public should be considered by designers.

Appendix 4.1

Number of users that expressed a vote intention for one of the candidates/parties that crossed the 5 per cent vote-share threshold

Country	Party/candidate	Type of voter	Number of respondents
Brazil	Dilma	Issue	1,374
		Non-issue	2,228
	Serra	Issue	1,052
		Non-issue	2,858
	Marina	Issue	2,285
		Non-issue	2,238
Cyprus	Akel	Issue	678
		Non-issue	243
	Dissy	Issue	595
		Non-issue	686
	Diko	Issue	173
		Non-issue	144
	Edek	Issue	149
		Non-issue	114
Greece	Pasok	Issue	405
		Non-issue	1,262
	New Democracy	Issue	658
		Non-issue	1,050
	KKE	Issue	937
		Non-issue	1,197
	Syriza	Issue	3,133
		Non-issue	2,506
	Dimar	Issue	1,067
		Non-issue	1,469
	Ind. Greeks	Issue	1,591
		Non-issue	1,978
	Golden Dawn	Issue	452
		Non-issue	1,559
Peru	Toledo	Issue	1,774
		Non-issue	3,817
	Fujimori	Issue	492
		Non-issue	993
	Castañeda	Issue	347

Country	Party/candidate	Type of voter	Number of respondents
		Non-issue	1471
	Kuczynski	Issue	6,029
		Non-issue	13,506
	Humala	Issue	1,262
		Non-issue	1,105
Scotland	SNP	Issue	1,234
		Non-issue	2,694
	Labour	Issue	964
		Non-issue	1,119
	Tory	Issue	481
		Non-issue	391
	Libdem	Issue	560
		Non-issue	343
Cyprus 2013	Anastasiadis	Issue	423
		Non-issue	3,199
	Malas	Issue	293
		Non-issue	1,066
	Lilikas	Issue	651
		Non-issue	1,154
Total number of respondents			79,449

Appendix 4.2

Average rank performance of issue voters versus non-issue voters across algorithms

Country	Party/candidate	Type of voter	Euclid	City Block	Scalar Product	Hybrid
Brazil	Dilma	Issue	1.2	1.33	1.77	1.46
		Non-issue	1.31	1.45	1.88	1.59
	Serra	Issue	1.61	1.69	1.69	1.66
		Non-issue	1.66	1.72	1.74	1.68
	Marina	Issue	2.09	1.9	1.37	1.71
		Non-issue	2.19	2	1.42	1.8
Cyprus	Akel	Issue	1.4	1.37	1.03	1.15
		Non-issue	2.22	2.1	1.16	1.64
	Dissy	Issue	2.7	2.6	1.83	2.36
		Non-issue	2.82	2.74	2.05	2.55

Country	Party/candidate	Type of voter	Euclid	City Block	Scalar Product	Hybrid
Greece	Diko	Issue	1.56	1.7	2.42	1.84
		Non-issue	1.58	1.68	2.54	1.89
	Edek	Issue	1.32	1.34	1.78	1.41
		Non-issue	1.55	1.58	2.01	1.64
	Pasok	Issue	1.73	1.73	1.73	1.69
		Non-issue	2.07	2.05	2.1	2.03
	New Democracy	Issue	1.88	1.94	2.08	2
		Non-issue	2.19	2.19	2.45	2.3
	KKE	Issue	2.16	2.04	1.74	1.86
		Non-issue	3.27	3.12	2.36	2.74
	Syriza	Issue	2.62	2.56	1.71	2.2
		Non-issue	3.32	3.28	2.16	2.86
	Dimar	Issue	1.83	1.88	2.32	1.97
		Non-issue	2.12	2.19	2.66	2.29
	Ind. Greeks	Issue	1.87	2.01	2.52	2.19
		Non-issue	2.01	2.17	2.67	2.37
	Golden Dawn	Issue	2.14	2.07	2.1	2.06
		Non-issue	2.39	2.35	2.3	2.33
Peru	Toledo	Issue	1.73	1.93	2.62	2.01
		Non-issue	1.84	2.01	2.76	2.1
	Fujimori	Issue	2.05	1.77	2.33	1.84
		Non-issue	2.12	1.87	2.4	1.94
	Castañeda	Issue	2.62	3	3.55	3.31
		Non-issue	2.62	3.01	3.5	3.27
	Kuczynski	Issue	4.14	3.88	1.67	3.14
		Non-issue	4.38	4.15	1.82	3.48
	Humala	Issue	1.43	1.36	1.41	1.3
		Non-issue	1.53	1.45	1.52	1.39
Scotland	SNP	Issue	1.66	1.6	1.4	1.48
		Non-issue	1.99	1.93	1.67	1.8
	Labour	Issue	1.89	1.92	2.24	2.05
		Non-issue	1.96	1.99	2.39	2.13
	Conservative	Issue	1.77	1.73	1.15	1.39
		Non-issue	2.19	2.12	1.29	1.66
	LibDem	Issue	1.23	1.31	1.76	1.45
		Non-issue	1.29	1.43	1.98	1.59

Country	Party/candidate	Type of voter	Euclid	City Block	Scalar Product	Hybrid
Cyprus 2013	Anastasiadis	Issue	1.74	1.68	1.43	1.59
		Non-issue	1.87	1.78	1.54	1.7
	Malas	Issue	1.18	1.19	1.09	1.14
		Non-issue	1.41	1.43	1.23	1.37
	Lilikas	Issue	1.06	1.09	1.28	1.13
		Non-issue	1.15	1.19	1.48	1.26

Chapter Five

Voting Advice Applications as Campaign Actors: Mapping VAAs' Interactions with Parties, Media and Voters

André Krouwel, Thomas Vitiello and Matthew Wall

While mass media remain essential channels of political communication within contemporary societies, over the last two decades the landscape of political communication has become more diverse, fragmented, and complex – with the most notable change being the advent of the internet. In this 'post-modern' campaign environment (Norris 2000), a multitude of non-party actors use the web to voice their policy positions to the electorate, and VAAs are one such non-party campaign actor (Farrell and Schmitt-Beck 2008).

As tools that are designed to assist citizens in taming the flood of political information that they encounter during campaigns, VAAs are located at the intersection of the communication flows between citizens, parties and media. For the users of such websites, VAAs 'belong to the media repertoire individuals have at their disposal in order to gather information about politics, parties and policies' (Garzia and Marschall 2012: 216). From the perspective of both politicians and journalists, VAAs are frequently seen as a campaign actor that can influence the opinions of voters (Walgrave *et al.* 2008).

In this chapter, we contribute to the growing literature on VAAs by exploring the nature of their relationships with the traditional key actors in political campaigns: parties, voters, and mass media. As we outline in the next section, we seek to establish not just how VAAs influence these actors, but also how these actors influence VAAs. We support our conceptual discussion with a descriptive analysis of two new datasets: the first is based on a content analysis of 51 VAA sites, and the second is based on responses to a survey of VAA practitioners (including several of our co-authors in this volume); out of 28 VAA teams contacted, a total of 15 responded to this survey.

Theoretical framework: A model of VAAs' interaction during electoral campaigns

In this chapter, we examine VAAs' relationships with parties, citizens and media. The chapter is thus informed by extant research regarding how these actors interact during political campaigns. For instance, several studies have noted that the attempts of political parties to set the agenda and to frame issues is filtered through media coverage, while, conversely, it has also been observed that media coverage of politics can be driven by the communication strategies of parties (Asp 1983; Brandenburg 2002; Hopmann *et al.* 2012; Walgrave and van Aelst 2006). Other analyses have focused on the fact that media play a crucial role in increasing public awareness of issues and/or contributing to public issue perceptions of how issues should be understood (McCombs and Shaw 1972; Scheufele and Tewksbury 2007). Political parties and the media play a particularly essential role in informing the public on issues that are technically complex (Popkin 1994; Page and Shapiro 1992).

The interaction between public opinion and party behaviour is another major theme within political science (Hellström 2008). Empirical evidence demonstrates that two types of linkages simultaneously exist between the public and parties: a top-down linkage in which public opinion is receptive to the policy ideas of political parties, and a bottom-up linkage whereby parties adjust their policies to public opinion (Wlezien 1995; Stimson 2004).

All of the above discussed research points to the existence of important and dynamic relationships between media, parties and voters. It also appears that, while they may often be somewhat unbalanced, such relationships are not unidirectional. We argue in this chapter that VAA projects can be conceived in this manner, and that VAAs vary in terms of the depth and reciprocity of their relationships with all three of these actors. The existence and reciprocity of these relationships are visualised in Figure 5.1.

We argue that VAAs have a direct effect on parties because the content analysis of the platforms that is performed in order to develop a VAA site may reveal ambiguous or vague propositions in parties' policy stance, 'forcing' the political parties to clarify their positions. However, this relationship can be reciprocal to varying degrees – some VAA projects involve parties in the design stage, while most depend on some form of party cooperation to maximise data quality when measuring party positions.

VAAs have been found to influence both participation and vote choice among site users, albeit with major variation across studies in the extent of influence observed. We focus here on the question of reciprocity in the VAA–voter relationship, arguing that VAA projects depend on users to both promote the site and to enter high-quality data. Finally, we note that VAAs can exert an 'effect' on media coverage of a political campaign (by making new information on parties and voters available to media outlets). However, VAA producers are typically more dependent on mass media to boost user numbers than mass media are dependent on VAAs to produce data, and we discuss the various media strategies adopted by VAA designers.

Figure 5.1: Dimensions of interaction between VAAs and actors of political communication: 1. the party dimension, 2. the voter dimension, 3. the media dimension

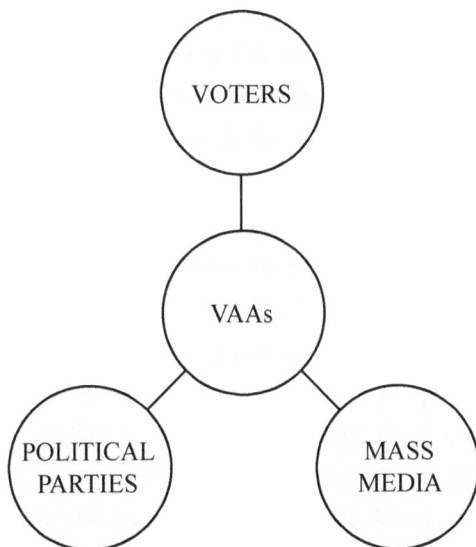

The Party Dimension: On the inclusion of parties and the resolution of conflicts of interest and opinion

Since the main purpose of VAA websites is to help voters pick the party or candidate that is closest to their own political preferences, VAA developers need information from parties on their issue stances. Table 5.1 reports the results of our survey of VAA practitioners regarding patterns of VAA–party interactions.

A first striking trend revealed in Table 5.1 is that communication with parties at some point in the VAA development process is the dominant norm, with 12 out of 15 respondents indicating that they did so. This engagement may begin early in the site's development, during the issue selection and statement development stages (Krouwel *et al.* 2012). We can see from Table 5.1 that this is the case with 7 of the 12 individuals who responded to this question. The Dutch VAA *Stemwijzer* is an example of a VAA team that engages in this practice (*see* Schuszler *et al.* 2003: 195). In other cases, contact with parties is only established after the issue statements have been formulated (as in the *Kieskompas* VAA methodology; *see* Krouwel *et al.* 2012). We can see from Table 5.2, however, that party policy platforms are the most common source for the development of issue statement lists – so the parties can exert an indirect influence over the development of VAA statements by emphasising issues in their platforms.

Table 5.1: Communication of the VAA team with parties/candidates during the development of the VAA

VAA teams contacted parties/candidates:	Yes	No
At any time during the development	12	3
In order to obtain their political manifestos	7	5
At the stage of issue selection and statement formulation	5	7
At the stage of their calibration on the issue statements	9	2

Table 5.2: Sources used by VAA teams for developing issue statements (note: several developers reported using multiple sources)

Party platforms	13
Experts/journalists	12
Journalists	7
Newspaper content analysis	9
Parliamentary debate content	7
Other	8

Table 5.3: Information used by the VAA team to position the parties/candidates on the issue statements of the application

Only self-placement of the parties/candidates	5
Only expert coding	1
Both self-placement of the parties/candidates and expert coding	9
Total	15

Table 5.4: Management of discrepancies between expert and party issue placements

VAA teams that used text sections from the political manifestos to justify the position of the parties/candidates on the issue statements	9
VAA teams that checked for discrepancies between the self-placement of parties/candidates and the content of their political manifestos	8
VAA teams that settled discrepancies by:	
Discussing them only within the academic team of the application	7
Discussing them with the parties/candidates	2
VAA teams that pointed to sections of political manifestos in discussing discrepancies	4
VAA teams that reached full agreement with all parties/candidates	7

Since the selection and framing of the statements included in a VAA is crucial for its quality and influential for the 'advice' given (*see* van Camp *et al.* in this volume), the methodology by which statements are developed and selected matters greatly. Moreover, as parties have a vested interest in putting certain issues on the agenda, while keeping others off the table, providing parties influence at this stage opens avenues for strategic and manipulative behaviour by party leaders and campaign managers (Praag 2007: 6–8).

Parties can be resistant to exclusion from the statement formulation stage of the process: some will request that they should be allowed to reformulate or delete certain questions, while others (usually small or new parties) may not even have issue positions on all the issues that VAA developers ask them to place themselves. The question format also triggers different responses from parties, as some VAAs frame questions in a binary yes/no format, while others use five-point Likert items.

Another important moment of VAA–party interaction is the measurement of parties' positions on the selected issues. Table 5.2 looks at the findings of our survey regarding the sources used to measure party position. Again, we find a norm of some form of VAA–party communication and interaction, with only one respondent using expert coding with no party input. Our content analysis of 51 websites revealed that half of the VAAs (26 out of 51) explicitly mention that they asked parties for a self-placement. Of course, parties differ in their response to such requests for collaboration and some refuse to respond, while others allow members of their campaign team who provide the answers. Depending on political culture and party type, VAA developers must decide who to contact within the party organisation.

Naturally, some parties attempt to manipulate their issue placements on VAAs in order to optimise their chances of being recommended to site users. The best documented case of a successful manipulation is the 2006 version of the Dutch *Stemwijzer* VAA. A Dutch Christian Democratic Party (CDA) spin-doctor decided not to give the party's issue positions according to the official manifesto, but choose to instead provide the answer that was most likely to be popular in order to boost the likelihood of winning more vote advices (Praag ibid.: 11). These events triggered a robust debate on the quality and methodology of VAAs in the Netherlands (De Groot 2002; 2003; 2004), illustrating the importance of managing VAA–party interactions for practitioners.

VAA developers differ in their methodological approach to extracting issue positions from parties or candidates and thus vary in their level of interaction with party elites (*see* Gemenis and van Ham in this volume). Some developers simply use publicly available sources, such as party platforms or websites, without having actual contact with the party leadership. Other VAAs interact more closely with parties. This is particularly the case for those developers who seek to combine party self-placement with expert coding. For instance, *Kieskompas* combines party auto-positioning with coder calibrations; when these sources clash, *Kieskompas* does not automatically accept the self-placements of parties, but enters into an extensive interaction with parties in order to clarify the party's position (*see* Krouwel and Elfrinkhof 2013).

Since there are many methodologies to determine the ideological or policy positions adopted by parties or candidates (Benoit and Laver 2006: 123–153; Gemenis 2013), having a baseline 'reality check' of parties' auto-positioning against official party documentation is a useful bulwark against error (Krouwel *et al.* 2012). We can see in Table 5.3 that the most prevalent approach (9 out 15 respondents) to coding party positions involves a combination of self-placement and expert coding.

Table 5.4 describes how developers using both expert coding and party self-placement have managed their relationships with the parties that they seek to locate when the experts and the party disagree about a placement. This process can impact on parties: in cases where the party and coding team disagree, the confrontation of parties with texts that were found by the coders can lock parties into a substantive policy debate which can serve to clarify issue stances. However, only two practitioners report engaging in such discussions in Table 5.4.

Oftentimes, party leaders, campaign staff and spin-doctors are unhappy that VAA developers do not automatically accept their auto-positioning. Party representatives have argued that VAAs reduce the complexity and multidimensionality of their stances too much, and thus blur their policy positions instead of clarifying them. Yet, overall, the interaction is constructive, levels of initial agreement are high (with 7 out of 9 respondents in Table 5.4 reporting that they were able to reach full agreement with all parties/candidates) and most discrepancies can be resolved quickly.

In conclusion, VAA developers can influence the behaviour of parties substantially in that they require them to clarify their policy positions. In some cases, VAA development has actually widened the scope of issues on which parties take a position. Parties have also learned to cope with VAAs and have sometimes seized the opportunity for propaganda or sheer manipulation. Through issue selection and question framing, VAA developers may impact on how parties are able to communicate their stances, which is sometimes perceived by the parties as manipulation of the public debate by VAA makers.

In countries where VAAs draw large numbers of users, party campaigns have adapted to them. The output provided by VAAs may alter the public perception of certain parties, especially if some of their policy positions were previously unclear. New and smaller parties – often neglected in the public debate – are usually very eager to participate, as VAAs provides them with an opportunity to reach voters and be seen on an equal footing with the dominant parties.

The media dimension: Models of VAA promotion

It is widely acknowledged that VAAs are dependent on mass media to attract high volumes of users (Walgrave *et al.* 2008). The example of the *EU Profiler*, which was launched in 30 countries for the 2009 European Parliament elections, illustrates this point. The site generated 919,422 advices (Trechsel and Mair 2011: 7), however, 45 per cent of these users were located in only two countries: Sweden and the Netherlands. These countries were the only instances in the *EU Profiler* project where there was a promotional partnership with a national newspaper (*Aftonbladet* in Sweden, and *Trouw* in the Netherlands).

Such media–VAA partnerships are based on a mutual exchange of services. The media fund (or partly fund) the VAA and promote the tool on their different outlets – most prominently by according it a place on their webpage. In exchange, the VAA developers provide an application that can help to drive site traffic, as well as furnishing the media partners with analyses of voters' and parties' issue positions, shifts in leadership evaluations and prospective voter behaviour on the basis of the data collected through the application during the campaign. Ideally, each media story based on such analysis further promotes the tool among the electorate, attracting further users and closing the feedback loop.

However, not every VAA project has established media partnerships, nor do all media partnerships fully incorporate analyses based on VAA data into their campaign coverage. Out of the VAA teams that answered our practitioner survey, two out of three established a media partnership. Among those VAA teams that established such a partnership, 90 per cent provided analyses using VAA data to their media partners and 70 per cent relied on the media partner for funding.

Instead of media partnerships, or in addition to them, some VAA developers devise their own public relations strategies. VAA makers may issue press releases; or organise promotional events, such as 'launch parties' or street events, with the aim of instigating media coverage of the tool; they may also invest in advertisement. Over 90 per cent of the VAA practitioners who we surveyed engaged in such activities and 80 per cent tried to promote their application in the mass media (TV or radio appearances, and newspaper publications). Since, for the most part, the individuals behind VAA projects are scholars, they may be invited to participate in radio or television debates, and can promote their sites through such channels.

VAA developers may also send data analysis reports to targeted journalists, in the hope that they will use such analysis in their campaign coverage, and cite the VAA as a source. Lastly, VAA teams can promote their sites via social media: more than 70 per cent of the VAA teams surveyed did so on Facebook and Twitter.

Therefore, many VAA developers run what Abold (2008) has called 'mini election campaigns' in order to reach users, but not all VAA teams do so. Out of these two variables – media partnership and mini-campaign – it is possible to identify four different configurations of VAA–media relationship, as illustrated below.

Neither media partnership nor mini-campaign

Some VAA sites are not involved in any formal media partnership and do not try to attract users beyond the personal networks of its developers. Such sites are usually made by a single person or a group of e-citizens. The 2012 French presidential election saw the emergence of several VAAs of this kind, such as: *Politest, Je Vote Qui en 2012, Pour Qui Voter en 2012* and *Qui Voter*.

Such VAAs are typically launched several months before the actual electoral campaign. Some may 'go viral' through social media sharing and thereby gain access to traditional media coverage, but most have very low numbers of users.

The *EU Profiler* site, developed by universities, is also an example of a VAA that featured, for the most part, neither media partnership nor mini-campaign, except in two countries (Sweden and the Netherlands). The result is that, once we take out these two countries, across the remaining twenty-eight countries covered by the site, 'only' half a million citizens used *EU Profiler*.

No media partnership, but a mini-campaign

Some institutionally based VAAs, such as the German *Wahl-O-Mat* or the Dutch *Stemwijzer*, receive coverage in national and local newspapers, however there appears to be no formal exchange or cooperation between the media and the VAA team. Therefore, we do not consider such media support as a partnership. However, such sites do actively promote their sites through press releases and media events. For instance, since 2002, *Stemwijzer* has participated in several television and radio programs where guests on the show – celebrities, journalists, and political leaders – take the test (de Graaf 2010). The audience is also invited to participate by taking the test and to interact with the show by email or SMS. In 2006, 526 media references (national and local newspapers, newswires and magazines) were made about *Stemwijzer*, and the site delivered 4.7 million vote advices.

The German VAA *Wahl-O-Mat*'s mini-campaign involved advertisements in popular computer and video games, and the posting of videos on a YouTube channel during the 2009 federal election campaign.[1] Despite only 57 media references during the 2009 campaign, *Wahl-O-Mat* delivered 6.7 million vote advices.[2] The institutional setting in which *Wahl-O-Mat* is developed may help to explain its success. *Wahl-O-Mat* is produced by the German Federal Agency for Civic Education,[3] a government agency whose civic education projects are designed to inform and mobilise voters (Marschall and Schultze 2012a). This agency actively engaged in a PR campaign to promote the application. Similarly, the *Stemwijzer* was developed as a collaborative project involving non-partisan organisations supported financially by the Minister of Interior Affairs (de Grafaf 2010).

An absence of media partnership may be the result of a deliberate strategy, but may also be the product of media refusal to engage in partnership with a tool that makes explicit political recommendations. The developers of the Turkish VAA *Oy Pusulasi* experienced this difficulty in the 2011 parliamentary elections. That VAA team was able to promote the tool through appearances in television news programs and to send analysis reports to targeted journalists, which resulted in several columns in national and local newspapers. In the four weeks of the election campaign, this strategy attracted about 200,000 users to *Oy Pusulasi*. Among the VAA teams surveyed, nine out of ten promoted the application in newspapers and on the radio, and two out of three also did so on TV.

---

1. Press release describing several of the public relation strategies of the '*Wahl-O-Mat*' team: http://www.bpb.de/presse/50105/du-hast-die-wahl, accessed on 22 April 2013.

2. Media references data have been collected through the search engine LexisNexis over a period of four weeks prior to election day.

3. *Bundeszentrale für politische Bildung*.

Media partnership, but no mini-campaign

The main objective of establishing a media partnership is to attract large numbers of users to the VAA. Some media may simply host the tool on their website, while others use VAA data to generate content-based stories. For example, the 2012 Italian VAA *Itanes-VoteMatch* was hosted for several weeks on the website of the national newspaper *La Repubblica,* however only one article was written that referred to the site, which simply presented the tool and explained its inner logic. The lack of the publication of additional articles by the newspaper may be related to the fact that *Itanes-VoteMatch* was not launched during a 'live' electoral campaign.

The 2012 French *La Boussole présidentielle* VAA was involved in a partnership with multiple media outlets: the largest French newspaper, *Ouest France* (which is also a regional newspaper), a free daily, *20 Minutes,* and an online platform (*2012 et vous*) which combined coverage from the television channel M6, the radio station *RTL,* and the online news site *MsnNews.* On a regular basis during the campaign, journalists from these media outlets received VAA data-analysis reports, covering the position of the candidates in the political landscape, the issue profiles of VAA users, the images of candidates according to the VAA users, and so on. Hence, over a six-week campaign, the newspaper partners published fourteen articles using VAA data analysis, mentioned the website in thirty-seven other articles and hosted the tool on their own website as well. Approximately 750,000 vote advices were produced by *La Boussole présidentielle.*

Media partnership and a mini-campaign

The Dutch VAA *Kieskompas,* which was first launched for the parliamentary elections of 2006, enjoys multiple media partnerships (with the newspapers such as *Trouw* and *Volkskrant,* with magazines such as *Elsevier* and *HP De Tijd,* and with radio stations such as Radio 1 and RNW), and also actively engages in a mini-campaign, with media events and appearances to promote the tool during each electoral campaign. *Kieskompas* provides analyses of the party-positioning data and user data to generate interest in key issues and party stances. In 2010, the year of its second-most-successful implementation with 1.5 million advices, *Kieskompas* was mentioned 181 times in the Dutch media (newspapers, magazines and newswires), among which 36 articles in *Trouw* were based on data analysis from the VAA.

VAAs and media – conclusions

Whether and how mass media report on VAAs depends on their news value and efforts of the VAA teams. VAAs' news value is influenced by their novelty, the climate of the election campaign, the fragmentation of the political offer, and the indecisiveness of the electorate. Considering all of these factors, one may ask: How are VAAs influencing election coverage in newspapers, radio and television?

A possible preliminary answer is that a distinction must be made between reporting coming from a VAA–media partnership that includes data analysis, and reporting from other media, which discuss or simply mention the VAA. These two types of coverage are evidently very different in nature and content.

As we have seen, the interactions that take place between media and VAAs are multiple and diverse. While some VAAs can attract many users without mass media partnerships (*see* the *Wahl-O-Mat* case), traditional media coverage is usually a key element of discrimination between successful and less successful VAAs. While it is difficult to identify a 'perfect' media strategy, it seems quite straightforward that a media partnership is very important in order to attract VAA users. This is especially true for newcomers in the VAA market; only well-established VAAs, such as *Stemwjizer* and *Wahl-O-Mat*, are able to attract a very large number of users without formal media partnerships. Table 5.5 summarises the campaign strategies of respondents to our survey of VAA practitioners.

The voter dimension

The political effects that VAAs exert on their users have been extensively studied (for a review, *see*: Garzia and Marschall 2012). As research on VAA effects on voters is reviewed and expanded elsewhere in this volume (*see* Andreadis and Wall; Garzia *et al.* in this volume), we simply note that scholars have amassed a wide array of evidence indicating that VAA-use does influence at least some users – both in terms of their levels of political participation and their choice of party when voting. The extent to which this relationship is reciprocal, however, is currently under-explored in the literature.

Generally, voters exert very little influence over the content of VAA sites. As discussed in the 'VAAs and parties' section, the design and selection of statements is usually carried out by VAA developers, in most cases with some form of interaction with political parties. One striking exception to this pattern is the German *Wahl-O-Maht* site, where first- and second-time voters are included in the site's editorial board (Garzia and Marshall 2012). Another example of voter-influenced VAAs is the small-scale sites developed by individual (non-expert) citizens, such as *Qui Voter* in France.

There is also limited scope for users to provide feedback on any aspect of VAA design once such sites are live. In some instances, such as the Canadian *Vote Compass* site, large numbers of users provided such feedback on the 'Comments' section of the media partner's (CBC) website. Also, in some instances voters send messages and comments to the developers through the contact details provided on the website. However, Twitter and Facebook messages, as well as blogs, provide a rich source of feedback on the statements and various other features of VAAs.

Ultimately, VAA projects are dependent on the actions of users for their success. Most obviously, VAAs require users to visit the site. In addition, many VAA developers seek to exploit users' social networking presence by encouraging them to post their outputs on Twitter or Facebook. Our survey of VAA practitioners indicated that over seventy per cent provided a facility for sharing results on Facebook or Twitter (*see* Table 5.5).

Table 5.5: Promotion and media strategies of VAA practitioners

Type of VAA promotion	
Media partnership	66.7%
Team promotion in the media	80.0%
Launching events	93.3%
	n=15
Media involvement in the making of the VAA	
Media gave input on VAA content	30.0%
Media financially contributed to the VAA	70.0%
Academic team provided analyses to the partners	90.0%
	n=10
How did the media promote the application to users?	
Hosting the application on the media partner's website	90.0%
Printed articles in media outlets	100.0%
On TV (ads or stories)	70.0%
On radio (ads or stories)	50.0%
	n=10
VAA team promotion in the media	
TV shows	66.7%
Radio	91.7%
Newspapers	91.7%
Magazines	16.7%
	n=12
VAA team promotion on social media	
Facebook	73.3%
Twitter	71.4%
Other (Google+, MSN)	26.7%
	n=15

More recently, VAA practitioners have begun to think about whether a collaborative filtering approach could be developed that would base output on data entered by other, similar users, rather than (or in addition to) a user–party comparison (Katakis *et al.* forthcoming).

Furthermore, VAA developers who employ VAA data for academic analyses (*see*, for instance, chapters by both Lander, and Wheatley and Mendez in this volume) depend on users to provide quality data. Users who visit the site enter responses of varying quality to the policy questions that are posed, with one indicator of quality being the time spent by users on each question (Andreadis, this volume).

Finally, many VAA site designs allow users to manipulate the type of feedback that they receive. In some cases, voters can decide how their policy positions are compared to those of parties – for instance, the *EU Profiler* VAA site allowed users to select an analysis from various comparison algorithms. In other cases such as *Kieskompas* the site design allows users to choose a subset of issues that are taken into account when comparing users to parties (Krouwel *et al.* 2012). Our content analysis of 51 VAA sites indicates that 58 per cent allow users to weight issues or issue areas for their outputs.

In conclusion, we contend that the user–VAA relationship is important for understanding the nature of VAAs as a campaign actor, and we recommend that future VAA projects should consider allowing users more influence over the development of VAA sites – both in the precampaign stage and once sites are live.

Conclusion

VAAs have the potential to deepen their relationships with parties, citizens and media. Parties, and particularly small parties, may use VAAs to both clarify and publicise their stances on issues. Voters may find in VAAs a useful time-saver for comparing parties' positions to their own, and this relationship could be bolstered by a more inclusive approach to considering the views of voters in VAA implementation. In order to maximise its utility for the democratic process, one of the concerns of VAAs is to reach undecided voters (*see* Marschall, this volume). To reach this target group, the strategies of VAA promotion and the choice of media-partnership is essential. Another concern is to reach as many political groups as there are in society, to have data capturing a range of opinions and issue positions as broad as possible. This task may be problematic where there exists a high level of political parallelism within the media system (Çarkoğlu *et al.* 2012), and VAA developers should be aware of this.

More generally, scholars studying VAAs should take into account all interactions described in the framework provided in Figure 5.1 when seeking to conceptualise the 'effects' that VAAs may exert on key political actors and when considering their role in political campaigns. We also feel that practitioners involved in developing such sites would benefit from considering this framework in order to plan their engagement with voters, parties and media.

Chapter Six

Data Quality and Data Cleaning

Ioannis Andreadis

Introduction

Although VAAs are different from web surveys in various aspects, the components that affect the quality of VAA data are very similar to the components that affect the quality of web survey data. According to Dillman (2007) the quality of a survey is affected by the overall survey error which consists of four components: coverage error, sampling error, nonresponse error, and measurement error. Coverage error is the error that occurs when some of the elements of the population cannot be included in the sample. Sampling error is the error (inaccuracy) in estimating a quantity based on the sample instead of the whole population. Nonresponse error occurs when some people in the survey sample do not respond to the questionnaire and there is evidence that they differ significantly from those who respond. Measurement error occurs when answers to survey questions are inaccurate or wrong.

The most significant errors associated with web surveys are coverage errors and measurement errors. Coverage errors occur in web surveys because a part of the population does not have internet access or they have internet access but they never use it. Moreover, people who use the internet more frequently are more prone to visit a VAA, and in a similar way they are more prone to participate in a web survey. Finally, even among frequent users there are differences regarding the type of use. For instance, internet users who go online having playing games as their primary task are less likely to visit a VAA than people who go online to search for information (*see* Andreadis 2013a; Fan and Yan 2010; Vicente and Reis 2012).

The probability of measurement error can be larger in all self-administered surveys due to the lack of interaction with a human (the interviewer) who could clarify the meaning of a question in case the respondent needs it. Finally, as Heerwegh and Loosveldt (2008) argue, web survey respondents might have a number of programs running concurrently with the web survey and they might devote their energy to multiple activities (multitasking). This multitasking could increase the probability of measurement error, and if the web survey is long it could also lead to drop outs (when another activity requires the entire attention of the user).

Of course, VAAs are different from web surveys with regard to two characteristics: access rules and respondent motivation. Access to a web survey is usually prohibited to the general public. In this case, only people who have been sent an invitation can participate in the web survey, by entering their unique pin code or token. On the other hand, VAAs are open to anyone with internet access. In addition, users can participate in a VAA as many times as they like. Web surveys that are open to the public (i.e. a pin/token is not required) may suffer from the same problem (multiple submissions by a single user). Some people may be motivated to participate in a survey multiple times by their intention to influence the findings of the survey by inflating the frequency of their views (e.g. to make their favourite political party appear more popular than it really is). We may observe this behaviour in users of unprotected web polls (usually with one question only) which publish the frequencies of the answers instantly. But when users complete a normal web survey, the only output they usually see is a 'Thank you for your participation' screen. In order to learn the findings, web survey participants have to wait for the publication of the analysis of the collected data. Thus, people participate in surveys (web or any other mode) through a sense of social responsibility. On the other hand, people use VAAs because their responses are evaluated immediately and the users get a personalised output, i.e. a personal 'voting advice'. This VAA feature motivates some users to complete the VAA questionnaire multiple times for various reasons. Some users give their true positions the first time they use a VAA, but then they become curious to find out the answers to various 'what if' questions. For instance, they wonder what the output would be if they had answered 'strongly disagree' (or 'strongly agree') to all sentences. Other users, the first time they complete a VAA questionnaire, use it as a game; they only want to see the available outcomes, not the outcome for their own positions. As a result, they do not pay too much attention to the questions, or they even give totally random responses without reading the questions. These users want to explore the tool and test how it reacts to their actions; their answers do not correspond to their true positions. This process of playing with the Voting Advice Application can be called VAA testing.

From the previous paragraphs it is obvious that the quality of VAA data suffers from two major shortcomings: i) lack of representativeness due to limited coverage, and ii) measurement error due to VAA testing. More information on the difference between the group of VAA users and the general population can be found in the following chapter by Marschall that presents the profile of VAA users. As internet use spreads to groups with lower access rates, the difference between the group of VAA users and the general population becomes smaller. The aim of this chapter is to address the error that results from VAA testing by answering the following questions: How can we discover the nonsense answers submitted by users who were just testing the VAA? How serious is the problem, i.e. what is the percentage of nonsense answers? What are the differences between VAA testing cases and the rest of the cases? The chapter concludes with implications and suggestions for VAA designers and researchers working with VAA data.

Response time

Item response time, i.e. time spent answering a survey question, belongs to a special type of data called 'Paradata'. These data do not describe the respondents' answers but the process of answering the questionnaire (*see* Stern 2008; Heerwegh 2003). Measuring response time is common in the survey literature. In fact, it is so common that many different measuring approaches have been proposed. For instance, there are two types of proposed timers depending on the mode of the survey: active timers and latent timers. Active timers are used when an interviewer is present; the interviewer begins time-counting after reading aloud the last word of the question and stops time-counting when the respondent answers. This approach assumes that the respondent starts the response process only after hearing the last word of the question. Latent timers are preferred when the questions are visually presented to the respondent (e.g. web surveys). This approach assumes that the respondent starts the response process from the first moment the question is presented to him/her. Another decision to be made concerns the location of time-counting. Should counting be done on the server side or the client side? Counting on the server side is feasible by recording a timestamp when a user visits a web page. This means that in order to count time spent on each question, we need to keep each question on a separate web page. Of course, this is not a problem for VAAs because usually VAAs present each question on a different page. But there is another problem with server-side time-counting. Server-side response time is the result of the sum of the net response time plus the time between the moment the user submits the answer and the moment the answer is recorded on the server. The second component depends on the type and bandwidth of the user's internet connection, but also on unpredicted, temporary delays due to network load, etc. On the other hand, client-side time-counting is done at the level of the respondent's (or client's) computer itself. Consequently, client-side time-counting should be preferred because it is more accurate and it does not include any noise. Of course, client-side time-counting depends on the settings of the user's browser, i.e. if the settings prevent the execution of any script, then it is not possible to run anything on the client-side. Thus, in order to minimise the number of cases with missing values, response time should be measured with the simplest and most widely installed scripting language.

Estimating the thresholds

Tourangeau *et al.* (2000) divide the survey response process into four major tasks:

1. comprehension of the question
2. retrieval of relevant information
3. use of that information to render the judgment, and
4. the selection and reporting of an answer.

For the common respondent, the time spent on comprehension and reporting components depends on the characteristics of the questions. Time spent on comprehension depends on the length and the complexity of the question. Time spent on reporting is affected by how many and what type of response categories are offered. For instance, previous results indicate that response times are longer when the negative rather than the positive end of the scale is presented first. Response time is longer for formats that are difficult for respondents to process (Christian, Parsons and Dillman 2009). For VAA items, reporting procedure is the same for all questions; thus, it is reasonable to expect a fixed time spent on reporting, and it should be short (clicking on a radio button is one of the simplest and fastest ways to report the answer).

According to Yan and Tourangeau (2008), retrieval and judgment may be determined by respondent characteristics (e.g. age, education level, etc.) but since I argue that some users give nonsense answers (and I want to study these users), I suppose that they would also give nonsense answers to the questions regarding their demographic characteristics. Thus, I do not use respondent characteristics in the analysis presented in this chapter.

Time dedicated to judgement depends on the existence or not of an attitude on the topic. People with a preexistent opinion/position are expected to answer faster than people who decide on the spot. Even between people who have an attitude, time will depend on the attitude strength. People with unstable positions need more time to finalise their answer than people with a stable position who do not need to spend more time than the time taken to retrieve their already processed opinion from their memory. Bassili and Fletcher (1991) have found a positive relationship between response latency and unstable positions (measured as changes of the answer after being exposed to the counterargument). Finally, it has been shown that attitudes expressed quickly are more predictive of future behaviour than attitudes expressed slowly. Bassili (1993) has provided logistic regression evidence supporting the hypothesis that response latency is a better predictor of discrepancies between voting intentions and voting behaviour than self-reported certainty about vote intention.

Much of the time spent on Task 1 (comprehension of the question) involves reading and interpreting the text. One component of this time is related to the complexity of the question. As Bassili and Scott (1996) have shown, badly expressed questions (e.g. double-barrelled questions or questions containing a superfluous negative) take longer to answer than nearly identical questions without these problems. Of course, a well-designed VAA should not include badly formulated statements (*see* van Camp *et al.* in this volume). Badly expressed statements should be corrected or replaced.

If all statements included in a VAA have similar complexity, then the most significant factor that affects time spent on Task 1 is the length of the statement. These two quantities (length and time) are proportional and their ratio defines the reading speed. VAA users need time to read the statement using a reading speed suitable for the comprehension of the ideas in the sentence. The unit used to measure reading speed in the related literature is 'words per minute' (wpm). This unit may be suitable to measure reading speed with large texts, but it is an inappropriate unit to measure reading speed of texts of limited size, like the sentences used in a VAA, because it is possible to have a sentence with a small number of lengthy words that is longer and requires more reading time than another sentence with more but shorter words. To avoid similar problems, I have decided to use the number of characters instead of using the number of words.

In the following paragraphs I will try to classify response times in order to find a way to reveal the cases where the response time was so small, indicating that the answer is not valid. Fry (1963) classifies readers as good (350 wpm), fair (250 wpm) and slow (150 wpm). Carver (1992) provides a table connecting reading speed rates and types of reading, and associates a reading rate of 300 wpm with a reading process named 'rauding', which is suitable for comprehension of a sentence, a reading rate of 450 wpm with skimming, i.e. a type of reading that is not suitable to fully comprehend the ideas presented in the text, and a reading rate of 600 wpm with scanning, which is suitable for finding target words. Thus, if we want to classify a reading rate as one of the three aforementioned categories, we can use the following rule:

- reading rate ≤ 375 wpm $\rightarrow$ rauding,
- 375 wpm $<$ reading rate ≤ 525 wpm $\rightarrow$ skimming
- 525 wpm$<$ reading rate $\rightarrow$ scanning

Using these rules, I try to estimate a threshold that will separate answers given after reading and comprehending the statement from answers given in so little time that there is strong evidence that the user was not able to read and comprehend the statement, i.e. the answer has no value and it should be discarded. A scanning reading speed is too fast for a VAA user to comprehend the statement. Thus, I use as a threshold the midway point between skimming and scanning, i.e. 525 wpm.

For English texts the average word length is 4.5 letters (*see* Yannakoudakis, Tsomokos and Hutton 1990). Thus, the above rules converted to characters per second (with 4.5 characters per word) give the following:

- reading rate ≤ 28.125 cps $\rightarrow$ rauding,
- 28.125 cps $<$ reading rate ≤ 39.375 cps $\rightarrow$ skimming
- 39.375 cps $<$ reading rate $\rightarrow$ scanning

If we divide the number of characters (without spaces) in each statement by the number 39.375, we can get the minimum time (in seconds) that is necessary to read the statement. Of course, users need some time for all other tasks (2–4) reported by Tourangeau *et al.* (2000), i.e. retrieval of relevant information, use of that information to render the judgment and the selection and reporting of an answer.

Bassili and Fletcher (1991), using an active timer, have found that on average, simple attitude questions take between 1.4 and 2 seconds, and more complex attitude questions take between 2 and 2.6 seconds. In their experiment, time-counting starts when the interviewer presses the spacebar after reading the last word of the question. Time-counting stops with a voice-key (the first noise that comes from the respondent's side triggers the computer to read the clock). For VAAs and web surveys, time-counting stops when the user clicks on one of the available buttons that correspond to answer options. This additional step requires some extra time. Thus, the minimum time reported by Bassili and Fletcher for simple attitude questions (1.4 seconds) can be used as the minimum time for Task 4 (selecting and reporting the answer).

Consequently, the item response time of scanning respondents should be less than: Threshold1=1.4+[Characters in statement without spaces]/39.375 and the corresponding time of skimming respondents should be between Threshold1 and Threshold2=1.4+[Characters in statement without spaces]/28.125. Users, who have spent on a sentence less time than Threshold2, are suspected of answering without understanding the statements. For most people the time given by the formula of Threshold2 is not enough, but there may be some VAA users who are very fast readers and they are capable of understanding the statement just by skimming the text. Thus, if a more strict rule is to be preferred, this is given by Threshold1: if a user has spent on a statement less than the time of Threshold1, the dedicated time was not enough for a valid answer; the answer was given either by randomly clicking on any of the available buttons or the user has clicked on a fixed button for all statements, e.g. the user was testing the application (e.g. to see the output it provides when all answers are 'Neither agree nor disagree'). Thus, Threshold1 will catch a smaller number of cases suspected of being invalid, but the probability of these cases being invalid is higher. Only extremely capable readers would be able to read and comprehend the exact meaning of a statement by just scanning the text.

Using the thresholds

In this section I apply the methodology described in the previous section to a dataset from the Greek VAA *HelpMeVote*, which was used for the Greek parliamentary elections of 2012. For the election of May 2012 *HelpMeVote* includes thirty statements displayed on separated pages, but all thirty pages are downloaded from the beginning to the users' browser. This means that there is no lag time between answering one question and viewing the next one. The time between clicks can be counted accurately. The response times are recorded in hidden input fields. Communication with the server is done at the end, when all questions have been answered and the user has clicked the 'Submit' button. When the respondent submits the web page, the content of the hidden fields is stored on the server. A presentation of all the technical details of *HelpMeVote* (including the statements that have been used) can be found in Andreadis (2013b). Table 6.1 shows the thresholds used to classify the answers to each question/sentence.

As an example of the output of this classification I use the second statement. As Table 6.2 shows, about 5 per cent of the answers have been given in less than 3.838 seconds, i.e. the users were scanning and the dedicated time was not enough

Table 6.1: Thresholds used to classify answers

Statement	Number of characters (without spaces)	Threshold 1	Threshold 2
1	68	3.127	3.818
2	96	3.838	4.813
3	127	4.625	5.916
4	73	3.254	3.996
5	83	3.508	4.351
6	62	2.975	3.604
7	72	3.229	3.960
8	83	3.508	4.351
9	105	4.067	5.133
10	78	3.381	4.173
11	80	3.432	4.244
12	94	3.787	4.742
13	67	3.102	3.782
14	61	2.949	3.569
15	87	3.610	4.493
16	84	3.533	4.387
17	148	5.159	6.662
18	73	3.254	3.996
19	46	2.568	3.036
20	69	3.152	3.853
21	76	3.330	4.102
22	120	4.448	5.667
23	96	3.838	4.813
24	134	4.803	6.164
25	65	3.051	3.711
26	107	4.117	5.204
27	67	3.102	3.782
28	62	2.975	3.604
29	73	3.254	3.996
30	38	2.365	2.751

Table 6.2: Distribution of time spent on Statement 2

	Frequency	Per cent
Scanning	25,095	5.3
Skimming	16,427	3.4
Normal	430,786	90.3
Unable to count	48,27	1.0
Total	477,135	100.0

Table 6.3: Valid and invalid cases according to response-time

	Frequency	Per cent
Normal	438,132	91.8
VAA testing	25,051	5.3
Unable to count	13,952	2.9
Total	477,135	100.0

Table 6.4: Distribution of answers given to Statement 2 by response-time category

	SD	D	NN	A	SA
VAA testing	23.8%	14.5%	17.6%	22.2%	21.8%
Normal	9.8%	15.1%	11.4%	37.1%	26.6%

Table 6.5: Distribution of answers given to Statement 18 by response-time category

	SD	D	NN	A	SA
VAA testing	21.2%	25.1%	23.2%	18.1%	12.4%
Normal	26.5%	37.2%	13.9%	18.3%	4.2%

to give a valid answer. The second category (3.4 per cent) consists of answers that were given in less than 4.813 seconds and more than 3.838 seconds. Users in this category were fast, but it is possible that some of these answers are valid. Most of the users (about 90.3 per cent) have spent more than 4.813 seconds. Finally, there are some users (1 per cent) for whom the time spent on Sentence 2 was not recorded for various reasons. The most common reason was that some users have tried to skip some questions, i.e. by modifying the URL of the address bar of their internet browser.

Up to this point I have used the thresholds developed in the previous section to classify a single answer in one of the following groups: scanning, skimming or normal. But if a user has answered only one or two questions with a scanning or skimming speed, this does not mean that all thirty answers are invalid. In order to classify a total row as invalid we need at least half of the answers to belong to one of the first two categories. Following this rule I find that more than one out of twenty cases of the dataset have been submitted by users who have not spent enough time reading and comprehending the VAA sentences (Table 6.3). The next question that should be answered is the following: Are these cases which are classified as invalid different from the rest of the cases?

What are the differences?

In this section I will try to reveal the differences between the answers given by people who have responded to the questions at a very fast speed (which I have classified as invalid or nonsense answers) and the answers given by people who have dedicated enough time to give a substantial response. Of course, the distribution of answers depends on the sentence itself. Some issues are widely accepted, i.e. the majority of the electorate supports them. On the other hand, there are statements which are faced with disagreement from the largest part of the electorate.

As Table 6.4 indicates, most Greek voters agree with the second statement (together, A and SA answers constitute more than 63 per cent of the total answers) and only 9.8 per cent answer that they strongly disagree. But within the invalid group we observe that the most frequent answer is SD (23.8 per cent) and all other options are selected with about the same probability (D: 14.5 per cent, NN: 17.6 per cent, A: 22.2 per cent, and SA: 21.8 per cent). This outcome could be the result of a primacy effect, i.e. increased likelihood of selecting the first of the available items. Psychologists argue that when we read the later response alternatives, our mind is already occupied with thoughts about previous response alternatives; consequently, the attention paid to later response alternatives is insufficient (later items are less carefully considered).[1] Psychologists also support that primacy could be a result of satisficing,[2] i.e. respondents choose the first acceptable answer instead of the optimal answer (*see* Simon 1956). Krosnick and Alwin (1987) have shown that response-order effects (both primacy and recency) are stronger among respondents low in cognitive sophistication. Order effects are present not only in the frame of surveys using the visual channel; these effects also occur when clicking behaviour is observed with regard to website or email links (*see* Murphy, Hofacker and Mizerski 2006). It seems that visitors click on the first link more frequently than any other link (primacy effect). The click-through rate decreases for all subsequent links except the last one, where it increases significantly (recency effect).

---

1. Response order effects depend on the channel used to present the response alternatives (visual presentation *vs.* oral presentation). When oral presentation is used, respondents are able to devote more processing time to the last item because interviewers pause after reading aloud the last available item and wait for respondents to give their answer. As a result, when the aural channel is used we observe recency effects instead of primacy effects.

2. A combination of 'satisfy' and 'suffice', i.e. to finish a job by satisfying the minimum requirements.

The findings from the distribution of responses to Statement 2 seem to support the hypothesis of a strong impact of primacy effects among the scanning group. But this hypothesis has to be double-checked by observing the distribution of responses to a statement when the majority does not agree with it (*see* Table 6.5, with the distribution of answers to sentence 18). In the Normal group the sum of SD and D responses to statement 18 is 63.7 per cent. On the other hand, only 4.2 per cent of the users select the answer SA. Within the VAA testing group the answers are distributed more uniformly and SA is selected by 12.4 per cent. It seems that among VAA testers, the distribution tends to look like a discrete uniform distribution with five outcomes, i.e. each of the five outcomes is equally likely to be selected (it has probability 1/5). If the hypothesis of the discrete uniform distribution is accepted, this means that the responses of the people in the testing group are random responses.

The usual test for the null hypothesis that a sample follows a particular theoretical distribution is the chi-square goodness-of-fit test. For the group of VAA testers, it seems that the observations tend to follow a discrete uniform distribution, i.e. all answers seem to occur with equal frequency. Since there are five substantial answers, the expected relative frequency of each category under the null hypothesis is 0.2. We can test both the Normal group and the VAA testing group against the null hypothesis and observe which of the two groups is closer to the theoretical distribution. If the number of cases was equal in both groups I could directly compare the chi-square values. But since the number of cases in the Normal group is much larger than the number of cases in the VAA testing group, it is better to compare the values of Cramer's V, which does not depend on the number of cases. In Table 6.6 I compare Cramer's V statistics calculated for the Goodness of Fit to the uniform discrete distribution between the Normal group and the VAA testing group. It becomes obvious that for all questions (except one where the coefficients are practically equal) the distribution of answers in the VAA testing group is closer to a uniform discrete distribution than the distribution of answers in the Normal group.

Pattern of answers and relation to response time

Another way to clean VAA data is to delete records submitted by users who (for various reasons) have given a constant answer to every (or almost every) question (provided that there are questions with opposite directions).

Table 6.7 indicates that there are 6,170 records that have the same value in all 30 fields, i.e. the user clicked on the same button for all 30 sentences. The most used constant answer is 'No answer' (57.4 per cent of the constant answer records). The next most used constant answer is the median 'Neither agree nor disagree' point (24.1 per cent). 'Strongly disagree' (11.6 per cent) and 'Strongly agree' (4.9 per cent) are next. The preference for 'Strongly disagree' can be attributed to the user interface of *HelpMeVote*: answering buttons are displayed vertically and the order of appearance is from 'Strongly disagree' to 'Strongly agree', and last comes the 'No answer' button. The other two buttons have been used as constant answers by a very limited number of users.

Table 6.6: Comparison of Cramer's V between Normal and VAA testing

	Cramer's V	
Statement	Normal group	VAA Testing
q1	0.326	0.194
q2	0.259	0.085
q3	0.153	0.160
q4	0.146	0.081
q5	0.206	0.078
q6	0.244	0.133
q7	0.212	0.115
q8	0.292	0.103
q9	0.352	0.188
q10	0.131	0.065
q11	0.174	0.049
q12	0.146	0.061
q13	0.356	0.134
q14	0.189	0.107
q15	0.322	0.096
q16	0.224	0.111
q17	0.235	0.081
q18	0.280	0.111
q19	0.304	0.255
q20	0.300	0.138
q21	0.139	0.090
q22	0.184	0.145
q23	0.152	0.074
q24	0.498	0.263
q25	0.304	0.166
q26	0.272	0.104
q27	0.358	0.163
q28	0.292	0.159
q29	0.352	0.156
q30	0.372	0.195

Table 6.7: Frequencies of fixed answers (rigid: 30 identical answers)

	Frequency	Per cent
Strongly disagree	715	11.6
Disagree	65	1.1
Neither […] nor	1,486	24.1
Agree	61	1.0
Strongly agree	300	4.9
No answer	3,543	57.4
Total	6,170	100.0

Of course, it is possible that some users had the intention to click on the same answering button for each question but while they were trying to do this at a high speed, they accidentally clicked once or more on a different button. VAA researchers, who want to have their VAA data as clean as possible, can follow a method to identify these cases that is available in Andreadis (2012). In the same paper it is shown that there are a lot of cases which are flagged as invalid by both time and pattern criteria. This shows a strong relationship between the two criteria. Still, there are additional cases that are flagged as invalid by time criteria which are not flagged as invalid by the pattern criteria. This means that if a voting advice application does not log the time spent on each statement, the collected data cannot be fully cleaned.

Discussion

The present results have both theoretical and practical implications. Theoretically, the results offer support to the importance of recording the time users spent to answer each of the questions in a Voting Advice Application. Recorded response times can be useful in many ways. They can help to identify questions with larger response times than the expected response time for their length. This could be a sign of a badly expressed statement that should be rephrased, replaced by another question or even totally removed. Response times can also help check if and when users get tired/bored and they start dedicating less time to answering the questions. Some of these ideas have been tested in the context of web surveys.

The main theoretical contribution of this chapter is the idea that response times can be used to identify non-valid, unconsidered, incautious answers to VAA statements in order to clean the dataset. Following the notion of four tasks reported by Tourangeau et al. (2000), I have tried to isolate the time requested for the first task and link it with the length of the statement, in order to classify the users according to their reading speed and total response time. The presented research provides a novel method to identify nonsense answers and demonstrates that VAA data cleaning based only on the pattern of answers is not adequate.

At the practical level, this research presents a series of findings regarding the frequency of the non-valid records and the distribution of answers in these records.

It is noteworthy that non-valid answers, identified by the response-time criterion, correspond to about 5 per cent of the total answers. With regard to the distribution of the answers in these invalid records, there is a tendency towards a discrete uniform distribution.

After presenting the aforementioned findings, one final question remains: 'If we analyse the data without removing the invalid cases, what will be the impact on findings and conclusions?'. In other words, what would be the impact if 5 per cent of a sample consisted of random answers? The answer to this depends on the analysis that has to be done. For instance, let us go back to Table 6.4 and suppose that we need to report the percentage of people who disagree strongly with Statement 2. If we used the total sample (without cleaning) we would report the figure 10.5 per cent, but if we used the 'normal reading speed' group (i.e. what remains from the total sample after removing the invalid cases), we would give the answer 8.5 per cent. This difference is not ver4y large, but it could change the outcome of (say) a chi-square test.

The bottom line is that recording response times can be implemented easily in a VAA environment and it can facilitate data cleaning by removing non-valid answers. Thus, I conclude this chapter by suggesting that all VAA designers record response times of their users, since this information could prove to be really valuable for data cleaning and further research regarding the behaviour of VAA users.

Chapter Seven

Profiling Users

Stefan Marschall

'Who Am I? And If So, How Many?'
(Richard David Precht)

Introduction

Usage and users have always been the core of research on Voting Advice Applications (VAAs). The 'success story' of VAAs has been linked not only to the spread of these applications across Europe and beyond but much more to the fact that in a lot of countries, Voting Advice Applications have become extremely popular with the electorates and have been used by large numbers of voters. This high demand is one – if not, the central – reason why Voting Advice Applications have attracted the attention of researchers over the last few years.

Meanwhile, VAA research has moved far beyond the questions of 'how many?' and 'who?' to questions concerning the specific effects of the tool on those using it with an emphasis on its impact on political behaviour, the likeliness to vote and electoral choice (for an overview *see* Garzia and Marschall 2012 and the chapters of this book). Another strand of research asks whether and how the design and methods of the tool make a difference regarding the usage and the results they provide – confronting the makers of Voting Advice Applications with ethical challenges. Additionally, VAA research takes an interest in the contents and data generated by the tools, e.g. on party positions, and how this abundance of data could be analysed and used for questions beyond VAA research in the narrow sense. In short, it has been more or less taken for granted that these tools are well established within the electorates and that they play a role within modern democracies, because 'apparently' numerous people have used Voting Advice Applications up to now and will use them in the future.

This chapter revisits the basic and seemingly conventional perspective of 'how many' and 'who' by applying a comparative perspective in order to learn more about the quantity and quality of the tools' users. A comparative approach might allow generating hypotheses regarding the factors which have an influence on the popularity of VAAs – factors which could for example be based in certain institutional settings. A comparative view can also help to identify and understand cross-national differences in the composition of the user groups – or whether there is something like a cross-nationally typical VAA user.

A sound knowledge of the quantity and qualities of the users can shed light on the role these web applications play within modern democracies and on the interactions between the users on the one hand and why/how they use them on the other hand. It might help us to gauge the capability of these tools to influence or even change election results – a capability which first of all depends on who exactly and how many use these applications. By profiling users, we might understand more about case-specific VAA effects, which could for example be rooted in the particular structure of a user group in a country. Finally, the makers of the tools might be able to draw lessons about the potentials and limits of reaching people with Voting Advice Applications or about which target groups should and could be addressed more intensively.

This chapter proceeds as follows: First, it focuses on the question of 'how many?'; on the basis of a survey, it takes stock of the user numbers of different VAAs in Europe, trying to set them into relation with certain system characteristics. Methodological options to measure the number of users/usages and their implications are discussed. Second, it presents data on the profiles of VAA users, presenting available and collected information regarding their demographics and other characteristics such as political interest. Again, the methodological challenges and deficiencies of such a survey and comparative analysis are addressed. Finally, this chapter discusses the findings and draws conclusions for future research on VAAs, advocating a coordinated cross-national research project on these tools, as the available data provide first descriptive information but do not allow sound comparative analyses.

How many?

From the perspective of the producers of the tools, VAAs are made to reach high numbers of people - whether the purpose is to educate citizens or out of research interests. As part of normatively fuelled citizenship education programs, these tools are designed to mobilise people to go to the polls, and to educate voters about the parties/candidates who are running for election and about their positions on salient issues so that their voting decision might be a more informed one (Fivaz and Nadig 2010; Marschall 2008). The larger the numbers of users, the more people can profit from this alleged benefit, as a result having an impact on the overall political and democratic culture of a country. In research-driven projects the makers of VAAs try to obtain large datasets that they could not acquire by traditional methods of data collection. The higher the number of cases, the more capacities research has for advanced statistical analyses and the more representative the sample might be – however, (*nota bene*) high figures do not guarantee the representativeness of the data.

Technically, being online tools, Voting Advice Applications are ready to deal with large amounts of usages. Early paper-and-pencil versions of VAAs could neither attract nor cope with many users in terms of giving out individual results, let alone with aggregating the output. As soon as these pre-election tools had been developed into internet applications with a high usability, the numbers went up rapidly (for the Dutch case *see* de Graaf 2010). Nevertheless, technical limitations could be set by the restricted size of available web and processing capacities.

In the literature on Voting Advice Applications, it has been mentioned time and again that these tools reach 'impressive numbers of users' (Cedroni and Garzia 2010: 9) or 'thousands' and 'millions' of visitors (Triga *et al* 2012: 195), or that they 'enjoy striking popularity among voters' (Ramonaite 2010: 122). In order to provide a comparative overview, we conducted a survey among the makers of European Voting Advice Applications as well as a review of the VAA research literature to learn more about the actual amount of users in different countries. We can draw on information provided for seventeen tools, i.e. covering only a part of all European VAAs.

Most of the data is based on self-reports of the respective makers of the tools and cannot be controlled for their accuracy. Apart from suffering from missing cases and the problem of relying on self-reported figures, analyses based on these data are confronted with substantial methodological problems. The crucial point is how the numbers of users are technically registered. Different methods have been applied to gauge the quantity of people resorting to VAAs: the data is based either on the number of visits (e.g. Portugal)[1], the number of unique-user sessions (e.g. *Wahl-O-Mat*, *HelpMeVote*), the amount of advices produced (e.g. *Stemwijzer*, *Wahlkabine*) or the number of users who completed an additional online survey (e.g. *Choose4Greece*). Some of the collected data indicate the difference between the amount of advices or the number of sessions and the actual number of users (e.g. *Bússola Eleitoral Portugal, Cabina Elettorale, Vote Match UK*).[2]

To refer only to the number of recommendations produced by the tool in order to estimate the total number of users could be misleading, as the amount of advices might significantly supersede the number of voters who resorted to the tool, given that a remarkable share of voters use these tools more than once. If only the number of sessions is documented, multiple-user situations (more than one user in a session) cannot be taken into account and bias the findings. To control for IP addresses does not necessarily solve the problem either, as users can change IP addresses easily and as it is still possible that more than one user has used the same address. If a compulsory online survey is conducted before the usage of the tool generating an individualised answer pattern, it might be easier to estimate the number of users. But also this method of controlling does not effectively prevent voters from using the tool more than once without being identified. To sum up, the providers of Voting Advice Applications cannot precisely provide the accurate number of VAA users.[3] This vagueness should be factored in when interpreting and comparing the data.

---

1. Only sessions lasting more than fifteen minutes have been counted.

2. Chapter Six in this book by Ioannis Andreadis proposes some ways to clean the data in order to identify a valid number of usages.

3. An alternative approach could be to rely on representative surveys including items on the use of VAAs (e.g. National Election Studies).

Table 7.1: Number of users of European Voting Advice Applications

Voting Advice Application	Highest score (HS)	Year of HS	Year of first use	Size of electorate (year of HS)	Voter turnout (year of HS)	Percentage HS/ voter turnout
BússolaEleitoral (Portugal)	175,000	2009	2009	9,519,921	5,681,258	3.1%
Cabina Elettorale (Italy)	2,916	2009	2009	50,276,247	32,748,675	0.0%
Choose4Greece (Greece)	92,007	2012	2012	9,949,401	6,476,751	1.4%
Do de Stemtest! (Belgium, Flandern)	840,000	2004	2002	4,568,250	4,284,656	19.6%
Help-MeVote (Greece)	480,000	2012	2012	9,949,401	6,476,751	7.4%
Help-MeVote (Iceland)	30,000	2013	2013	237,957	193,792	15.5%
Kieskompas (Netherlands)	1,500,000	2010	2006	12,524,152	9,442,977	15.9%
KohoVolit CZ (Czech Republic)	150,000	2010	2006	8,415,892	5,263,822	2.8%
KohoVolit SK (Slovakia)	60,000	2012	2006	4,392,451	2,596,443	2.3%
Mano Balsas (Lithuania)	100,000	2008	2008	2,696,090	1,309,965	7.6%
smartvote (Switzerland)	437,000	2011	2003	5,124,034	2,485,403	17.6%
smartvote (Luxemburg)	15,100	2009	2009	223,876	203,535	7.4%
StemWijzer (Netherlands)	4,900,000	2012	1994	12,689,810	9,462,223	51.8%
Vaalikone (Finland)	1,000,000	2007	1996	4,083,549	2,772,799	36.1%
Valijakompass (Estonia)	111,535	2011	2011	913,346	580,264	19.2%
Vote Match UK (UK)	1,200,000	2010	2008	45,597,461	29,691,380	4.0%
Wahlkabine (Austria)	850,000	2008	2002	6,333,109	4,990,952	17.0%
Wahl-O-Mat (Germany)	13,300,000	2013	2002	61,946,489	43,726,856	30.2%
Who should you vote for? (UK)	900,000	2005	2005	44,245,939	27,148,510	3.3%

Source: Own calculations; for single data *see* Appendix 7.1.

Looking at the numbers of Table 7.1, and at this point putting aside the methodological problems, several findings are striking: first, given the spread of VAAs and the numbers in the countries, we can proceed from the assumption that by this time tens of millions of voters in Europe have already used a Voting Advice Application before an election.

Second, the numbers differ significantly between countries. In absolute figures, VAAs like *Wahl-O-Mat*, *Vote Match UK*, *Vaalikone*, *Kieskompas* and *Stemwijzer* are each able to attract more than one million users each (or to give more than one million advices). The highest absolute score was delivered by the German *Wahl-O-Mat*: during the federal election of 2013, about 13 million usages were documented.

However, after factoring in the turnout rates in the countries and setting them into relation with the number of usages (as a proxy for the amount of users), so far the *Stemwijzer* of 2012 appears to be the most popular version of a VAA within a country, reaching a value of about 50 per cent. Already in 2007 the Finish *Vaalikone* accounted for 36 per cent. The 'champion' in terms of absolute figures, the German *Wahl-O-Mat*, scores clearly above the average of 13 per cent with a value of about 30 per cent.[4]

Are there any patterns discernible within the group of the most successful VAAs which might explain why Voting Advice Applications have been demanded more in some countries than in others? To start with, time seems to make a difference: although several tools have already been offered for years, the point of time for the highest score for most of the successful cases (*Vote Match UK*, *Wahl-O-Mat*, *Stemwijzer*) is the last election. And within the group of successful tools, many of them are from before 2005. The longer their existence and the more often these tools have been implemented within a country, the more users they attract – possibly independent of the characteristics of the country they have been applied in. Obviously, VAAs need time to become popular and demanded.

It has been argued that the election and party system might make a difference regarding the popularity of VAAs (Garzia and Marschall 2012). However, the documented cases do not give clear evidence of this assumption. The tool works successfully in systems with candidate voting and open lists (Switzerland, Finland) as well as in systems with party voting (Germany, Netherlands). Moreover, it has been assumed that VAAs might prosper especially in proportional representation systems in which voters have to choose among a higher number of parties (Garzia and Marschall 2012). However, even in a country like Great Britain, with a plurality formula (Lijphart 2012), a VAA meets a high demand. So at least there is no straightforward relationship between the electoral system and the popularity of VAAs. Still, it could be argued that VAAs tend to perform especially well in fragmented party systems (Krouwel *et al.* 2012).

---

4. The Netherlands is a special case, having two VAAs which are both in strong demand. In the Dutch case, the establishment of a second tool has obviously not affected the demand for the first one in a negative way; to the contrary, these tools might have even promoted each other.

Finally, the countries with a high degree of voter volatility have been supposed to be more likely to have high user numbers. Although aggregate-level data suggest that VAAs are used the most in those countries where electoral volatility is higher, this finding is also not straightforward. Moreover, it has been assumed that cross-media effects could be a factor for the success of these tools, as in the countries with highly demanded VAAs there has been TV shows covering the Voting Advice Application or mass media promoting the respective tool (for Finland *see* Ruusuvirta 2010: 54–55, and for Belgium *see* Walgrave *et al.* 2008). Finally, the success could also be based on the kind of organisation which offers the tool, as this determines the resources which could be used for marketing (Garzia and Marschall 2012).

In general, more and deeper analyses seem to be necessary to understand the variance in the demand for VAAs in different settings. The number of cases with the relevant information turns out to be too low and the cases themselves vary in so many respects that so far a comparative analysis does not produce meaningful results – also because data on the numbers of users is based on different calculation methods.

Who are they?

What can be said about those using VAAs? Again, makers of the tool might have certain expectations regarding the composition of the group of people they would like to reach. From a citizen education perspective the idea is to provide information and mobilise those who tend to be apolitical. Then again, researchers producing VAAs might be interested in generating representative samples of the electorates.

What do we know about the users of these tools? Apart from the figures on usage and users, information has been provided for some of the aforementioned Voting Advice Applications on certain demographic characteristics as well as on the political interest of their users. Again, a comparative analysis of this information is confronted with methodical problems, since the data have been gathered in different ways. Data collection is either based on onsite surveys (e.g. Italy, Lithuania and Estonia) or refers to surveys representative of the whole electorate such as national election studies (e.g. in Germany, Luxembourg and Switzerland). In particular, the onsite survey collection of data on users has been heavily criticised for delivering findings which are not representative of the whole VAA user group, much less for the population (Pianzola and Ladner 2011; Vassil 2012). Another problem: the reported data was collected in different years and the answer categories are not standardised between the surveys. Still, the findings could give us first indications about what could be called a typical VAA user.

a) Age

Whenever data has been collected on the age distribution within the groups of VAA users, a clear tendency emerges: the users of these tools are relatively young.

—   *Cabina Elettorale* (Italy, 2009): 43 per cent of the users of this Italian VAA are younger than 30 years of age, and 14 per cent older than 60 (*see* De Rosa 2010: 191).

—   *Mano Balsas* (Lithuania, 2008): 62.8 per cent are younger than 39, and only 1.8 per cent are 60 and older (*see* Ramonaitė 2010).

—   *smartvote* (Luxemburg, 2009): about 19 per cent of the users are between 18 and 24 years old; the proportion of users older than 64 accounts for 8 per cent (*see* Dumont and Kies 2012: 397).

—   *smartvote* (Switzerland, 2007): 35 per cent of the users of *smartvote* are younger than 30; only 6 to 7 per cent are 60 years of age and older (*see* Fivaz and Nadig 2010: 181).

—   *Wahl-O-Mat* (Germany, 2009): 37.5 per cent of the *Wahl-O-Mat* users are younger than 30; only 7.1 per cent are older than 60 (*see* Marschall and Schultze 2012b: 11).

For some cases these user characteristics were set into comparison with the age distribution of the population and the online community (*see* e.g. Marschall and Schultze 2012b). Such analyses show that users of VAAs are on average significantly younger than the internet users and even more so than the population.

Table 7.2: Gender distribution in VAA user groups

VAA	Male (%)	Female (%)	Internet population (male/female, in %)	Total population
Cabina Elettorale (Italy, 2009)	55	45	57.0 *vs.* 43.0 (2010)	48.5 *vs.* 51.5
smartvote (Luxemburg, 2009)	60	40	N/A	49.9 *vs.* 50.1
smartvote (Switzerland, 2007)	65 to 75	25 to 35	54.6 *vs.* 45.4	49.3 *vs.* 50.7
Valjakompass (Estonia, 2011)	48.3	51.7	46.5 *vs.* 53.5	46.1 *vs.* 53.9
Wahl-O-Mat (Germany, 2009)	59.7	40.3	54.0 *vs.* 46.0	49.1 *vs.* 50.9

Source: Own calculations, for total population: http://epp.eurostat.ec.europa.eu/tgm/table.do?tab =table&init=1&language=de&pcode=tps00001&plugin=1; for single data *see* Appendix.

However, the share of elderly users might increase over time. At least for the German *Wahl-O-Mat*, it could be documented that the number of elder users has expanded within the ten years of its frequent application.[5] Either the widening of the user community has changed the composition, or the VAA user group has become older over the years.

b) Gender

Research has also identified a pattern concerning the gender distribution within the VAA user group (*see* Table 7.2). Considering the respective gender distributions within the population, indeed in all VAA user groups male persons are overrepresented – however, to a different degree. Moreover, in the German case for which we have detailed information, we could observe a high variation within the gender distribution over different VAA versions within the country.[6] So not only the system framework but also situational factors within a system might have an influence on the share of male *vs.* female users.

c) Education

Research on several Voting Advice Applications has provided information on the degree of formal education of the users:

— *Cabina Elettorale* (Italy, 2009): 60 per cent of the users of the Italian tool have a baccalaureate or an academic degree, 31 per cent a high school diploma, and only 1 per cent a middle school diploma (*see* De Rosa 2010: 192).

— *Mano Balsas (Lithuania, 2008): 77 per cent have a higher educational attainment, and 23* a lower or medium one (*see* Ramonaitė 2010).

— *smartvote* (Luxemburg, 2009): 70 per cent of the users have a higher education, 6 per cent a first-level secondary education and 24 per cent a second-level secondary education (*see* Dumont and Kies 2012: 397).

— *Valjakompass* (Estonia, 2011): only 1 per cent has a basic educational attainment, 5.8 per cent completed elementary school, and 37.1 per cent the secondary level. A majority – 56.1 per cent – of the Estonian VAA users have a higher formal education (*see* Vassil 2012).

— *Wahl-O-Mat* (Germany, 2009): about 38.7 per cent have a high formal education ('Abitur', university degree), 35.8 per cent a medium formal education and 20 per cent a low one (*see* Marschall and Schultze 2012b: 11).

---

5. *See* the survey results on the *Wahl-O-Mat* homepage: http://www.phil-fak.uni-duesseldorf.de/wahl-o-mat/en/results-of-the-online-surveys/.

6. A list of different VAA versions can be found at http://www.wahlomat-research.de/wahl-o-mat/en/links/.

Although it certainly is a problem to match and analytically compare the different degrees across countries, the overall picture is that a majority of the users of VAAs belong to the rather well-educated segments of the respective population, which again are strongly overrepresented compared to the respective population but also to the national online communities (for Germany *see* Marschall and Schultze 2012b).

d) Political Interest

Concerning the question whether or not users of VAAs belong to the group of politically interested persons, information has been provided at least for three cases:

— *Cabina Elettorale* (Italy, 2009): 59 per cent of the Italian VAA users say that they are interested in politics (*see* De Rosa 2010: 193).

— *Wahl-O-Mat* (Germany, 2009): also about 59.2 per cent of the users consider themselves politically interested (*see* Marschall and Schultze 2012b: 12).

— *smartvote* (Switzerland, 2007): 79 per cent of the *smartvote* users report they have rather high or high political interest (Fivaz and Nadig 2010: 181).

Although we do not have that much information about the political interest of VAA users, at least based on the surveys mentioned there is a clear indication that these tools are primarily used by voters who belong to the group of politically interested citizens.

To sum up: the typical VAA users seem to be rather young, male, highly educated and politically interested. This is a pattern which can be found in different systems. However, the available data does not allow for more in-depth causal analysis, under which conditions there might be a variation in the composition of the user groups.

Conclusions and open questions

What do we know about the users of the tools? First, beyond reasonable doubt there are millions of them. In some countries VAAs are able to reach a large share of the respective electorate, especially in those systems where Voting Advice Applications have become an established pre-election element, as it is the case, for example, in the Netherlands, Finland and Germany. Since in some other countries VAAs have only been implemented for the first time just recently, we might expect an overall increase of VAA users over the next few years. This raises the question of when the end of the flag pole could be reached: what is the maximum number of users who could be attracted by these tools within a country – and within Europe? And what are the conditions which determine and change the maximum value (e.g. the respective degree of internet penetration)?

Due to the low number of cases, other success factors beyond time are not easy to identify. Some assumptions had been articulated in VAA literature: the number of parties, the electoral system or the degree of voters' volatility could make a difference. Still, there could be more case-specific factors contributing to the popularity of these tools. For example, it might make a difference what organisation produces a VAA, depending on its resources and its reputation. Then again, design aspects could contribute to the success of a tool as it might have an impact on the attractiveness of the application. Finally, the respective internet culture could make a difference, i.e. the degree to which the public sphere of a country is shaped by online communication. Facing the low number of cases and the high degrees of freedom, a statistical test of the aforementioned assumptions is rather difficult. With the data at hand we cannot explain the value of the dependent variable, i.e. the variance in the popularity of VAAs. Eventually, the hypotheses could be tested in a number of case studies or by applying statistical methods which can deal with small numbers of cases such as Qualitative Comparative Analysis (QCA) (Ragin 2005).

Concerning the question whether there is something like a typical VAA user, some baseline characteristics can be identified: whenever data on users has been collected and analysed, the picture emerges that VAA users are on average male, young, highly educated and politically interested. Especially the fact that the users belong to the group of well-educated politically engaged persons once again brings up the question whether these tools primarily 'preach to the converted', i.e. that they carry political information and mobilisation to those who are already politically informed and involved (Marschall and Schmidt 2008). From a citizen education perspective in particular, this raises the question how to reach persons who are considered 'apolitical'. However, if only to a lesser degree, VAAs *are* able to reach uninformed and politically uninterested voters – perhaps even more than other tools of citizen education. Research is needed to understand why and how and with what effect.

Further questions await being answered concerning the quantity and the quality of the VAA user group. As there might be a relationship between the size and the composition of the group of VAA users, research on these tools could address how the increase of usage numbers changes the structure of the user group. It could be hypothesised that the larger the user group becomes, the more representative of the online community and the population it might become. Apart from cross-national comparison it might be helpful to conduct comparative analyses within systems, in order to keep the number of independent variables controllable.

The problems of comparing the figures from different tools show that there is a need for more standardised research designs and even a common research project profiling the users of Voting Advice Applications. An important first step would be to find an agreement on how to count the users; reflections on data cleaning (*see* Chapter Six) could serve as one point of departure.

Appendix 7.1

Sources for tables

Voting Advice Application	Sources for Table 7.1 and Table 7.2
BússolaEleitoral	Lobo/Vink/Lisi 2010: 145, and http://eleicoes.cne.pt/raster/detalhe.cf m?eleicao=ar&dia=27&mes=09&ano=2009&codreg=0&local=0
Cabina Elettorale	Email communication with Diego Garzia, and http://elezionistorico. interno.it/index.php?tpel=E&dtel=07/06/2009&tpa=Y&tpe=A&lev0 =0&levsut0=0&es0=S&ms=S; De Rosa 2010: 193, and http://www. freedomhouse.org/sites/default/files/inline_images/Italy_FOTN2011. pdf
Choose4Greece	Email communication with Fernando Mendez and http:// de.wikipedia.org/wiki/Parlamentswahl_in_Griechenland_Mai_2012
Do de Stemtest!	Walgrave *et al.* 2008, and http://verkiezingen2004.belgium.be/nl/vla/ results/results_graph_etop.html#
HelpMeVote	Email communication with Ioannis Andreadis, http://de.wikipedia. org/wiki/Parlamentswahl_in_Griechenland_Mai_2012, and http:// de.wikipedia.org/wiki/Parlamentswahl_in_Island_2013
Kieskompas	Garzia/Marschall 2012: 206, and http://www.verkiezingsuitslagen.nl/ Na1918/Verkiezingsuitslagen.aspx?VerkiezingsTypeId=1
KohoVolit CZ and KohoVolit SK	Email communication with Kamil Gregor, http://volby.cz/pls/ ps2010/ps2?xjazyk=EN, and http://app.statistics.sk/nrsr2012/sr/tab1. jsp?lang=en
Mano Balsas	Email communication with Rokas Salasevicius, and http://www. vrk.lt/2008_seimo_rinkimai/output_en/rezultatai_daugiamand_ apygardose/rezultatai_daugiamand_apygardose1turas.html
smartvote	http://blog.smartvote.ch/?p=1005, and http://www.bfs.admin. ch/bfs/portal/de/index/themen/17/02/blank/key/national_rat/ wahlbeteiligung.html; Fivaz/Nadig 2010: 181; own calculations, sources: http://www.bfs.admin.ch/bfs/portal/de/index/themen/16/04/ key/approche_globale.indicator.30106.301.html?open=4#4 and http:// www.bfs.admin.ch/bfs/portal/de/index/themen/01/02/blank/key/ frauen_und_maenner.html
smartvote.lu	Dumont/Kies 2012: 399, and http://www.elections.public.lu/fr/ elections-legislatives/2009/electeurs-inscrits/index.html; Dumont/ Kies 2012: 397
StemWijzer	Garzia/Marschall 2012: 206, and https://www.kiesraad.nl/sites/ default/files/BIJLAGE%20bij%20nieuwsbericht%20uitslag%20 TK2012.pdf
Vaalikone	Garzia/Marschall 2012: 206, and http://192.49.229.35/E2007/e/ aanaktiivisuus/aanestys1.htm

Voting Advice Application	Sources for Table 7.1 and Table 7.2
Valijakompass	http://www.ut.ee/kristjan.vassil/wp-content/uploads/report.pdf and http://www.vvk.ee/?lang=en, http://pub.stat.ee/px-web.2001/dialog/varval.asp?ma=IC32&ti=COMPUTER+AND+INTERNET+USERS+AGED+16–74+BY+GROUP+OF+INDIVIDUALS&path=../I_databas/Economy/20Information_technology/04Information_technology_in_household/&search=INTERNET&lang=1, own calculations
Vote Match UK	Homepage: http://www.votematch.org.uk/faq.php and http://www.parliament.uk/briefing-papers/RP10-36.pdf and http://news.bbc.co.uk/2/shared/election2010/results/
Wahlkabine	Mayer/Wassermair 2010: 178, and http://www.bmi.gv.at/cms/BMI_wahlen/nationalrat/2008/End_Gesamt.aspx
Wahl-O-Mat	Hompage: http://www.wahlomat-research.de/wahl-o-mat/en/facts-about-the-wahl-o-mat/, and http://bundeswahlleiter.de/de/bundestagswahlen/BTW_BUND_09/ ergebnisse/bundesergebnisse/index.html; Marschall/Schultze 2012b: 11; AGOF internet facts 2009-IV
Who should you vote for?	Email communication with Andrew Chapman, http://www.parliament.uk/documents/commons/lib/research/rp2005/rp05-033.pdf and http://en.wikipedia.org/wiki/United_Kingdom_general_election,_2005

Chapter Eight

The Impact of Voting Advice Applications on Electoral Participation

Diego Garzia, Andrea De Angelis and Joelle Pianzola

With the growing number of voters resorting to VAAs at election time, interest has arisen concerning the potential effect of these tools on the political behaviour of the users (Garzia 2010; Garzia and Marschall 2012). In this chapter, we focus on one of the crucial questions in this strand of literature, namely: What is the effect of VAA-usage on users' patterns of electoral participation? We begin by outlining a brief theoretical framework for the analysis. The available literature is then reviewed and critically assessed against our research design. Data and measures are presented before the statistical analysis. The results are discussed along with their aggregate-level implications in the last section.

Theory and methods

The available works on VAA effects on users' political behaviour have usually been framed within issue-voting theories (Garzia 2010). Simply put, issue voting refers to the assumption that vote choice is driven by the voter's proximity (or distance) to the position of the parties on the relevant issues (Downs 1957). The precondition for voters to link their policy preferences to party positions is obviously to have developed preferences in the first place. In order to be meaningful, however, issue voting also requires voters to have developed a sufficient amount of information with respect to the policy stances of the various parties taking part in the election (Carmines and Huckfeldt 1996).

Consistent with low-information rationality theories, the individual-level probability to cast a vote is inversely proportional to the effort required to gather enough information (Popkin 1994). A number of costs are involved in the process of becoming sufficiently informed about a particular political matter, namely: procurement (i.e. gathering the relevant data), analysis (i.e. undertaking a factual analysis of the data), and evaluation (i.e. relating data and/or factual analysis to specific goals) (Carmines and Huckfeldt 1996: 245). On the basis of these strands of literature, contemporary reasoning voters are expected to cut the cost of casting a vote by relying on whatever 'free' or inexpensive information can be picked up. In this respect, VAAs represent a potentially relevant source of political information for their users. By comparing the voter's position on the various issues with that of the parties', VAAs can significantly lower the costs related to the procurement, analysis and evaluation of information. Research on the impact of political knowledge on turnout provides evidence that higher levels of political information correspond to a higher likelihood of turnout in elections (Delli Carpini and Keeter 1996). In this sense, the usage of VAAs can be thought to reduce the cost of getting informed about politics and political parties, thereby increasing the chances of voting *vis-à-vis* abstention.

The providers of VAAs bear great confidence in the mobilising capacity of these tools (Ruusuvirta and Rosema 2009). Indeed, some VAAs are actually developed as an explicit attempt to mobilise voters and increase turnout (Marschall 2005). The few available analyses of VAA effects on turnout would seem to support this expectation. Studies of the impact of *Wahl-O-Mat* usage in German federal elections consistently find one *Wahl-O-Mat* user out of ten declaring feeling more motivated to turnout because of having used that VAA (Marschall 2005; Marschall and Schmidt 2010; Marschall and Schultze 2012a). Further evidence in this direction comes from the Swiss case. An analysis of *smartvote* 2007 data found about 40 per cent of respondents declaring that using the VAA had a 'decisive or at least slight influence on their decision to go to the polls' (Ladner and Pianzola 2010). According to Fivaz and Nadig (2010), the overall turnout in that election could have been about 5 per cent lower had the *smartvote* platform not been made available to Swiss voters. Similar conclusions are reported in Ruusuvirta and Rosema's (2009) analysis of the Dutch election of 2006. According to their study, the massive usage of VAAs among the voting population increased turnout at that election by 3 per cent (Ruusuvirta and Rosema 2009: 18). VAAs have also been found to exert a significant effect in supranational elections. An analysis by Dinas *et al.* (2014) shows that even after controlling for a wide set of socio-structural, attitudinal and behavioural variables, the individual-level probability to cast a vote in the EP election of 2009 was 14 percentage points higher for VAA users as compared to non-users.

This relatively short inventory of analyses of VAA effects on turnout highlights commonalities in terms of their exclusive focus on national case studies. Clearly, the lack of an integrated framework for analysis made previous research on VAAs unable to serve the scientific goal of knowledge accumulation. Indeed, the employment of widely different operational measures across countries led to hardly comparable results. A further shortcoming of these analyses comes from the way in which effects are measured. Virtually all the aforementioned studies (yet with very few exceptions) rely on opt-in surveys administered to users right after having been exposed to the VAA. In other words, the influence exerted by the VAA on users is measured through self-assessment and only among those who are willing to fill in the opt-in survey. Apart from being subject to a heavy self-selection bias, this kind of data does not even ensure that subjective estimates of impact will match with actual changes in terms of preferences and behaviour. Survey research has widely demonstrated that self-reported intentions are a rather unreliable source of information as to the actual influence of the treatment on the dependent variable. Indeed, Walgrave *et al.* (2008) found that the reported intention of changing behaviour as a result of having used a VAA is not always (nor often) matched with actual changes in voting behaviour.

Against this background, the aim of the analysis that follows is to provide a comparatively reliable assessment of VAA effects on their users' patterns of electoral participation across countries and time. In particular, we are interested in estimating (i) the causal impact of VAA usage on the individual-level probability to cast a vote in the election, and (ii) the aggregate contribution brought about by VAA usage in a country on the overall electoral turnout in that election.

The lack of comparable estimates that characterises the available literature will be addressed using standardised cross-national measures of VAA usage as made available by the growing amount of national election studies asking voters not only whether they did cast a vote in the election, but also whether they have used a VAA during the campaign. The availability of these measures will allow going beyond users' self-assessment of the effect that the VAA had on their decision to turnout. Our multivariate analysis will also take into account possible selection biases due to unobserved heterogeneity between VAA users and non-users. There are reasons to hypothesise that using a VAA and casting a ballot in elections represent two behavioural decisions that are associated beyond known or measured characteristics (Pianzola and Ladner 2011). In order to incorporate the possibility of systematic differences between the two groups of interest in the model specifications, we will rely on treatment effect models (Maddala 1983).

Data and measures

In the statistical analysis, we will employ eight datasets from four different countries: Finland (2007, 2011), Germany (2009), the Netherlands (2003, 2006, 2010), and Switzerland (2007, 2011). The dependent variable of the analysis is a dummy indicating whether respondents have voted in the election under analysis. The key independent variable of the analysis is another dummy, measuring whether respondents used a VAA (or more) during the campaign.

Table 8.1 presents the percentage of respondents that declared to have used a VAA during the campaign in each election study. According to these data, VAA-usage is most spread in Finland and the Netherlands, where over one voter out of three declares to have used a VAA during the campaign. In Germany and Switzerland, this proportion amounts to about one voter in ten. For all the countries in which more than one data source is available, it is interesting to observe an unambiguous upward trend in the proportion of VAA users over time.

Table 8.2 presents a bivariate analysis comparing the turnout rates across users and non-users in each sample. As it can be easily observed, VAA users are constantly more likely to cast a vote in the election as compared to non-users. The correlation of these variables is weak in magnitude (mean $r = .10$) but highly significant and signed as expected, and so are the various t-tests (last row in the table).[1]

---

1.   In the Dutch and Swiss studies, the whole sample has been asked directly about VAA usage during the campaign. However, in both the 2006 and 2010 Dutch studies, the 'direct' VAA-usage

Table 8.1: Percentage of VAA users across studies

	Finland 2007	Finland 2011	Germany 2009	Netherlands 2003	Netherlands 2006	Netherlands 2010	Switzerland 2007	Switzerland 2011
Users within sample	416	558	202	819	903	897	358	496
Valid N	1410	1297	2064	2556	2356	2151	4377	4379
% of VAA users	29.5%	43.0%	9.8%	32.0%	38.3%	41.7%	8.2%	11.3%

Table 8.2: Turnout rates across users and non-users

	Finland 2007	Finland 2011	Germany 2009	Netherlands 2003	Netherlands 2006	Netherlands 2010	Switzerland 2007	Switzerland 2011
% Voters (non-users)	80.2%	83.8%	77.4%	94.8%	90.6%	87.9%	67.5%	72.7%
	(796)	(614)	(1413)	(1647)	(1317)	(1102)	(2713)	(2812)
% Voters (users)	91.9%	92.6%	96.0%	98.3%	97.0%	92.1%	86.3%	87.3%
	(381)	(510)	(192)	(805)	(876)	(862)	(308)	(432)
T-test (Df)	-5.43	-4.76	-6.21	-4.16	-5.97	-6.74	-4.76	-7.04
	(1406)	(1282)	(2023)	(2554)	(2354)	(2149)	(1282)	(4363)

Individual-level analysis

Over time scholars have developed various individual-level explanations for voters' propensity to cast a vote in elections, ranging from the rational, incentive-based perspective, to the inclusion of the role of sanctions and social norms, and the consideration of social elements such as generational effects. The purpose of the present analysis is to test whether it is correct to attribute a genuine effect to

question was asked only to those who declared in a previous question that they 'know one or more tests of political preference on the internet, where people can find out which party they agree with the most'. In this analysis, we coded '0' all those who answered negatively to the 'filter' question. Also, the German study features a direct question of VAA usage. However, only a subsample of users has been asked this question – namely, all those who reported to have used (at least) once a week the internet (at least) once a week to inform themselves about political parties during the federal election campaign (i.e., those who declare to have never used the internet to gather information about political parties during the campaign have been coded '0'). With respect to Finland, there is no direct question regarding VAA use. We then decided to resort to an indirect measure based on how much did respondents follow the election campaign on 'Candidate Selectors on the internet' (i.e., VAAs). The possible answers are: 'A great deal', 'Quite a lot', 'Not very much', '"Not at all' and 'Can't say'. All the respondents picking any of the first three answers are coded '1', with all others coded '0'.

Table 8.3: Multivariate analysis of VAA effects on turnout

	Finland 2007	Finland 2011	Germany 2009	Netherlands 2003	Netherlands 2006	Netherlands 2010	Switzerland 2007	Switzerland 2011
Age	1.571**	0.850	-0.636	2.441**	2.423***	1.650***	0.054	-0.121
	(0.770)	(0.736)	(0.710)	(1.127)	(0.768)	(0.618)	(0.342)	(0.351)
Age sq.	-1.000	-0.359	0.558	-1.943	-1.992**	-1.606***	0.336	0.462
	(0.778)	(0.758)	(0.715)	(1.202)	(0.782)	(0.612)	(0.351)	(0.365)
Education	0.279**	0.394***	0.052	-0.246	0.264**	0.218+	0.164***	-0.019
	(1.999)	(0.153)	(0.138)	(0.224)	(0.134)	(0.113)	(0.062)	(0.063)
Gender	-0.016	-0.120	-0.213+	-0.006	-0.062	0.018	0.016	-0.012
	(0.119)	(0.121)	(0.138)	(0.206)	(0.137)	(0.121)	(0.054)	(0.055)
Income	0.124	0.310**	0.214+	0.279	-0.101	0.058	0.223***	0.104+
	(0.141)	(0.138)	(0.124)	(0.190)	(0.161)	(0.144)	(0.062)	(0.062)
Belongs to a religion	-0.060	0.002	0.119	0.392+	0.024	0.226+	0.013	0.128**
	(0.126)	(0.123)	(0.112)	(0.217)	(0.131)	(0.118)	(0.054)	(0.054)
Trade union member	0.020	n/a	0.042	n/a	0.144	0.053	n/a	n/a
	(0.123)		(0.123)		(0.144)	(0.115)		
TV news exposure	0.021	0.266**	0.227**	-0.191	0.111	0.168	-0.034	0.013
	(0.130)	(0.134)	(0.116)	(0.204)	(0.118)	(0.104)	(0.057)	(0.058)
Partisanship	0.427***	0.233**	0.459***	n/a	0.082	0.227***	0.342***	0.436***
	(0.120)	(0.119)	(0.127)		(0.183)	(0.166)	(0.060)	(0.057)
Interest in politics	0.174	0.786***	0.805	0.431**	0.272	0.525**	0.650***	0.587***
	(0.153)	(0.176)	(0.131)	(0.210)	(1.128)	(0.106)	(0.060)	(0.060)
Ideology	-0.094	-0.034	-0.013	-0.206	0.132	0.080	-0.063	-0.138**
	(0.126)	(0.136)	(0.121)	(0.201)	(0.130)	(0.111)	(0.057)	(0.059)
Satisf. with democracy	0.155	0.001	0.308***	0.341+	0.112	0.075	0.012	0.049
	(0.114)	(0.127)	(0.117)	(0.180)	(0.118)	(0.101)	(0.055)	(0.059)
Past turnout	0.829***	0.519***	0.602***	0.797***	0.829***	0.607***	0.909***	0.926***
	(0.086)	(0.085)	(0.117)	(0.099)	(0.077)	(0.065)	(0.048)	(0.046)
VAA Usage	0.527***	0.237*	0.147	0.650**	0.463***	0.591***	0.256***	0.323***
	(0.155)	(0.149)	(0.174)	(0.270)	(0.151)	(0.138)	(0.066)	(0.070)
Constant	-5.33***	-4.36***	-1.741	-5.727	-5.024***	-4.218***	-3.543***	-3.094
	(1.302)	(1.237)	(0.126)	(2.037)	(1.245)	(1.030)	(0.589)	(0.650)
BIC	631.92	600.487	711.213	299.778	621.199	760.462	2489.362	2397.825
McFadden adj. R^2	.294	.245	.278	.287	.269	.221	.336	.332
Adj. count R^2	.246	.285	.234	.103	.096	.207	.403	.378
Valid N	1062	1030	1181	1016	1793	1693	3127	3254

Note: table entries represent standardised logit coefficients. Standard errors in parentheses.
***p<.001, **p<.01, *p<.05, +p<.10.

VAAs on turnout levels. Hence, our task implies the consideration of statistical controls that include the main explanations of electoral participation. Given the cross-sectional, individual-level nature of the present analysis, we proceed by abstracting from contextual explanations (i.e. the institutional and socio-structural ones) to focus on the individual determinants. We thus identify three main accounts of turnout rates (for a more elaborated discussion of various explanatory models of turnout, *see* Smets and van Ham 2013). The resource approach focuses on the resources needed to cast the ballot in terms of time, resources and cognitive skills. One of its most basic propositions is that more resources corresponds to a higher likelihood of turnout in elections. To separate the effect of VAAs from the resource explanation we introduce controls for age (including possible quadratic effects), gender, educational attainment, and income level. Secondly, the mobilisation approach expects higher turnout rates when citizens are mobilised by interest groups and social actors. We thus further control for the belonging to a religious group and for trade union membership, as well as for the mobilisation potential of media (as measured by the frequency of TV news consumption). Thirdly, we consider various psychological determinants of turnout that are especially relevant in terms of cognitive and identification mechanisms. We include variables controlling for the strength of party identification, ideological attitudes (self-placement on the left–right scale), interest in political matters and sense of satisfaction towards democracy. Finally, we include a control capturing past turnout behaviour in order to control for the effect of voting habits. As the dependent variable (turnout) is dichotomous, logistic regression has been preferred to traditional OLS estimation (linear probability models).

The results presented in Table 8.3 provide strong confirmation of our research hypothesis. With only the exception of Germany, VAA usage is always significantly related to turnout at the individual level even after the introduction of our extensive set of statistical controls. Indeed, VAA usage would seem to appear one of the strongest predictors across the various models. The results of our analytical effort are summarised in Figure 8.1, where we plot the increase in predicted probabilities to cast the ballot (individual-level) between VAA users and non-users. The strongest effects can be found in Switzerland – VAA users are about 10 per cent more likely to cast a vote as compared to non-users. As a bottom line, there is a 2% increase in Germany, Finland (2011) and the Nether-lands (2003).

Treatment effect models

As outlined earlier, a regular regression model might not suffice for adequately comparing VAA users to non-users in terms of electoral participation. If the decision to become a VAA user and the decision to go to the polls have common determinants that are either unobserved or unknown, estimates from a regular regression model will be biased. Observational studies generally suffer from a lack of random treatment assignment (Morton and Williams 2010), hence from the fact that it is the respondent, rather than the researcher, who decides whether to use

Figure 8.1: Percentage increase in predicted turnout probability (individual-level)

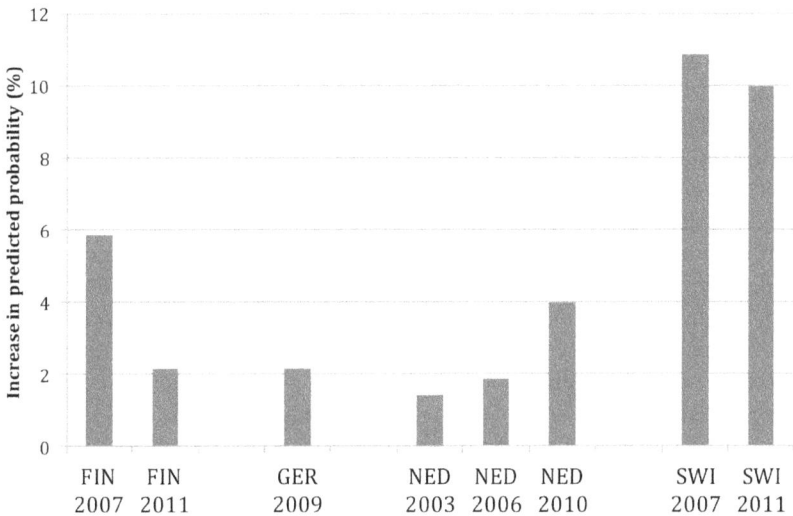

Table 8.4: Treatment effect models of VAA effects on turnout for specific countries

	Finland 2007	Finland 2011	Germany 2009	Netherlands 2003	Netherlands 2006	Netherlands 2010	Switzerland 2007	Switzerland 2011
VAA-usage	0.395	1.120*	1.073***	0.063	0.817	0.800*	0.342	0.853**
	(0.95)	(2.55)	(3.62)	(0.07)	(0.72)	(2.20)	(1.15)	(2.67)
Rho	0.088	-0.587	-0.521**	0.295	-0.250	-0.193	0.066	-0.179
	(0.38)	(-1.61)	(-2.62)	(0.53)	(-0.34)	(-0.86)	(0.48)	(-1.08)

Note: Cell entries are (recursive) bivariate probit estimates. Standard deviations in parentheses. Dependent variable: Turnout. Rho indicates correlation coefficient of the two simultaneously estimated equations (Outcome equation: Turnout predicted from VAA usage, Age, Education, Income, Belongs to a religion, Trade union member, TV news exposure, Partisanship, Interest in politics, Ideology, Satisfaction with democracy. Selection equation: VAA usage predicted from Age, Education, Gender, Income, Belongs to a religion, Trade union member, TV news exposure, Partisanship, Interest in politics, Ideology, Satisfaction with democracy). Exclusion restriction used: Gender and Ideology. *** $p < 0.001$ ** $p < 0.05$ * $p < 0.1$.

a VAA for the elections or not, thus self-selecting themselves into the 'treatment condition' (in this case, using a VAA). The selection process might systematically distinguish VAA users from non-users, and if those differences are also predictive of electoral participation then regular regression methods will provide biased and inconsistent results (Wooldridge 2002). To tackle the issue of self-selection and possible unobserved heterogeneity in our data we employed treatment effect models (Maddala 1983). A treatment effect model simultaneously models both decisions (i.e. VAA usage and electoral participation) and further models the expected correlations between these two decisions, thereby eliminating possible selection biases in the estimation procedure (Greene 2002). The results of this effort are presented in Table 8.4. According to our model specifications, it turns out that our results for Finland, the Netherlands and Switzerland do not suffer from hidden selection biases in comparing the participatory behaviour of VAA users to non-users. However, our model specifications do indicate a systematic selection bias in the German data. It is interesting to note that unlike in the regular regression setup, the effect of VAA use on electoral participation in Germany becomes significant when controlling for unmeasured systematic differences between VAA users and non-users.

Figure 8.2: Aggregate effect of VAA usage on turnout (%)

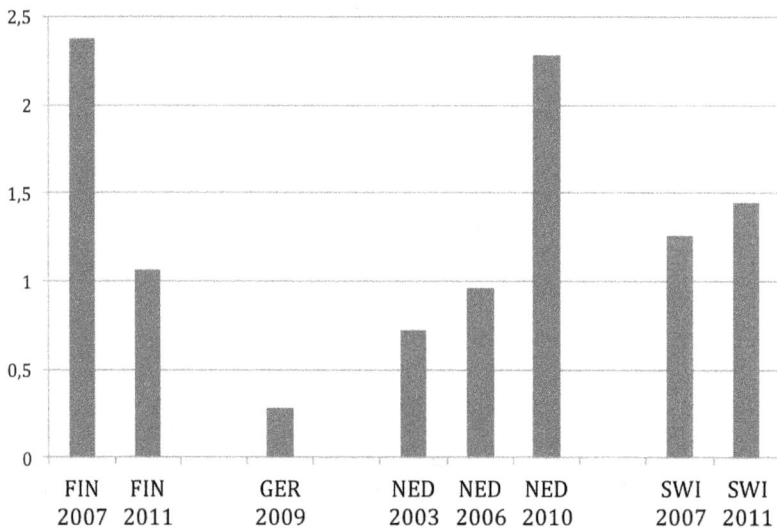

Aggregate-level implications and concluding remarks

The final question we address in this chapter relates to the aggregate-level implications of VAA usage. As an ever-growing number of voters are resorting to VAAs during election campaigns, and to the extent that VAAs are able (as we showed in the section above) to motivate users to turnout in the election, a tangible effect of VAAs on the aggregate turnout rate can be envisaged. To test this expectation, we performed a number of logit simulations. In particular, we estimated how the turnout shares in each of the elections under analysis would have decreased had no one (in the sample) made use of a VAA during the campaign. The estimated aggregate VAA effect in each country and election is reported in Figure 8.2. As one can see, the effects are not spectacular in magnitude but yet remarkable in aggregate terms – the effect being quantifiable in about a 1 percentage point increase throughout time and countries with peaks above 2 per cent in Finland (2007) and the Netherlands (2010).

Overall, VAAs would seem to exert an impact on democratic elections. By providing information about political issues to their users, VAAs make contemporary reasoning voters more likely to cast a ballot. In turn, the massive growth of users among the electorate has led VAAs to bear a measurable effect on turnout rates in national elections. The findings presented in this chapter show that VAA users are in every instance more likely to cast a ballot as compared to non-users. Even after controlling for a wide range of alternative explanations, VAA usage remains a highly significant predictor of turnout at the individual level. Interestingly, we found that in the majority of countries under analysis self-selection into VAA use was of no concern for the estimation procedure. In other words, whatever causes people to use VAAs prior to the elections is not a driving force for electoral participation. Rather, the engagement with the VAA itself is what leads people to turnout more at the polls. The only country where self-selection mechanisms seem to play a role is Germany: the country, among those under analysis in this chapter, where VAAs are comparatively less spread. This indicates that a growing expansion of VAAs in election campaigns might diversify the user base, diminishing the stark differences between those who use VAAs versus those who do not use them – and with that, reducing the possibility of unobserved heterogeneity that might have an impact upon the effects of interest.

Appendix 8.1

List of control variables included in the regression analysis

Resources model	
Age / Age sq.	in years
Education	interval-level scale from 0 (lowest) to 1 (highest)
Gender	female=0; male=1
Income	interval-level scale from 0 (lowest) to 1 (highest)

Mobilisation model	
Belongs to a religion	no=0; yes=1
Trade union member	no=0; yes=1
TV news exposure (FIN)	How much attention did you pay to media coverage of the parliamentary elections: television news and current affairs programs? [No attention at all=0; Only a little attention=1; A fair amount of attention=2; A great deal of attention=3]
TV news exposure (GER)	Weekly frequency with use of TV news programs: ARD [Scale from 0 (never) to 7 (weekly)]
TV news exposure (NED)	Frequency watching NOS/RTL4 TV newscasts (Average value) [Less than once a week=0; 1–2 times a week=1; 3–4 times a week=2; daily=3]
TV news exposure (SWI)	How many days/week R watches news on TV? [Scale from 0 (never) to 7 (weekly)]

Psychological model	
Partisanship	no partyID=0; not very close=1; somewhat close=2; very close=3
Interest in politics (FIN, SWI)	not at all=0; not very interested=1; somewhat interested=2; very interested=3
Interest in politics (GER)	not at all=0; not very=1; middling=2; quite interested=3; very interested=4
Interest in politics (NED)	not interested=0; fairly interested=1; very interested=2
Ideology	scale from 0 (left) to 10 (right)
Satisfaction with democracy (FI, NET, SWE)	not at all=0; not very satisfied=1; fairly satisfied=2; very satisfied=3
Satisfaction with democracy (GER)	0=very dissatisfied; 1=fairly dissatisfied; 2=neither/nor; 3=fairly satisfied; 4=very satisfied

Voting Habit Model	
Past turnout	no=0; yes=1

Chapter Nine

The Impact of Voting Advice Applications on Vote Choice

Ioannis Andreadis and Matthew Wall

In this chapter, we re-examine one of the best-investigated aspects of VAAs: their effects on the vote choices of users. We focus on whether VAA use is associated with an increased likelihood of vote switching using an integrated dataset comprising nine national election studies that include items on VAA use. We explore the strengths and weaknesses of these data – noting that they are structured in a manner that makes it difficult to definitively distinguish causation from correlation, but that they do offer a high level of external validity – making it possible to make inferences about the impact of VAAs on electorates. We find that VAA use is associated with an increased likelihood to 'switch' between parties, controlling for an array of confounding factors. This finding is robust to several modelling strategies that were employed in order to account for epistemologically problematic data structures. We conclude with recommendations for future national election studies seeking to capture the effects of VAA use.

Introduction

Given their constantly increasing global reach and popularity (Rosema, this volume), it is important to know whether VAAs have an impact on users' vote choice. As Bartels (2006: 134) reminds us,

> the primary aim of participants in electoral campaigns is to produce politically significant changes in the attitudes and perceptions of perspective voters. The primary aim of scholarly observers of election campaigns is to measure and explain those politically significant changes.

While, as Garzia *et al.* (this volume) elaborate, several scholars have focused on turnout as a dependent variable; the question of whether VAA use affects vote choice is also the subject of several research papers (Marschall and Schmidt 2010; Pianzola *et al.* 2012; Ruusuvirta and Rosema 2009; Walgrave *et al.* 2008; Wall *et al.* 2012).

This paper takes up the question of VAAs' effects on vote choice, but adopts a novel methodological approach – we seek to test for a VAA 'effect' across several political systems (Switzerland, Germany, the Netherlands and Finland) using data collected in national election studies. Because all of these studies include questions about respondents' use of VAAs, we combine these datasets and perform a pooled analysis of the link between VAA use and voters' propensity to switch allegiance between parties. We outline our theoretical understanding of VAA effects on vote choice, elaborating a testable hypothesis. We then discuss the epistemological challenges of inferring 'effects' on the basis of survey data, before presenting our data, methods and analysis. We conclude with a discussion of best practice for future national election studies that seek to capture the effects of VAA use.

Why would we expect VAA use to influence vote choice?

In a context of growing voter–party dealignment in established democracies around the world (Dalton 2000), the importance attributed to political campaigns by both practitioners and academics has grown rapidly in recent years (Farrell and Schmidt-Beck 2002), resulting in a scholarly focus on short-term determinants of voting behaviour, including *inter alia* party issue stances (Franklin *et al.* 1992; McAllister 2007; Carmines and Stimson 1980; Erikson and Tedin 2007). We proceed from the presumption that issue-based voting represents a reasoned attempt by voters to use party policy positions to guide their electoral decision (Downs 1957). During campaigns, candidates and parties announce positions on issues in order to win votes, and voters choose from alternatives that best represent their interests on those issues. If we adopt this conceptualisation of political campaigns, VAAs represent a uniquely personalised and directed source of issue-based political information that voters can access during campaigns.

Walgrave *et al.* (2008) argue that the potential for VAAs to influence electoral behaviour lies in their informative effect. A major function of VAAs is to substantially reduce the cognitive cost needed for a voter to engage in informed issue-voting. Wall *et al.* (2012) further argue that the 'recommendations' issued by VAAs have a powerful heuristic quality given that modern campaigns are often suffused with tracts of indigestible data coming from a baffling array of political and media actors. Thus, it is anticipated that VAA use may influence voter behaviour by making voters more likely to vote for the party that is recommended to them.

What are the observable implications of this theoretical approach? The most obvious hypothesis is that voters should be more likely to vote for the party that was 'recommended' to them by the VAA. Indeed, Wall *et al.* (2012) find that this was the case for a group of Dutch VAA users. However, not all public opinion datasets that measure VAA use include a variable describing the specific recommendations received by users, and, even where they do, a user's recall of their recommendation is not always reliable (Wall *et al.* 2012). A second, more analytically tractable implication of the argument can be stated in the following hypothesis:

H1: VAA users are more likely to switch parties (either between elections or during campaigns) than non-users.

The logic underlying this hypothesis is that, in cases where they are recommended a party that they had not previously voted for or considered as a potential vote choice, voters are more likely to give consideration to that party (Pianzola *et al.* 2012; Walgrave *et al.* 2008). It is this empirical contention that we will explore. We begin this exploration with a discussion of the challenges involved in identifying VAA 'effects'.

The epistemological and methodological challenges of identifying VAA 'effects'

Differentiating causation from correlation is a challenge that unites social scientists across a wide array of specialisations – and one that has long been acknowledged as being of fundamental epistemological importance (*see*, for example: Wright 1921). This is particularly the case for advocates of a 'scientific' approach to the social sciences, with the foundational epistemological work on the topic holding that a definitional criterion of scientific social research is that 'the goal is inference' (King *et al.* 1994: 7). King *et al.* go on to elaborate that scientific inference can be either descriptive or causal, with the latter defined as 'learning about causal effects from the data observed' (8).

However, in seeking to arrive at causal inferences about the social/political world, we confront a fundamental problem: the impossibility of observing the counterfactual (Imai *et al.* 2011). Because human events cannot be replayed with a certain variable altered and everything else held constant, we can never be fully certain when we seek to infer causal relationships by observing data drawn from the social/political world.

Several studies investigating the effects of VAAs on their users' vote choices have employed post-election surveys of users (sometimes as part of larger surveys which also include non-users), where respondents provide their own subjective evaluations of whether their choice was influenced by their visit to a VAA site (Carlson and Strandburg 2005; Aarts and van der Kolk 2007; Ladner *et al.* 2010; Marschall and Schmidt 2010; Walgrave *et al.* 2008). These surveys have varied dramatically in their estimates of the importance attributed by users to VAA sites. Estimates of percentages of users who feel that their eventual decision was influenced by their visit to a VAA vary from a low of 6 per cent (Marschall 2005) to a high of 67 per cent (Lander *et al.* 2010). Unfortunately, a lack of standardisation in the field to date means that the specific questions used to elicit estimates of site influence vary across studies, which may help to explain some of the disparity of the findings.

From an epistemological point of view, subjective evaluations of the extent to which an event or recommendation was influential after the fact, while informative are regrettably not totally reliable sources of information as to the actual influence that the event may have exerted. The agenda-setting, priming and framing literatures in communications and media studies, for instance, have uncovered the existence of politically influential behaviours that rarely register in the consciousness of voters (Scheufele and Tweksbury 2007). More generally, post-election surveys provide limited analytical leverage over the impact of any single campaign event on voting patterns, which is why dynamic designs, such as survey panels and rolling cross-sections (Bartels 2006), have been employed by researchers interested in campaign effects. Finally, surveys of VAA users rely on the cooperation of those users, and it is likely that those VAA users who respond to survey requests from VAA designers are more likely to have a positive perception of VAAs (Andreadis 2013a). We note here that Vassil (2012) presents a promising approach to dealing with this issue for user surveys, using a Heckman selection model in his re-analysis of Swiss *smartvote* user survey data.

The ideal scenario from an epistemological and methodological standpoint is random assignment of a treatment (in this case, VAA use). Given random assignment, one can simply compare treatment and control groups. Indeed, this approach was adopted by Pianzola *et al.* (2012) – subjects were randomly assigned to treatment and control groups, where the treatment was an email invitation to use the *smartvote* VAA. The resultant analysis indicates that, as our research hypothesis implies, those exposed to the treatment were more likely to consider multiple parties as viable vote choices.

However, experimental studies are of limited external validity when the experimental subjects are not randomly drawn from a representative sample of society. Furthermore, the attribution of VAA participation across a society by a research team is ethically questionable, given the purported role of VAAs as a source of politically useful information for voters (Marschall and Schmidt 2008). Finally, if access to a VAA is open to the public, we cannot be sure that the subjects selected for the control group have not followed the treatment (i.e. used the VAA), because even if they have not got an email invitation, they could learn about the VAA from their peers. This means that analysts must engage with observational survey data based on representative sampling if they wish to generate inferences about the effects of VAAs on electorates.

The difficulty that cross-sectional survey data poses relates to causal inference. VAA use is not randomly assigned to individuals (*see* Marschall, this volume), and VAA sites can attract high numbers of unaligned or wavering voters (Ladner *et al.* 2010). Analyses of whether users of VAA sites exhibit higher in-campaign or between-election volatility than non-users may therefore tell us more about the type of audiences that VAAs attract than about the effects that they may be said to exert. As such, a bivariate analysis may report a VAA 'effect' that is little more than spurious correlation.

One strategy for addressing this difficulty involves using panellised survey data, where the same individuals are tracked at several time points, so that the causal effect of VAA exposure between these time points is identifiable (Ruusuvirta and Rosema 2009; Walgrave *et al.* 2008; Wall *et al.* 2012). Unfortunately, panellised data structures are the exception, rather than the rule, for national election studies, and we therefore cannot draw on such methods in our analysis. Even if we had panel data, we would not be absolutely sure that the users switched their vote choice because of VAA use. It is possible that they switched their vote before visiting the VAA due to some other event. The only way to learn about vote intention before VAA use is to ask users on the VAA site immediately before presenting their 'recommendation' output.

Therefore, in this article we adopt the following analytical strategy when testing for the existence of VAA 'effects' using national election study data that captures responses at a single time point. We firstly control for possibly confounding variables – i.e. variables that are likely to affect both the probability of VAA use and vote switching. Secondly, we test the robustness of our analysis to multiple model specifications, including models that are specifically designed to account for endogenous causal relationships between independent and dependent variables. Finally, we analyse both pooled models capturing data from multiple studies and analyses that separate out the individual studies.

Data, variables and methods

Data – National election studies with VAA-use questions

In order to test our research hypothesis, at a minimum we need a variable that describes vote switching and a variable that describes VAA use. All national election studies include questions regarding vote choice both for the current and the previous election, and several include an item about in-campaign switching.

On the other hand, items regarding VAA use have appeared in a very limited number of national election studies questionnaires. We were able to find such items in studies from Finland,[1] Germany, Switzerland and the Netherlands. In our pooled dataset there are three election studies from Finland (2003, 2007 and 2011), one from Germany (2009), three from the Netherlands (2003, 2006 and 2010) and two from Switzerland (2007 and 2011). None of these datasets includes a variable for in-campaign vote switching, but all of them include variables regarding vote choice in the current and in the previous election. In order to analyse vote switching, we therefore consider only those respondents who named the political party they have voted for in both elections. For these respondents we calculate a new variable that describes vote switching coded with the value of 1 when the two vote choices are different and 0 when the two vote choices are the same.

For VAA use, the situation is more complicated. For instance, in Finland information on VAA use was extracted by a question asking Finnish voters

1. Karvonen, L. and Paloheimo, H. Finnish National Election Study 2003 [computer file]. FSD1260, version 1.1 (2012–01–05). Espoo: TNS Gallup Finland [data collection], 2003. Elections and Representative Democracy in Finland research group [producer], 2003. Tampere: Finnish Social Science Data Archive [distributor], 2012; Paloheimo, H. Finnish National Election Study 2007 [computer file]. FSD2269, version 1.1 (2012–01–05). Helsinki: Taloustutkimus [data collection], 2007. The Political Participation and Modes of Democracy: Finland in a Comparative Perspective research group [producer]. Tampere: Finnish Social Science Data Archive [distributor], 2012; Finnish National Election Study (2003) [codebook]. Tampere : Finnish Social Science Data Archive [producer and distributor], 2012; Finnish National Election Study 2007 [codebook]. Tampere : Finnish Social Science Data Archive [producer and distributor], 2012.

whether they followed the election campaign via online candidate selectors. The German study includes a direct question on VAA use, but this question is asked only to a subset of survey participants, because another question (about frequency of internet use) is used as a filter. The Dutch study includes a direct question on VAA use but it is asked only to respondents who have indicated that they know one or more VAAs. Table 9.1 shows the rates of VAA use and vote switching per study.

Variables to be controlled for

VAA use is only one of a number of factors that could have an impact on vote switching. Based on the established literature on vote choice and on the constraints imposed by the availability of the suitable variables in all datasets we have in our hands, we can construct a regression model to estimate the impact of VAA use on vote switching while controlling for other factors that can affect vote switching. Thus, in addition to VAA use, we have included the following control variables: age of respondent; strength of party identification; evaluation of the economy; left/right self-placement; and level of satisfaction with the way that democracy works in the country. In the pooled analysis, we also include country/year dummies for each election study.

Age is a particularly important control in an analysis of vote switching because it has been argued that as people get older, they accumulate political experience and become more confident about their party identification and less likely to change it. In addition, older people are more likely to forgive mistakes made by their parties. As Franklin and Jackson (1983: 960) put it:

> [A]n older Republican in 1964 or an older Democrat in 1972 may easily discount the platforms of their party in those elections as not being truly representative of the party. On the other hand, younger voters with less experience and fewer observations may not be so sure of future party positions.

As a result, younger voters are expected to switch their votes more often. [2] Similarly, Carrubba and Timpone (2005) find that older people are less likely to defect from governing coalition parties.

Strong party identification is the best-known factor that makes voters remain loyal to their party (Campbell *et al.* 1960; Herrnson and Curry 2011; Evans and Chzhen 2013), thus we expect to find party identification to have a negative relationship with vote switching.

With regard to left/right self-placement, right-wing voters (being conservatives) are less likely than left-wing voters to change their votes. Marsh (2009), using data on the elections for the European Parliament, finds that left-wing voters are more likely to switch. Similarly, on the other side of the Atlantic, Herrnson and Curry

---

2. In fact, Franklin and Jackson (1983: 965) conclude that the effect of past identification on current identifications increases by 0.13 for each ten years of age.

Table 9.1: VAA use and vote switching per study

Study	N	VAA use	Vote switching
Switzerland 2011	1698	12.5%	22.9%
Switzerland 2007	1883	9.3%	19.8%
Netherlands 2010	1713	43.0%	44.0%
Netherlands 2006	1963	38.9%	37.6%
Netherlands 2003	2355	33.1%	28.2%
Germany 2009	1260	12.5%	24.0%
Finland 2011	845	45.0%	34.8%
Finland 2007	944	30.4%	22.8%
Finland 2003	603	26.5%	19.2%
Total	13264	27.4%	29.0%

(2011: 296) find that 'Republicans on the liberal end of the spectrum (roughly 2 per cent of all identifiers), were about 37 percentage points more likely to cross party lines than the most conservative Republicans'.

As far as the evaluation of the economy is concerned, a negative evaluation would make voters of the government party/parties more likely to switch their votes (*see* Erikson 1989; Evans and Chzhen 2013). Furthermore, Carrubba and Timpone (2005) show that unemployment and low GDP have a negative impact on voting for governing coalition parties.

Finally, with regard to satisfaction with democracy, we expect unsatisfied voters to be more likely to switch their vote. According to Zelle, political dissatisfaction is a potential predictor of volatility: '[F]loating voters on average are somewhat less satisfied with the political system, less trusting in parties, and less happy about their favoured party' (2005: 340).

With regard to the profile of VAA users, analyses that focus on user demographics have consistently shown that VAA users are younger, more affluent and more educated than national populations as a whole (Çarkoğlu *et al.* 2012; Hooghe and Teepe 2007; Marschall, this volume; Ruusuvirta and Rosema 2009; Wall *et al.* 2009). However, there are indications that the gap between VAA users and the rest of the population is narrowing over time (Fivaz and Nadig 2010; Garzia *et al.* this volume). We thus use these socio-demographic variables as predictors of VAA use. We also control for political interest, because it is expected to have a positive relationship with VAA use (Marschall, this volume). Finally, we have included the strength of party identification as an independent variable in order to test if it has a positive or negative impact on VAA use.

Methods: Modelling VAA effects

Since our dependent variable (vote switching) is a binary variable, we can assume that the observed outcomes (0, 1) are determined by a latent regression on a continuous variable and that the errors are distributed according to the Normal distribution $N(0,1)$, i.e. we have a probit model. If all the aforementioned independent variables were exogenous, we could use a simple probit model for vote switching.

But, as we discussed above, VAA use is not randomly attributed across the population, so we also need to employ a model where VAA use is not considered to be exogenously determined. Following the approach of Greene (2002: 715–718) and Greene and Hensher (2010: 90–93), we can model VAA effects on vote choice as a recursive simultaneous-equations model and, to be more specific, as a recursive bivariate probit model. A recursive bivariate model is a more complex specification than a probit, which accounts for unobserved heterogeneity that affects both independent and dependent variables. This is similar to 'Model 6' analysed by Maddala (1983: 122–123).[3] Bivariate probit is the extension of the probit model to allow more than one equation, with correlated disturbances, as in a seemingly unrelated regressions model. We also note that this modelling strategy is advocated by Pianzola and Ladner (2011) in order to analyse the effects of VAAs on the vote-switching propensities of users employing data that includes both treated and non-treated respondents (i.e. a mix of those who have and have not used VAAs).

In applying a bivariate probit model to a dataset there are two issues that require special attention: i) testing the goodness of fit of the model to the dataset, and ii) testing if the correlation coefficient ρ equals zero. If the goodness of fit fails then the model does not perform well in describing the data we have in our hands. For our model, which is based on maximum likelihood estimation, it is necessary to test for the goodness of fit because maximising the joint density of the observed dependent variables does not guarantee a good fit (Greene 2002: 686). The goodness of fit is tested using Murphy's score test of normality in bivariate probit models (*see* Murphy 2007; Chiburis *et al.* 2012). The correlation coefficient ρ measures the correlation between the disturbances in the equations. According to Greene: 'ρ measures (roughly) the correlation between the outcomes after the influence of the included factors is accounted for' (2002: 717). If ρ equals zero the model consists of independent probit equations, which can be estimated separately (712). The hypothesis $\rho=0$ is tested by the likelihood ratio chi-square test (comparing the likelihood of the full bivariate model with the sum of the log likelihoods for the univariate probit models).

---

3. Following Maddala, we should clarify that our model is not a sequential model. Our model would be sequential if the occurrence of VAA use was a precondition for vote switching (i.e., if we could not measure the vote switching or if it was always 0 when VAA use was 0). If the model was sequential, the proper estimation procedure would be to estimate the first model (VAA use) using the entire set of data, and estimate the second model (vote switching), but using the subset of observations for which VAA use =1.

In the analysis below, we employ recursive bivariate probit models for cases where ρ is statistically significant, indicating that the exogeneity assumption cannot be met. This is the case for our pooled analysis of all datasets. However, apart from the 2011 Swiss election study, ρ is not statistically significant in any of the models for individual election studies, so in these cases we employ probit models.

Analysis

Table 9.2 reports the results of an analysis of a pooled dataset comprising our nine national election studies. The results reported in bold in the first column indicate that VAA use has a positive and significant effect on users' likelihood to engage in vote switching, with 99 per cent confidence. This finding provides support for the relationship between VAA use and vote switching that we elaborated in Hypothesis 1.

In order to estimate the average treatment effect of VAA use on vote choice we have calculated the average value of the differences of the conditional probabilities P(vote switching = 1 | VAA use = 1) – P(vote switching = 1 | VAA use = 1) to get $ATE_{biprobit}$=0.209. This means that on average the probability of switching vote after using a VAA is 0.21 higher than the probability of switching vote without using a VAA. If we have used the univariate probit the estimated average treatment effect would be ATE_{probit} =0.073; i.e. it would be considerably smaller (though still positive and statistically significant).

The correlation coefficient of the bivariate probit model (reported in the third column of Table 9.2) is significant and negative (ρ=-0.247**), indicating that this modelling approach is necessary for these data. We note that Pianzola and Ladner (2011: 12) inform us that '[a] negative rho indicates that the treatment effect is underestimated by an ordinary probit model where the selection bias is not considered', and indeed the coefficient for 'VAA use' is considerably smaller for the probit specification which is consistent with the corresponding findings on the average treatment effects.

Age has a negative effect both on VAA use and on vote switching. The bivariate probit model provides a better understanding of the impact of age on vote switching: age affects vote switching both directly and indirectly (through VAA use).

However, in post-estimation analysis we noted that this biprobit model gives a Murphy's score test result of $X^2_{(9)}$ = 43.27 and sig<0.001, indicating that the model fit is not good for these data. Specifically, this result indicates that the assumption of bivariate normal distribution of the error terms, which underlies the bivariate probit model, does not hold. Using biprobit models in each individual study we found that the Murphy's score indicates that the bivariate probit model does not fit well to the data of the Dutch 2010 and 2006 and the Swiss 2007 studies. Thus, as a robustness check we exclude these three studies from the pooled analysis reported in Table 9.3. We note that the substantive findings discussed above (i.e. the coefficient of VAA use and the correlation coefficient ρ) do not change for this

Table 9.2: Recursive bivariate probit model of vote switching, pooled data

Variables	Switching	VAA Use	ρ
VAA use	0.628***		
	(0.134)		
Age	-0.004**	-0.031***	
	(0.001)	(0.001)	
Party identification	-0.349***	-0.027*	
	(0.015)	(0.016)	
Evaluation of the economy	-0.037*		
	(0.021)		
Left/Right Self-placement	-0.022***		
	(0.006)		
Satisfaction with Democracy	-0.055***		
	(0.015)		
Finland 2007	0.294***	0.183**	
	(0.088)	(0.085)	
Finland 2011	0.381***	0.593***	
	(0.096)	(0.087)	
Germany 2009	0.201**	-0.448***	
	(0.080)	(0.081)	
Netherlands 2003	-0.013	-0.0938	
	(0.077)	(0.080)	
Netherlands 2006	0.166**	0.146**	
	(0.076)	(0.074)	
Netherlands 2010	0.265***	0.223***	
	(0.079)	(0.075)	
Switzerland 2007	0.078	-0.893***	
	(0.074)	(0.079)	
Switzerland 2011	0.332***	-0.690***	
	(0.075)	(0.078)	
Education		0.665***	
		(0.062)	
Income		0.248***	
		(0.063)	
Political interest		0.153***	
		(0.016)	
Constant	-0.091	0.075	-0.247***
	(0.130)	(0.094)	(0.086)
Observations	9,685	9,685	9,685

Reference study: Finland 2003
Standard errors in parentheses *** $p<0.01$, ** $p<0.05$, * $p<0.1$

Table 9.3: Recursive bivariate probit model of vote switching, pooled data (restricted sample)

Variables	Switching	VAA use	ρ
VAA use	0.653***		
	(0.178)		
Age	-0.005***	-0.028***	
	(0.002)	(0.001)	
Party identification	-0.350***	0.068***	
	(0.0219)	(0.024)	
Evaluation of the economy	-9.32e-05		
	(0.0294)		
Left/Right Self-placement	-0.0372***		
	(0.00895)		
Satisfaction with Democracy	-0.0569***		
	(0.0209)		
Finland 2007	0.293***	0.133	
	(0.0889)	(0.086)	
Finland 2011	0.401***	0.533***	
	(0.102)	(0.088)	
Germany 2009	0.231***	-0.460***	
	(0.0844)	(0.081)	
Netherlands 2003	-0.0229	-0.035	
	(0.0788)	(0.086)	
Switzerland 2011	0.365***	-0.782***	
	(0.0789)	(0.082)	
Education		0.748***	
		(0.082)	
Income		0.421***	
		(0.096)	
Political interest		0.159***	
		(0.023)	
Constant	0.0633	-0.352***	-0.260**
	(0.155)	(0.119)	(0.113)
Observations	5,163	5,163	5,163

Reference study: Finland 2003
Standard errors in parentheses *** p<0.01, ** p<0.05, * p<0.1

Table 9.4: Univariate probit models of vote switching for each study

Variables	Election Study								
	FIN 03	FIN 07	FIN 11	GER 09	NET 03	NET 06	NET 10	SWI 07	SWI 11
VAA use	0.428***	0.324**	0.202	0.247**	0.137	0.262***	0.241***	0.101	0.202*
	(0.144)	(0.139)	(0.135)	(0.124)	(0.089)	(0.072)	(0.075)	(0.119)	(0.104)
Age	-0.004	-0.016***	-0.015***	-0.013***	-0.007**	-0.005**	-0.009***	-0.001	-0.005*
	(0.004)	(0.004)	(0.004)	(0.003)	(0.003)	(0.002)	(0.002)	(0.002)	(0.002)
Party Identification	-0.342***	-0.629***	-0.490***	-0.332***	-0.218***	-0.423***	-0.442***	-0.274***	-0.310***
	(0.069)	(0.074)	(0.072)	(0.046)	(0.041)	(0.037)	(0.039)	(0.031)	(0.040)
Evaluation of the economy	0.099	0.001	-0.198**	-0.033	0.023	-0.177***	-0.091*	0.155***	0.067
	(0.073)	(0.093)	(0.077)	(0.080)	(0.061)	(0.046)	(0.047)	(0.058)	(0.058)
Left/Right Self-placement	-0.010	0.014	-0.079***	-0.088***	-0.018	0.015	-0.011	-0.020	-0.017
	(0.032)	(0.029)	(0.028)	(0.024)	(0.019)	(0.016)	(0.015)	(0.014)	(0.014)
Satisfaction with Democracy	0.054	-0.151**	-0.098	-0.088*	-0.049	-0.115***	-0.072*	0.075*	0.018
	(0.068)	(0.069)	(0.062)	(0.046)	(0.043)	(0.035)	(0.037)	(0.039)	(0.038)
Constant	-0.450	1.427***	1.747***	0.980***	0.078	0.357**	0.711***	-0.685***	0.087
	(0.351)	(0.348)	(0.371)	(0.201)	(0.218)	(0.178)	(0.200)	(0.183)	(0.208)
Observations	578	617	526	1,175	1,170	1,721	1,537	1,787	1,645

Standard errors in parentheses

*** p<0.01, ** p<0.05, * p<0.1

restricted sample, and Murphy's score test for biprobit indicates a much improved fit: $X^2_{(9)} = 15.94$, and $sig= 0.0682$.

Finally, we present study-by-study analyses in Table 9.4, controlling for the same independent variables as was the case in the pooled analysis. As discussed above, for the nine studies, ρ was not statistically significant, hence we report the results of probit models in Table 9.4. We note here that, for the case of the 2011 Swiss election study, where ρ was significant, the substantive results presented here are robust to a bivariate probit specification.

We can see that, of the nine election studies analysed, all report a positive coefficient for the 'VAA use' variable. For seven of the nine studies, this coefficient is statistically significant with at least 90 per cent confidence. As with our pooled analysis, these findings lend support to the relationship between VAA use and vote switching that we outlined in Hypothesis 1.

Conclusion

This chapter has examined whether VAA 'effects' on users' vote choices are discernible in a pooled dataset comprising representative samples from nine national-level elections. While, as we acknowledge, the structure of the data militates against being certain of cause–effect relationships, we nonetheless argue that our findings indicate that VAAs do influence the vote choices of a significant portion of those who use them. This finding chimes with several published papers and work in progress on the effects of VAA use on vote choice. The finding also serves to reinforce a theme that is common in discussions among VAA practitioners: the importance of values of impartiality, transparency and academic rigour in VAA implementation (*see* The Lausanne Declaration, this volume).

An important problem with the analysis in the previous section is that with the variable 'VAA use', we cannot discriminate VAA users who have been advised to vote for a different party than they previously voted for from those who have been advised to vote for the same party they had previously voted for. VAA effects on vote choice can run in both directions: enhancing voter loyalty or provoking voter defection. The direction of the effect is determined by the nature of the advice. In fact, if a VAA suggests more than one party, there are more possibilities: i) the previously-voted-for party appears first in the list of VAA results (absolute matching), ii) the VAA shows that the voter is close to his/her pre-selected party, but there is another party that appears first in the list (partial matching) and iii) VAA advice differs significantly from the previous voting behaviour (significant deviation). In the first case, the potential impact of using a VAA is to enhance the user's intention to vote for the pre-selected party. In the third case, the possible effect of the VAA will be in the opposite direction, i.e. the VAA recommendation would undermine the user's initial selection, and if the influence is strong enough, it can lead to a change of voter's position. In the second case, the possible impact could be towards both directions because it depends on how the voter interprets the output. More details on these three types of impact are presented in Andreadis

2013b (*see* Andreadis 2013b). Thus, the leverage that we can get over VAA effects is limited by both substantial variation in question wording across studies and the absence, in most cases, of a question asking voters to recall the party that was recommended to them.

This is a very significant factor that changes the role VAA use has for vote switching. In order to better measure the impact of VAAs on vote choice, we would recommend that future studies should consider the following options:

i) Follow the paradigm of Dutch parliamentary election studies of 2006 and 2010, which ask respondents to indicate the parties that VAA(s) recommended to them.

ii) (For those analysts who are also VAA practitioners) ask VAA users to indicate their vote intention before the presentation of the advice and either follow up with an exit survey and collect vote intention or collect email address and follow up with a post-election web survey.

We would urge fellow scholars to further investigate the effects that we have observed in this chapter – there are particularly rich pickings to be found in investigating the national and individual-level variables that condition VAA effects, and these data are well-disposed to uncovering such conditioning variables. While the field to date appears to have established that VAA use does affect vote choice, the next step is understanding the factors that exacerbate or minimise these effects, and feeding such findings back into the design and implementation of VAA websites.

Chapter Ten

Social Representations of Voting Advice Applications: A Comparative Analysis

Vasiliki Triga

Introduction

The last decade has witnessed the growing use of Voting Advice Applications (VAAs) in various national and transnational electoral contexts. The increasing popularity of VAAs has opened up a fruitful research agenda in many disciplines. However, despite this popularity, the existing body of literature is structured upon a top-down approach. To put it more explicitly, the way in which lay social actors themselves account for their experience of using VAAs still remains rather unexplored. Thus, VAAs are understood and evaluated largely on the basis of the ideas of researchers and involve limited direct feedback from the VAA users. To date, there is limited research as to whether one of the major goals of VAAs, which is to help citizens be informed about the parties' positions, is achieved or not from the users' perspective.

To try and fill some of this gap, this chapter undertakes a bottom-up qualitative analysis with the aim of unfolding the users' views of VAAs. More specifically, the chapter explores the ways in which the users of three VAAs (Greece, Spain and Cyprus) talk about and evaluate the use of the respective online applications in their electoral contexts. The analysis is focused on two levels: firstly, to explore users' experiences of specific VAA applications, and, secondly, to consider lay accounts that reflect on the nature and limitations of VAAs in general. The comparative analysis is based on focus groups that were conducted with VAA users in the three countries during the respective electoral campaigns.

Part of the rationale behind the selection of the three cases is that they are all settings where VAAs are not institutionalised. In one of the cases (regional elections in Spain) this was the first time a VAA had been deployed. Although the elections concerned different levels – namely parliamentary, regional and presidential – they were all salient and critical. Moreover, all selected cases are from Southern Europe and occurred in the midst of the financial crisis. The context in which the elections took place was characterised by a manifested distrust towards the political elites and the breakdown of traditional political alignments with the emergence of new extremist parties. Finally, another similarity concerns the fact that all selected VAAs were embraced by thousands of users while portrayed by the media as an alternative source of political information, suited mostly to undecided voters.

The aim of the analysis of the focus groups discussions is to provide users' repertoires on the use of VAAs and their importance concerning the electoral procedure, the formation of voters' preference, and, more generally, the positive and negative implications of VAAs' use during an election. Unlike most of the VAA literature that draws on political science, this chapter's theoretical point of departure is social psychology. Specifically, it draws on the theory of social representations. This framework is considered well-suited for investigating whether there is consistency between the scientific rationale behind VAAs and the perceived utility of a VAA as represented by the users themselves.

The chapter is organised in four parts. The first part discusses the theoretical framework that guides the analysis, namely social representations. The second part presents the methodology on which data collection and analysis was based. In the third part the results of the thematic content analysis of the focus groups discussions are outlined, and, finally, in the last part the discussion of the results as well as the overall conclusion is provided.

Theoretical framework

The theory of social representations is an interpretative approach in social psychology that focuses on the way the perception of an individual's social world is structured. The founder of this theory, the French researcher Serge Moscovici (1976), identifies the basic goal of social representations as the study of thought in its socio-historical context. The conceptual roots of this theory are found in the notion of collective representations developed by Durkheim in order to explain social change and, more particularly, how people understand new phenomena and give meaning to them. This latter component makes it a useful framework for investigating the recent phenomenon of the VAA.

An important contribution of this theory is its focus on the relation between scientific knowledge on the one hand, and common sense or lay people's knowledge and thought on the other (Moscovici 1961, 1976). This is especially relevant to VAAs where the nexus between academic scientific knowledge and its penetration of lay discourse has not been the subject of enquiry. To this end, social representations provide an explanation of the way science becomes the object of communication and influence in society through its transformation into a representation. The theory has its origins in Moscovici's study of how psychoanalysis penetrated everyday life and discourse in France during 1950s. In his book *La psychanalyse son image et son public* he underlined how scientific thought penetrated everyday (non-scientific) knowledge and was transformed into what is known as 'common sense'. Scientific ideas thus acquire another meaning as they are accommodated by 'common sense'. This transformation of scientific thought into everyday knowledge takes place through the cognitive mechanism of 'anchoring' (Moscovici 1976), which refers to the cognitive process by which the assimilation of new social objects is connected (anchored) to a network of already-known representations.

Social representations provide a code of communication among people, found at the centre of public interest and discussion constituting some stable basis of understanding (Abric 1994). According to the theory, people acquire knowledge of social phenomena through collective, inter-subjective processes. The social world acquires a meaning through the representations formed in everyday social interactions and communication processes. Meaning is produced as a common and collective outcome rather than a personal account. This shared meaning attributed to social phenomena serves for developing a common 'language' that allows people to communicate and understand each other (Moscovici 1984). In this sense, Moscovici's theory could provide a useful framework for studying how VAA users perceive, construct and evaluate the VAAs. Social representations of VAAs would constitute the vehicle through which users can understand and give meaning to these tools, on the one hand, and reconstruct scientific knowledge and the rationale behind these tools, on the other. By studying users' social representations of VAAs, the aim is to investigate the extent to which the basic academic principles and goals of a VAA's design are interpreted as 'common sense'.

Methodology

The study is based on data collected from focus groups conducted in Greece, Spain and Cyprus. Focus groups, as a tool for data collection, are considered appropriate since they allow interaction and eventually disagreement between participants (Morgan and Krueger 1993).

In total 29 focus groups were conducted with 144 participants. More specifically, in Greece focus groups comprised 46 participants, of which 21 were men and 25 were women, aged between 20 and 63 years old, with an average age of 30 years. All participants had filled in the *Choose4Greece* VAA[1] before the 6th May 2012 Greek national elections. These participants formed ten focus groups. In Spain, ten focus groups were also conducted on the occasion of two different regional elections, namely in Galicia and Catalonia. In Galicia 20 participants formed four focus groups, whereas in Catalonia 26 participants formed six focus groups. All participants had previously used the relevant voting advice applications, that is the *Horizonte Galicia* VAA[2] for the Galician parliamentary elections on 21st October 2012 and the *Horizonte Catalunya* VAA[3] for the Catalonian parliamentary elections on 25th November 2012. The 47 Spanish participants had an average age of 34 years with a range from 18 to 64 years old. Finally, in Cyprus nine focus groups were conducted consisting of 51 participants, of whom 18 were men and 33 were women. The average age of the participants was 24 years old. As in the previous cases, before participating in the focus groups, participants had already

---

1.   http://www.choose4greece.com

2.   http://www.horizontegalicia.com

3.   http://www.horizontecatalunya.com

used the *Choose4Cyprus* application[4] that was active for covering the Cypriot presidential elections (17 and 24 February 2013). Table 10.1 provides an analytical overview of the participant characteristics in the three cases. In observing Table 10.1, it is clear that an attempt was made to include participants with various demographic characteristics (e.g. age, sex and professional occupations), with the goal not to ensure representativeness but rather variety, which, according to the analytical approach followed, can also lead to the production of a variety of arguments and representations covering a wide spectrum of users' views on VAAs. All focus groups consisted of four to six participants who had used the respective application before the elections (usually one week). The duration of focus groups was from approximately 35 minutes to one hour. All discussions were recorded (with the permission of the participants) and were then transcribed.[5]

In the focus group discussions, participants were encouraged to evaluate the respective VAAs and discuss their experience of using the particular application. At the same time, they were also invited to discuss the importance, function and socio-political implications of VAAs more generally. In all three cases the same research structure was followed that was based on a specific number of open questions. The themes that guided the discussions were the following:

- General impressions after using the VAA

- Comments on the Questions, Answer Categories, Graphs (difficulty, importance, etc.)

- Utility and Matching Result (Voting Advice function)

- Potential problems and risks entailed in VAAs

- Contribution of VAAs to the overall political process

The transcribed material was then analysed based on qualitative content analysis (Ahuvia 2008; George 2008; Smith 1995). Specifically, the objective in this analytical approach is to unfold the dominant themes that appear in the content of the discussion, to search for the variety of issues and, finally, to produce interpretations of these themes. This is why it is also known as thematic content analysis. When we refer to dominant themes, this is not understood in quantitative terms (frequencies) but rather in terms of commonalities of the accounting practices in the discourse of the participants (Condor and Gibson 2007: 121). Unfolding the dominant themes involves repeated readings of all the transcripts with a view to identifying the themes in which the content of discussions was classified.

---

4. http://www.choose4cyprus.com

5. During the transcription process, emphasis was drawn on the content rather than other linguistic characteristics.

Table 10.1: Personal characteristics of participants (N=144)

Professional occupation				
	Students	Employees (public or private sector)	Unemployed	Retired
Greece	20	22	4	-
Spain	13	22	10	2
Cyprus	38	10	3	-
TOTAL	*71*	*54*	*17*	*2*

Age						
	18–25	26–33	34–41	42–49	50–57	58–64
Greece	22	16	1	4	1	2
Spain	12	14	13	2	2	4
Cyprus	45	1	1	4	-	-
TOTAL	*79*	*31*	*15*	*10*	*3*	*6*

Gender		
	Male	Female
Greece	21	25
Spain	30	17
Cyprus	18	33
TOTAL	*69*	*75*

Results

This section analyses the themes that were discussed in the focus groups. Five themes emerged and are related, on the one hand, to the design and methodology of VAAs and, on the other, to a more general evaluation of the VAAs regarding the utility of this tool as perceived at the individual level and its broader implications at the societal level.[6]

6. All selected extracts from the transcribed focus groups discussions are provided in an online annex downloadable at https://www.dropbox.com/s/dhxdcwfli8b5o0z/Annex.pdf?n=5481747

Issues related to methodology and design of VAAs

Thematic content analysis of the discussions revealed three themes that are related to the design of a VAA. These are the statement selection and formulation, the answer categories of a Likert scale, and the graphical representation of the results. Below, each one of these themes is discussed in more detail.

Statement selection and formulation

Participants discussed extensively in focus groups issues regarding the selection and formulation of the policy statements of a VAA. Their representations are both positive and negative.

Starting from the positive representations of the policy statements, we should underline that these were framed around two dimensions: a) the content, and b) the variety of themes. Regarding the content of the policy statements, there were participants in all focus groups that identified the questions as simple, comprehensive and easy to understand and answer. Moreover, questions were described as clear and concise in terms of formulation as well as content since the topics were related to everyday life. Such attributions were then related to the fact that users of VAAs do not need to have specialised knowledge to be able to answer the questions.

Concerning the variety of themes, participants provided accounts that constructed the questions as actual, concrete, pertinent to the electoral campaign and therefore interesting for all users. Policy statements were related to classic political cleavages, current issues or new topics altogether. The latter was represented as an asset of VAAs since the new topics inserted in the political debate (e.g. gay marriage, the role of the church, etc.) had an informative function for users and stimulated a learning process. An innovative aspect was deemed to be the fact that the policy statements also tackled issues that political parties as well as the mainstream media avoid discussing (e.g. decriminalisation of marijuana). Additionally, the questions were portrayed as 'key' and relevant for the calculation of the proximity with the parties in order to produce more valid results. Finally, participants suggested that even more issues could be included but they recognised that this would have made the application too lengthy.

The positive representations can be contrasted with the negative accounts, which were also framed around the dimensions of content and variety of topics. However, in this second case the arguments are reversed. In relation to the content of statements, there were participants in all focus groups that constructed the questions as general, vague and unclear. They underlined the need to have simpler and more specific questions, which would help users take a position. Questions were described as difficult due to the use, for instance, of acronyms or technical and political terminology, with which respondents were unfamiliar. This led to the argumentation that VAAs were excluding certain groups of citizens since the questionnaire was only suitable for the well-informed or users with high educational attainment. In addition, participants characterised the formulation of the questions as rigid or absolute and in need of extra explanatory information for allowing users to respond (e.g. whether all pensions should be cut and by how much, whether all categories of civil servants should be prone to austerity measures, etc.). Special reference was made to questions that involved a trade-off or a dilemma (e.g. monarchy *vs.* republicanism, or economic development *vs.* widening the gap between poor and rich). In these cases, respondents had a problem in taking a position which led them, in some cases, to position themselves on the basis of what they guessed would be their preferred party's position. This was portrayed as a problem since users were perceived to be pushed to answer in a superficial manner based on what they believe the parties' positions are and not on their true opinions. In this regard, some participants disputed the value of having certain questions included (e.g. the duration of military service, etc.) and were concerned about such questions' effects on the final results.

Concerning the variety of topics covered by the questions of VAAs, in the negative accounts the participants identified topics they felt were missing that were related to everyday life and citizens' problems. For example, in the Spanish focus groups participants wanted more attention to issues related to the reform of the electoral system, environmental and social issues such as health, education and employment, as well as questions focused on immigration and nationalism. Similarly, in the Cypriot focus groups participants wanted a greater focus on issues concerning what is called the 'Cyprus problem', education, unemployment and the exploitation of gas resources. Finally, in the Greek focus groups participants wanted the inclusion of more national issues, MPs' rights and duties, the crisis of the political system or questions regarding the quality of democracy and accountability, to name but a few. It is important to note that in most cases there were indeed policy statements on all of these issues in the respective VAAs; what the participants were arguing was that there should have been a greater focus (i.e. more statements) on some of those issues.

The two main representations of the VAA users regarding the statement selection and formulation are based on positive as well as negative evaluations of the content as well as the themes included in the selected questions. The implications of both representations can be identified in the scientific literature on VAAs. Statement selection and formulation constitutes one of the most important methodological issues of the VAA design. This is further elaborated in the chapter by van Camp *et al.* included in the present volume. In particular, participants relate the issue of statement selection (and whether this is biased towards specific parties, covers a wide spectrum of themes, etc.) to the production of valid matching results. This is the basic argument of the paper by Walgrave *et al.* (2009) that reveals that the vote recommendations generated by a VAA are to a large degree dependent on the type of questions. In addition, participants recognise that the formulation of the questions and whether this is concrete, to-the-point and containing one instead of many issues is inextricably linked to the ability of the users to provide their answers. This argument is underscored in the paper by Gemenis (2013) in which he provides a list of rules for the formulation of VAA statements that can facilitate the provision of accurate answers. Regarding the variety of the issues that a VAA needs to include, it appears that participants reproduce the academic debate. On the one hand, focus groups participants are fond of the fact that a large variety of policy issues are included in the VAAs, which follows the general trend of most VAA designers. On the other hand, other participants doubt the value of some specific issues and prefer only issues relevant to the campaign, which is the argument of Wagner and Ruusuvirta (2012). However, this is in contradiction to the overall perception of participants, according to which the statement selection of VAAs is associated with a 'pedagogic' function since they provide the opportunity to the users to learn and reflect on new policies. This is pointed out by the literature as a general characteristic of VAAs that may contribute to enhancing the civic competence of their users (Garzia 2010; Garzia and Marschall 2012).

Answer categories

The answer categories were represented in more negative than positive terms across the focus groups. It is important to note that the same five-point Likert scale was used for all VAAs: 'completely disagree', 'disagree', 'neither agree nor disagree', 'agree', 'completely agree'. A 'no opinion' was also included as an answer category. Accounting for the negative representations were grounded in various arguments. A first one constructed the answer categories as constraining for users to express their views, especially for some specific types of questions (e.g. difficult policy questions, or those that included trade-offs or dilemmas). For these policy items participants would have preferred different answer categories even if this had entailed difficulties for the calculation of the results. Another interesting account that emerged was that the lack of alternative answer options downgraded the VAA into a tool similar to other surveys rather than something more unique and innovative. These participants used their previous knowledge and experience of participating in surveys to justify the negative representation of Likert scales by pointing to instances when these scales attract random answers. This, in effect, could undermine the validity of the VAA matching function.

Turning to the meanings participants attributed to the middle category of 'neither agree nor disagree', the respondents provided multiple interpretations. A striking account concerned the fact that many participants avoided using the middle category since they thought this might influence the result. In most cases, the middle category was understood and used as the intermediate category between agree and disagree. Users justified the choice of this answer as being in a dilemma, not knowing exactly how to position themselves, or being reluctant to take a position. They further qualified that the choice of this answer category did indicate the existence of an opinion, albeit one that is not crystallised either due to missing information, lack of knowledge or lack of understanding the question. A number of participants attributed their selection of the middle category to indifference to the question at stake, while some also described it as a neutral position. In general, the 'middle category' was differentiated from the 'no opinion' answer based on the argument that in the first case respondents have an opinion whereas in the second they do not. Nevertheless, there were a few participants that disagreed and considered both answer categories as declaring an opinion. The general perception of the meaning attributed to the 'no opinion' answer was the absence of an opinion because of ignorance, indifference and lack of understanding the question.

The meanings attributed to the 'middle category' as well as the answer category of 'no opinion' by the focus groups participants were various and in a way echo the arguments from the scientific literature dealing with Likert scales. We came across accounts that construct the middle answer category as conveying dilemmas (Baka *et al.* 2012) but also indifference, fatigue or ignorance (Krosnick 1991). Similarly with the 'no opinion' answer category, both strands of academic claims were found in the representations of focus groups participants. It was described as a missing value as well as a non-clear opinion (Baka *et al.* 2012). These findings do suggest a need for greater attention to the meaning attributed to Likert scales and its specific consequences for VAAs.

Graphical representation

The VAAs deployed in the three different country settings all used the same graphical representation of results. There were three types of graphs for presenting the matching results: 1) bar charts to represent the overall similarity with parties, 2) two-dimensional spatial maps (scatterplots), and 3) a radar chart to show proximity with every party separately across multiple dimensions. As expected, participants represented the usefulness of the graphs as both user-friendly and difficult. There were accounts that found the overall appearance and presentation of the graphical results easy to understand, interesting to observe and complete in information. However, there were also accounts that constructed the additional graphs (i.e. those beyond the simple party/candidate match) as an extra feature of the application that was tiring and confusing.

Although the goal of the analysis is not to present the dominant themes in terms of frequencies, in this case it is worth mentioning that the vast majority of the accounts evaluate the graphs across the three cases in very similar terms (in line with the findings presented by Alvarez *et al.* 2014 based on *EU Profiler* user data). In particular, it was a common perception that the easiest and most useful graphical representation was the simple bar chart that presented proximity between the user and the party/candidate in bars and conveyed the actual percentage of similarity (in line with the findings presented by Alvarez *et al.* 2014 based on *EU Profiler* user data). On the other hand, in all focus groups there was agreement among the participants (apart from a few exceptions) that the most confusing and difficult-to-understand graph was the radar chart (spidergram). Participants reported that they had a problem in understanding the distance and closeness with the party/candidate in pragmatic terms. Interestingly, this was also the case, though to a lesser extent, with regard to the complexity of the political map (two-dimensional matrix). The scatterplot was portrayed as a specialised graph that is not suited to the level of knowledge and competence of all VAA users.

These arguments could have an important bearing for VAA designers. There are various VAA developers that also include two-dimensional maps (*Kieskompass*) and multi-dimensional radar charts (*smartvote*). Indeed, for *Kieskompass* the primary matching result is based on the two-dimensional scatterplot.

Issues related to VAAs' utility and effect

In this section we present two more themes that were discussed in focus groups and these concern the implications of VAA users at the individual level and also at the broader societal level.

Utility of the matching function

For the participants in focus groups, the utility of a VAA is connected with its matching function. In all focus groups we came across participants who claimed that the results coincided with their vote intention, but also those who claimed that they were surprised by the result since this was not anticipated or expected. In both cases, this was evaluated in positive terms. However, not surprisingly, there were also negative accounts that were predicated on attributions of the limitation of the VAA application.

Starting from the positive evaluations of the matching function, participants describe it as useful for particular categories of voters, such as indecisive or disappointed voters, young voters and those that are open-minded rather than partisans, as well as those who are not well-informed about politics. A feature of the matching function that was positively evaluated by the participants was that there was no perfect match with one party. Rather, users were positioned in ideological spaces and were provided with a direction instead of a position. This was constructed as extremely helpful since users a) get to know parties' positions on a list of policy issues in a much more concrete manner than when these are presented in the mainstream media, b) have the opportunity to familiarise themselves with new parties, and c) feel privileged to explore alternative options. Interestingly, one common positive argument was the possibility to reconfirm a users' vote intention after a successful matching result. This had a reinforcing effect on a user's confidence in his/her intended vote choice.

In cases in which participants received an unexpected matching with parties that differed from their vote intention or their ideological orientation, the evaluation of this function was still positive in many cases. The 'unsuccessful matching' did not lead to doubts regarding the validity of the application but instead it was reconstructed as an opportunity for reflection, critical thought and a reconsideration of voting criteria. Participants, in other words, perceived the 'unsuccessful matching' as a challenge that motivated them to find more information, but also reinforced their willingness to participate in the elections.

The cases in which the matching function was questioned tended to occur when participants did not receive the expected matching result. Multiple reasons were constructed as responsible for this outcome. One of these was attributed to the fact that there were missing parties, or that parties unknown to the participants were included. Another line of argumentation was linked to the method of coding parties' positions, or that parties had lied about their positions. A similar line of argumentation suggested that the undesired match was the result of including 'bizarre' or 'targeted' questions. There were also accounts that doubted the validity of the result in the sense that this was characterised as a 'mechanical calculation that can be wrong'.

In general, utility (providing information/matching) was accounted for through recourse to characteristics of voters (participants maintained that VAAs are more useful to young/indecisive voters), through recourse to the specific electoral context in Spain, Greece and Cyprus (participants pointed out that VAAs may be more useful in contexts characterised by uncertainty, the appearance of new parties and coalitions, etc.) and through recourse to users' need for confirmation of their vote intention. All of these accounts led to positive evaluations of the matching function that were also connected to either increased participation (turnout) or enhanced voter competence regarding knowledge of party positions. In addition, we come across a so-called 'third-person effect', i.e. users that represented themselves as more resistant and immune to the influence of a VAA in comparison to (unspecified) others.

The representations of the utility of VAAs' matching function for the users is a common topic in the respective literature on VAAs. Many of the arguments that emerged in the analysis are commonly found in academic studies too. Scholars have associated the utility of VAAs with the provision of information and help for undecided voters, especially in political contexts with high electoral volatility, in which VAAs are very popular (Garzia and Marschall 2012), as well as swing voters (Ladner *et al.* 2012) and younger voters (*see* the chapter by Marschall in this volume). Others have focused on the accuracy of matching algorithms (Mendez 2012). Even researchers who doubt the direct effect of VAAs on voting behaviour still recognise as the principal goal of VAAs the provision to the users of a reconfirmation of their vote intention (Walgrave *et al.* 2008), an argument that was commonly mentioned in the focus groups. In the case of 'unsuccessful' matching results, researchers underscore that VAAs offer the potential to the user to reflect, think critically and get more information on parties' positions (Fivaz and Nadig 2010; Nuytemans *et al.* 2010; Marschall 2008). These contribute to increasing the political motivation of the users to become more informed (Garzia 2010; Garzia and Marschall 2012) and more prone to participate in the elections (Marschall and Schultze 2012a; Ladner and Pianzola 2010; Ruusuvirta and Rosema 2009). Even though the arguments about the necessity of transparency in the methodology regarding calculating the results are always present in the academic literature, the representations presented by the users could bring to the fore the need for a more focused approach on this issue.

Implications for political processes

This theme refers to the implications of VAAs for the social and political context. In discussing this theme participants mainly referred to the dangers and risks entailed by VAAs, which were structured around four dimensions: 1) the possibility of manipulating VAAs; 2) VAAs' effect on voting; 3) VAAs' contribution to the overall political dialogue; and 4) the inclusion of all citizens.

Departing from the discussion regarding VAAs' potential to manipulate voters, VAAs were constructed as tools that can manipulate voting intentions so as to direct electoral preferences towards a specific political party. In these accounts voters were represented as the victims of improper political influence and the parties as the main actors orchestrating the intervention. Along the same lines, the objectivity and political neutrality of the researchers who design VAAs was also questioned. For instance, there were participants in the Spanish and Greek focus groups who found that the respective VAAs favoured left-wing parties. Similarly, in the Cypriot focus groups a generalised suspicion was expressed regarding the goals of a VAA, with arguments about the choices of including certain issues over others and the fact that science can always be used to manipulate instead of truly serve the society. Some participants particularly insisted on expressing an overall suspicion towards VAAs through recourse to previous experiences with similar tools, such as opinion polls, which were portrayed as known to serve particular political interests. Other preoccupations were expressed with respect to potential security issues related to preserving users' anonymity and the use of the data collected.

The second dimension concerned the potential of VAAs to exert an influence on their users' voting behaviour. Participants' views were divided. On the one hand, VAAs' influence was accounted for through recourse to the context of the crisis, which makes voters more critical towards political parties and their previous choices. In these accounts, voters were represented as potential issue-voters, rational thinkers rather than emotional agents, who are aided by the VAAs. On the other hand, for other participants VAAs' influence on voters' behaviour was doubted and this was accounted for through recourse to the characteristics of voters, such as older voters with crystallised political views and voters with strong partisan affiliation and indifference to politics. In other words, these accounts pointed to the dominance of alternative voting criteria (other than issue-voting) such as socialisation effects, party identification and tradition as the key determinants of vote choice. In these accounts, voters were represented as active agents, fully responsible for their political choices that are rooted in specific cultural and context-related factors. Furthermore, VAAs were constructed as 'psychological tests' which fail to embrace the complexity of political reality and the public sphere.

The third dimension was built upon the criticism of VAAs as reproducing the mainstream political agenda by forcing their users to take a position in a limited spectrum of political topics and by excluding political parties or views that may be peripheral. These accounts, however, even within the same focus group discussion, were counter-posed by others which denied the potential of VAAs to shape the political agenda. The latter represented VAAs as a sign of the times which mirrors, rather than restricts, the political dialogue.

Finally, the fourth dimension pointed to the restricted potential of VAAs to attract all types of citizens. In the respective accounts, VAAs were represented to be of limited access due to the digital divide and the fact that the technological knowledge needed for participating was rather high – so users who were not familiar with the technology were automatically excluded. Participants associated the digital divide with a generation gap and pointed out that those who are most excluded are the older citizens. Following the same line of argumentation, other participants underscored that citizens with basic political knowledge are also excluded, since effective participation in a VAA requires a rather high level of political knowledge.

The arguments discussed around this theme are also found in the academic literature on VAAs, representing a more critical stance. For example, the issue regarding the purported neutrality of VAA researchers identified by focus group participants is also addressed by Anderson and Fossen in this volume. Their major concern is whether and to what extent VAA designers can be neutral when making their choices for their VAAs. In addition, the arguments regarding the effects of VAAs on voting behaviour and the representation of users as issue-voters are parallel to the arguments in the scientific literature which consider VAAs as able to provoke a change in users' vote choice (Wall *et al.* 2012; Ladner *et al.* 2010; Ruusuvirta and Rosema 2009). In contrast, the arguments produced in focus groups which dispute the effect of VAAs on voting behaviour also coincide with some more sceptical approaches (Walgrave *et al.* 2008). Regarding the representation of VAAs as unable to raise new political issues or change the political debate, we can interpret it as a plea on behalf of the users for a differentiated version rather than just a matching VAA. In a way, it might be parallel to a contestatory VAA, as conceptualised by Anderson and Fossen (in this volume) whose primary goal is to challenge the status quo and change the political agenda. Finally, the criticisms raised by participants regarding specific categories of users who are excluded from using VAAs can be related to the literature regarding the profile of VAA users, who are young, highly educated (which presupposes the use of technology) and politically engaged (for a further discussion, *see* the chapter by Marschall in this volume).

Conclusion

Based on a comparative qualitative content analysis of focus groups discussions, this chapter followed a social psychology framework in order to explore the users' social representations of their use of VAAs. The theoretical framework guiding this research was based on the theory of social representations. The latter was deemed appropriate for exploring how a community (in our case the VAA users) attributes meaning to the world as well as the content of this meaning. What was discovered is that most of the representations of VAAs neatly dovetail the debates that exist in the academic literature. Drawing on the ideas of Moscovici, this was an expected outcome since there is an interaction between scientific and everyday knowledge. More specifically, the analysis brought to the fore a variety of representations of VAAs organised around five topical issues. Three themes concerned the design and methodology of VAAs, namely the statement selection, the answer categories and the graphical representation of the results. The other two themes focused on the wider implications of VAAs either at the individual or social level.

The analysed VAAs all constituted cases in which a VAA is not an institutionalised feature of the political landscape. The trials could therefore be considered as rather innovative tools in their respective electoral campaigns. Drawing on the theory of social representations we argued that for social actors to be able to represent new concepts, in our case VAAs, they have to connect them to an already-known network of representations through the mechanism of anchoring. We found evidence of this in the fact that when lay people are asked to evaluate scientific applications, they attribute meaning to them as a result of their previous knowledge, personal experience and communication. The analysis brought to the fore two distinct elements in this connection. Firstly, where VAAs were represented in negative terms across all the five themes, they were considered similar to tools such as opinion polls and other types of surveys. In the most negative (and conspiratorial) cases, VAA users were represented as potential victims of manipulative practices. The criticism based on the opinion-poll analogy ought to be considered by VAA designers. It could be argued that VAAs as currently designed are little more than a data-gathering tool for researchers interested in mass public opinion. VAA designers should devote more attention to developing more interactive features to their presently rather static platforms.

By contrast, where VAAs were represented positively they were portrayed as innovative tools that can transform the electoral process. The argument here coincides with many of the more positive academic analyses. VAAs are considered as based on rational, scientific practices that offer citizens the potential to become more informed about the policy issues at stake and party positions, with the end result that they are able to subsequently make more-informed vote choices. Users in this case are represented as active and politically engaged. Both representations draw on various scientific claims in the respective VAA literature but at the same time they also point to some elements that need to be further addressed. Specifically, how do the mechanisms of enhanced voter competence operate and how could they be improved? The current approach to these questions is through a number of limited questions typically included in an opt-in survey of the VAA, and typically completed by a small proportion of VAA users. More focus group research on this question could lead to the formulation of new hypotheses, which may then be amenable to more experimental designs – even among smaller groups of VAA users.

One of the dominant themes which emerged from the focus groups in all cases is directly related to ongoing research on statement selection and formulation as well as the meanings attributed to the answer categories of the Likert scales. Alternative answer categories may be an idea that can be tested in future VAAs. This is already the case for VAAs – some such as *smartvote* use a four-point scale without a middle category, whereas other VAA families (e.g. *Stemwijzer*) use an agree/disagree scale. There is certainly more room to investigate which types of answer scales are best suited to which particular types of statements. Again, here there is great scope for experimental designs on smaller numbers of VAA users. The graphical representation of the results clearly constitutes an area that, unlike some of the themes just mentioned, is not very well studied. An evaluation of the utility of graphs is needed that will address the cognitive capacities of the users. Here the discipline of psychology is likely to yield many insights and should be considered by VAA designers. This can also be linked to more systematic analyses of the processes of opinion formation by the users of VAAs. On the other hand, the study of the effects (or not) of using a VAA on political participation is a theme that is already being taken by political scientists. Finally, a series of shortcomings and risks of VAAs have also been pointed out, such as the purported neutrality of VAA designers. Users are certainly concerned about security and data-protection issues. For the moment, this is a topic which appears not to be addressed by the academic community, though it may be more suited to legal scholars or computer scientists interested in security issues.

Regarding the limitations of the present study, we recognise that it is confined to very specific electoral and political contexts. This does not mean that due to sample limitations any of its findings are not generalisable to other VAA settings. Many of the insights ought to be applicable to even some of the institutionalised VAA settings. They are certainly relevant to new VAA settings, particularly outside the Western European setting. What emerges from this particular research agenda is that there is much scope for qualitatively probing the user experience, and that doing so could provide insights for more experimentally focused research. The end result would be an improved VAA design and enhanced user experience.

Chapter Eleven

Being a VAA-Candidate: Why Do Candidates Use Voting Advice Applications and What Can We Learn From It?

Patrick Dumont, Raphaël Kies and Jan Fivaz

Introduction[1]

The advent of the internet and its success story have raised questions regarding its potential impact on politics and more specifically brought about a growing literature in political science and communication studies on how this technological change may affect electoral campaigns. The issue at stake is whether web applications have led to a new campaign era – that some coin 'post-modern' (Norris 2000; Vergeer *et al.* 2013) – corresponding to a more interactive, bottom-up, personalised and competitive electoral contest. This hypothesised wide-ranging effect, that has so far mainly been tested for the initial online presence of political parties and candidates through 'traditional' websites, is currently being gauged for the social media (e.g. Facebook, Twitter, and YouTube) that has emerged and become very popular in recent years. In this chapter we consider whether Voting Advice Applications (VAAs) can be seen as belonging to this family of new and widely used online applications that contribute to reducing the political parties' and traditional media's monopoly over the electoral agenda.[2]

While research on the various aspects of VAAs, such as their architecture and methodological choices (Baka *et al.* 2012; Gemenis 2013; Krouwel *et al.* 2012; Walgrave *et al.* 2009), their usage and impact on voting behaviour (Dumont and Kies 2012; Fivaz and Nadig 2008; Ladner *et al.* 2012; Marschall and Schmidt 2010; Walgrave *et al.* 2008), as well as data they generate on party positions or voter–party congruence (Wheatley 2012), is ongoing, the question of the perception and usage of such applications by parties and candidates is still under-explored. Our objective in this chapter is twofold. First, we lay down the rationale for a candidate-centred research agenda allowed by the development and popularity of VAAs, by arguing that they open avenues for comparative and longitudinal

1. This article benefitted from the financial support of the Luxembourgish Chair in Legislative Studies and the Luxembourgish National Research Fund.

2. Note that parties and the traditional media are moved by distinct motivations and logics that are so far only imperfectly translated in the online context.

analyses of candidates' behaviour in an increasingly personalised and connected political world. Second, we provide an exploratory research on the determinants of the acceptance of this medium by candidates when such an instrument is first introduced. What can account for their decision to apply this new instrument as part of their campaign strategy? The analysis of candidates' reaction to the first implementation of VAAs is relevant for two main reasons. The first is that it offers an evaluation of the instrument by the political actors themselves. The existing literature on VAAs has focused on the perception and behaviour of voters and so far largely ignored those of the political agents – parties and/or candidates – involved (*see* however, Ladner *et al.* 2010; Trechsel and Mair 2011). It is however clear that one cannot explain the success of VAAs that in the majority depend on the collaboration of these political agents (*see* Ladner and Fivaz 2012) by referring only to the 'demand' side. Secondly, such a study can improve our understanding of the behaviour and strategies of candidates facing the emergence of any technological innovation in electoral campaigns. In an era where online electoral tools are continually evolving whilst their utility and effects are uncertain, this is a topic that appears to be particularly relevant to understanding how candidates' electoral strategies are evolving through time and especially in recent years.

To this end, and in the absence of dedicated empirical research on candidates' propensity to use VAAs,[3] we build our expectations on the existing literature on candidates' usage of Web 2.0 tools (such as Facebook, Twitter and YouTube) and related theories on Web 2.0 campaigns. The actual hypotheses derived for our empirical analysis also owe to works on incentives to cultivate a personal vote in open-list electoral systems, as our data concern the first implementation of the *smartvote* platform in Switzerland for the federal elections in 2003 and the introduction of a similar instrument for the national elections in Luxembourg in June 2009. The remainder of this chapter is divided into five sections. Section one presents the importance of a candidate-centred analysis of VAAs. Section two refers to the expectations we can derive from theoretical and empirical analyses of candidates' use of other social media for our research question. The following section moves on to the specification of hypotheses, owing to these broad expectations as well as to more general literature on electoral systems and campaign strategies. Finally, sections four and five present and discuss the findings of our explorative empirical analysis.

Candidate-centred analysis of VAAs

To date, the majority of existing VAAs are party-centred, that is they provide exclusively a matching between positions of voters and parties. There are VAAs designed for presidential elections (such as in France and the US) but to our

---

3. The only known exception is Fiechter and Leuenberger (2009) but in their working paper the authors mainly looked through descriptive statistics at the representativeness of the candidates running for Swiss elections in 2007. Since this second edition of the *smartvote* VAA already assembled no less than 84 per cent of all candidates, this study is of limited use for our purposes here.

knowledge for legislative elections only Switzerland, Luxembourg, Finland, Lithuania and Denmark offer online platforms that allow candidates to make their personal positions known.[4] This comes as no surprise. In countries using an electoral system where preferential voting is allowed and even facilitated, the 'objects of electoral choice' can be either parties or candidates (Carey and Shugart 1995; Marsh 2007). Preferential votes can still reflect primarily a partisan motivation, not least because candidates are expected to be committed to party policy in order to be on a given party list (*see* Müller 2000; van Holsteyn and Andeweg 2010), but it is also well-known that other factors more or less aloof from policy proximity, such as the oft-mentioned charisma of candidates, or their socio-demographic characteristics (*see* McDermott 1997; Cutler 2002; Shugart *et al.* 2005), may also guide voting choices. Nevertheless, even in the case of lower-stakes elections (compared to presidential ones), it is a reasonable expectation owing to the Downsian proximity model that when deciding to vote for one or several candidate(s) voters will be more likely to choose candidates who appear to share their own views than those who do not. In electoral systems with preferential votes, information on the policy positions of candidates should therefore matter in voters' choices.[5] This is obviously the case when the electoral system provides candidates with incentives to cultivate a personal vote, as in Switzerland and Luxembourg. In these two countries, preferential votes (which can be cast for candidates of different lists – what is termed 'inter-party panachage' – and cumulated up to two votes per candidate) and list votes are first pooled at the level of the party in the constituency to determine the number of seats devolved to each list, and then the candidates' personal scores decide on who will fill those party mandates. In countries using multi-member constituencies, incentives to cultivate a personal reputation exist as long as the ballot allows for preferential votes – i.e. the electoral system is not of a closed-list type – and increases in size the number of MPs to be elected or rather the number of co-partisans on the list (Carey and Shugart 1995). This is obviously the case for open-list and Single Transferable Vote systems, but even for the more widespread flexible-list systems, where the ordering of candidates made by party leaders can hardly be overturned by voters, the possibility offered to express preferential votes makes for a personal popularity contest among candidates of the same list that may be consequential for the latter's

---

4. A transnational project (mypolitiq.eu) run in Poland, Lithuania and Latvia for the 2009 European elections also allowed candidates to register, but the proportions of those who did, probably due to the lower stakes of the election and electoral systems in use, were disappointing, ranging from 11 per cent in Poland to 33 per cent in Lithuania, which had already experienced a VAA for its national elections (Dziewulska 2010; Ramonaité 2010). Note that some VAAs in Germany also provide a matching with the candidates (for first vote in the German mixed electoral system), like www.abgeordnetenwatch.de, but prove much less successful than the party-based one(s).

5. For instance, an interview in the media may reveal a candidate's personal preference on a specific issue that does not match with that officially taken by their party, making their rate of preferential votes rise or fall according to how this distance from the official party position is received by the electorate at large, that is both voters who traditionally vote for that party of the candidate and those who do not.

political career.[6] In a variety of electoral systems, therefore, the availability of information regarding candidates is an important issue for the crucial democratic exercise of making an informed electoral choice, and candidate-centred VAAs can be seen as contributing to this goal. They may even be 'the only systematic way to gain knowledge about individual candidates' policy positions' (Hansen and Rasmussen 2013: 191) for the media, interest groups and of course voters. As, in addition, a trend of electoral reforms in Europe leading towards a greater scope and weight for preferential votes has been observed especially since the 2000s (Renwick 2011), we can expect that the personalisation of politics will make candidates even more eager to publicise their opinions and make voters and media interested in knowing them in an increasing number of electoral contexts, leading to a corresponding expansion of candidate-centred VAAs.

From an academic perspective, such a development is very welcome, as the analysis of the usage of VAAs by candidates offers important innovative avenues of research. First, their adoption is relevant to further explore to what extent 2.0 techniques can favour a greater personalisation of politics. The decision to be visible on a VAA and the nature of the information they provide on the website is indicative of the types of personalisation candidates want to promote. Research on VAAs allows, for instance, to gauge whether candidates focus their campaign on their competencies and political views (professional sphere) rather than on their personal life and preferences (intimate sphere).[7] Second, it permits to improve our understanding of vote-choice models in an era of growing personalisation of electoral choices (Garzia 2014) by studying voter–candidate policy congruence. Third, research combining VAAs and an analysis of the legislative behaviour of elected candidates also allows for evaluating to what extent MPs commit to their individual preelectoral positions and therefore the accountability of the political personnel (Schwarz *et al.* 2010; Schädel 2011; Fivaz *et al.* in this volume). Fourth, VAAs can give indications regarding the political competencies of candidates, for instance when candidates copy-paste the official positions and justifications of their party on all items. Alternatively, such behaviour could be a sign of candidates' subordination to their party, and it is indeed probably in the field of intra-party politics, and in particular issues regarding party discipline and policy cohesion (*see* Hansen and Rasmussen 2013), that candidate-centred analyses of VAAs can be of greatest use for political science scholars. On all these questions the VAAs provide new and powerful data that could hardly be measured with traditional research instruments. In particular, VAAs can become a research tool complementary to candidate surveys that typically suffer from low response rates, as these new instruments provide candidates with electoral incentives to deliver their personal views and therefore can be expected at some point – once the system has been experimented with at least once and proved to be both reliable and popular – to cover most of the individuals running for an election.

---

6. Crisp (2013) show that in Slovakia parties reward their preference-vote-earning candidates with better positions on their lists at future election.

7. Gulati and Williams (2010) performed such an analysis of personal candidate websites.

Table 11.1: Hurdles and incentives for using VAAs and Web 2.0 tools, respectively

	Hurdles		Incentives	
	Knowledge accessibility	Undesired exposure	Electoral gain	Civic potential
Facebook	+	+	?	+
Twitter	+	+	?	+
YouTube	+	+	?	+
VAA	++	++	++	++

Finally, as we will see in the following section, a candidate-centred analysis of VAAs can also enlighten us on the strategies of candidates in a 2.0 electoral campaign era.

Attractiveness of VAAs compared to other 2.0 technologies

The appearance of the new social media gave e-campaigning a significant boost. Vergeer (2009) describes the transformation from Web 1.0 to Web 2.0 as the passage from the web as a mass medium to the web as a networked community medium. In the context of elections Web 2.0 applications allow politicians to develop personalised and individualized campaigns, more or less detached from their party's, in comparison to the early days of web campaigning.

Indeed, with the large diffusion of the new social media, candidates nowadays have a larger array of offline and online instruments at their disposal than ever before. Facing successive technological innovations and constrained by a limited amount of time, resources, competencies and knowledge about the electoral potentialities of each of these novel techniques, they have to go through a pro-cess of selection in order to determine which one(s) could be the most useful for their personal campaign. This selection is based on the characteristics of the technology and the personal advantages and disadvantages of its adoption. Table 11.1 that follows identifies four factors that are likely to influence this choice and that can help us understand the attractiveness of VAAs compared to the most popular 2.0 applications currently used in electoral campaigns: Facebook, Twitter and YouTube.

VAAs share many similarities with 2.0 techniques, but strongly differ on the definition of the electoral agenda. While 2.0 applications allow candidates to freely choose and discuss any issue (political or personal), VAAs constrain them to take a more-or-less blunt position (from binary to five-point-scale answer categories) on a fixed menu of political issues selected and formulated in statements by an external actor (the VAA designers). This very outsourcing of the electoral agenda may dissuade some candidates from participating in VAAs. This is likely to be the case for inexperienced candidates who do not have an opinion on all the matters. Some of these candidates may just renounce to publicise their personal views in order to avoid giving uninformed answers, while others could privilege heuristic shortcuts such as copy-pasting the answers and justifications of their colleagues or the official answers of their party.[8] Depending on the comprehensiveness (broad coverage of issues), length and complexity of the questionnaire, the effects of the instrument's level of knowledge accessibility may be more or less strong. The other categories of candidates that could be reluctant to use a VAA are those who feel confident of being (re)elected, since participating imposes upon them to take a position on a wide array of issues, including sensitive ones that could lower their personal appeal. Top candidates who planned to focus their campaign on specific issues (by carefully avoiding others, in accordance with the saliency theory of political competition) and those who would prefer to capitalise on their personality and private life rather than on issues are the ones who most likely are affected by this hurdle.[9]

Counterbalancing the negative effect of these hurdles, the instrument's perceived potential of electoral impact may act as an important incentive for candidates to adopt it, even in the context of a first implementation of a VAA. It is useful here to refer to research carried out on the '1.0 phase' of web campaigning, which was generally characterised by political websites offering top-down information. In these earlier days of the internet, the environment was characterised by a high level of uncertainty regarding their electoral impact but also confined to smaller proportions of connected voters seeking political information, and mostly larger parties could afford dedicating some of their resources to the building of websites. Research on the electoral effects of campaign websites therefore often indicated a 'normalisation' of the aggregate in terms of the existing balance of power among parties, and also pointed at a 'reinforcement' at the individual level in the sense of a confirmation of voting preferences for self-selected politically interested website visitors (who had made their voting choice before consulting their preferred party's online material; *see* Margolis and Resnik 2000; Dumont *et al.* 2006; Jankowski *et al.* 2005; Kluver *et al.* 2007). Other research showed a positive relation between online presence and electoral results, but authors remained sceptical of any direct effects occurring and the potential for 1.0-type instruments to reach and convince undecided voters (Ward 2012). These results challenged the expectations of an 'equalisation' of political competition through, and a direct net electoral impact of, web campaigning. In turn, this may have changed with the advent of Web 2.0 tools. Such applications are easier to implement for individual candidates and appear to be efficient to create a network and, in certain cases, to foster a larger

---

8. Note that among our two cases this can only happen, strictly speaking, in Luxembourg where the official position of the party is asked to the top party officials on behalf of their organisation. In the case of Switzerland the official position of a party corresponds to the average of the answers of all the party's candidates on the different items. Less-experienced candidates can nevertheless copy-paste the answers and justifications of their fellow party candidates.

9. These characteristics extend to the parties the candidates belong to. Candidates of policy-seeking parties that concentrate on a limited number of issues (e.g. single-issue, niche parties) and candidates of vote- and office-seeking parties (e.g. contemporary cadre parties and populist ones that capitalise on the charisma of their personnel and/or leader) would be less likely to take part in a VAA.

involvement of users supporting candidates in the political campaign. Short of attracting a significant amount of undecided voters, personal Web 2.0 applications are not expected to have a large direct effect on voting behaviour (*see* however, Spierings and Jacobs 2013). But these tools reach activists who can easily relay candidates' messages to their own online social networks (Hermans and Vergeer 2013). The extent of this indirect effect would then largely depend on how capable small and homogeneous networks of followers are to persuade new people to vote for specific candidates (Verger *et al.* 2013: 497). In addition, what candidates decide to share with their 'friends' or 'followers' on the social media, through short messages, pictures or videos, may also lead to a negative evaluation of their political competencies: the echo given outside of their core supporters' networks by interested observers monitoring candidates' online activity may actually turn out to be detrimental to the latter's electoral performance.[10]

The electoral cost–benefit calculus of participating in a VAA appears different in several respects. First, the scope of consequential campaigning 'gaffes' is more limited as the repertoire is limited to personal views on a fixed list of political issues. Second, VAAs directly appeal to a wider audience as these are instruments undecided voters may find useful to express an informed electoral choice.[11] Third, contrary to Twitter for instance, where candidates' networks are largely disconnected and the vast majority of users only follow one candidate (Verger *et al.* 2013: 497), VAAs allow – on the very same platform – for a simultaneous comparison of candidates' positions on a wide variety of issues (that can further be disaggregated by users themselves to offer advices on the issues they are most interested in). Participating in a VAA therefore makes it possible for candidates to show personal views distinct from these fellow party candidates in the hope of getting more preferential votes. Finally, VAAs provide voters with a ranking of the parties and candidates present in the system and that match their own political positions. The results returned to them often invite them to consider, on the basis of their policy proximity, parties and candidates they would have never considered as a potential electoral choice otherwise. Hence, not only undecided or volatile voters who are seeking relevant electoral information can be expected to follow the advice given by the instrument but even party identifiers may reconsider and eventually modify their voting choice due to their unexpected closeness of views with some parties or candidates (*see* Andreadis and Wall *et al.* in this volume).

---

10. The success and viral quality of Web 2.0 applications has indeed also widened traditional media sources of information. Journalists can therefore contribute to the indirect effect on voting behaviour by relaying candidates' centred information through their own social media networks and, more importantly, by their professional offline reporting.

11. There is indeed a marked difference between users of VAAs and those of Web 2.0 applications. Previous research classified the former amongst 'information-seekers', who represented four times more people than the latter, labelled as 'net activists' in the 2007 national electoral campaign in Denmark. VAAs were the single most popular political facility on the internet for this campaign, and their users were more likely to be politically interested but also undecided voters (*see* also, amongst others, Dumont and Kies 2012 on the characteristics of VAA users).

This stands in stark contrast to 2.0 applications, which typically only directly reach a circle of convinced voters whose belonging to a candidate's social network can only lead to a reinforcement of original voting choices. These expectations in terms of gains in visibility and electoral rewards indeed figure prominently in the decision of candidates to participate in VAAs (Ladner *et al.* 2010). Overall, owing to the 'equalisation' hypothesis, candidates who may derive the greatest benefit in terms of preferential votes from the usage of VAAs are the lesser-known ones, either competing for the first time or on smaller lists and therefore largely absent from the traditional media. Since in open-list systems even marginal differences in personal appeals can decide who will be elected, candidates who perceive their chances to gain a seat as being fair (neither null nor very high) could be the most interested in participating in such a new and potentially electorally rewarding tool.

But VAAs have much more than a purely strategic appeal for candidates. A well-elaborated VAA offers information on a large variety of electoral issues and allows voters to elaborate a more complex and refined electoral opinion as they are confronted to topics and candidates they may not have considered relevant otherwise. VAA builders generally provide a description of the issues at stake, with references to the current or proposed legislation and sometimes with pros and cons arguments. Candidates may qualify and justify their own positions on the statements. Hence, the civic potential of VAAs may also motivate candidates to participate and thereby contribute to displaying all the diversity and potential richness of one's election political offer to the voters. Candidates calling for a greater openness, transparency and participation in politics are likely to be more sensitive to this feature of VAAs.

In this section we derived a number of broad expectations regarding the candidates' adoption of technological innovations in electoral campaigns, looking at the distinctive incentives (civic potential and expected electoral gain) and hurdles (knowledge accessibility and undesired exposure) that pertain to the use of VAAs and Web 2.0 applications. In the next section we move on to specifying testable hypotheses and describe the operationalisation of relevant variables for an illustrative and exploratory empirical study of candidates' participation in the *smartvote* VAA first implemented for the 2003 federal elections in Switzerland and the 2009 national elections in Luxembourg.

Hypotheses and operationalisation

We draw on our previous discussion of hurdles and incentives for candidates' participation in VAAs and on the more general literature on electoral systems and the personalisation of electoral campaigns to devise four hypotheses to be tested in a first, exploratory analysis of the determinants of the adoption of information technology innovations. In addition, we spell out two expectations with regard to distinct relationships in the Swiss and Luxembourgish cases, owing to the timing of the first implementation of *smartvote* and differences in the average level of competition facing candidates.

We alluded earlier to the differential incentives of VAA participation across incumbents and non-incumbents. The former, especially when they are almost sure of their re-election, may find adopting the instrument unnecessary or even a risky move as this could cause an undesired exposure of political views that may be detrimental to their personal appeal. These candidates indeed managed to get elected without it in the first place and could even see these tools as dangerous toys. Challengers in general do not benefit from the visibility (and image of competence) of MPs and would, according to the equalisation theory of the internet, be keener on improving it by using all tools at their disposal. However, newcomers and candidates who do not expect to be elected in particular may face the knowledge-accessibility hurdle or would not consider investing in personal campaigns at all. Hence, it is mainly amongst candidates who stand a fair chance of being elected, for instance those who hold a local political mandate and therefore can count on some level of visibility and political legitimacy, therefore that we can find the highest incentives to further cultivate a personal vote that could eventually lead to their election by participating in an instrument such as a VAA.

H1: Given their *a priori* perceived probabilities of getting elected, candidates with very high (incumbents) and very low visibility (those without any political mandate) are less likely to use a VAA than those with some visibility (candidates with a local mandate)

How competitive candidates feel depends also on the electoral context they face. Both incumbents and challengers develop constituency-level expectations regarding this competition. According to Carey and Shugart (1995), in electoral systems allowing for preferential votes, the incentives to cultivate a personal reputation increase with district magnitude as the number of co-partisans to distinguish from also goes up.[12] Crisp *et al.* (2007) concur with this idea but improve on its operationalisation: in order to tap more closely the 'co-partisan crowdedness' perceived by a candidate, one should take into account both the actual number of co-partisans on the list (C) and the number of seats won by the party in the previous election (P), the latter reflecting the current strength of the party in the constituency and a reasonable expectation of the number of seats the party could win in the present election. For these authors, as the C:P ratio gets larger so does the intra-party competition for the seats the party could hope to secure. According to us, this index offers the advantage of reflecting both the size of the party in the constituency and the degree of competition for preferential votes each candidate faces on their list. However, in systems like Luxembourg and Switzerland where list votes and preferential ones are pooled to determine

---

12. We can further hypothesise that a 'reactive' mechanism could be at work in larger constituencies. Just as incumbents' personal campaign spending may rise in majoritarian electoral system races as a response to high levels of spending of challengers, we can expect that the presence of competitors (from the list or from other lists) on a VAA may induce candidates to adopt it as well. The diffusion of this reactive mechanism is likely to be exponential in larger constituencies.

the number of seats to be allocated to each party, the probability of winning seats also depends on the overall success of the list. Hence, smaller parties in particular are more likely to play the collective-identity card by promoting list voting than bet only on the popularity of their candidates in their campaign to collect enough votes to secure a seat. From a more rational-individualistic perspective, since most of the candidates on these lists consider that they have no chance of being elected, they will also be less likely than candidates from larger parties to participate actively in the electoral competitions by using a VAA.[13] Given this, where the index reaches large numbers – that is, when a party is only expected to win one seat in a large constituency – as well as when it is set as zero – when a party had no seat in the constituency in the previous election – we would expect an average's candidate on the list to have a smaller probability to cultivate a personal vote than in contexts where the C:P index has more moderate values. In other words, we would hypothesise a curvilinear rather than a linear relationship between this index and the propensity of candidates to participate in a VAA.

> H2: Candidates facing moderate to high levels of intra-party competition are more likely to participate than those facing extreme (lowest and highest) levels of intra-party competition as measured by C:P

Aside from the strategic considerations that we assume to loom large for candidates seeking election, we also consider other sources of motivations that may account for the variance observed in their responses to the VAA innovation. Personal views on the openness of democratic participation and on the civic potential of VAAs may lead to more or less positive assessments of the instrument. The general orientation of the party they belong to may have the same effect, as party organisations may encourage or, to the contrary, prevent their candidates participating. Instead of assuming a link with broad ideological orientations, such as the left–right or cultural liberalism *vs.* social conservatism, that are only very indirectly related to the issue, we would hypothesise that candidates belonging to parties that favour greater democratic participation would either share this concern or would be more or less explicitly pressured by their organisation to collaborate with this novel source of political information.

> H3: Candidates belonging to parties that call for high levels of democratic participation are more likely to respond to a VAA

Among the hurdles to VAA participation, we mentioned the knowledge-accessibility one that may discourage some candidates from adopting the tool.[14] More fundamentally, the digital gap between generations constitutes another barrier for older candidates who have grown, worked and perhaps also fought electoral

---

13. Recall that we here refer to party strength at the constituency level (parties may be comparatively performing better or worse in other constituencies and thus may be a large or small party at the national level).

14. Data on the education level of the candidates could serve as a proxy to study this issue.

campaigns in a purely offline environment. For those candidates, the mere lack of personal experience with this technology, which may feed into a persisting image of the unruly nature of the internet and its unpredictability, acts as a disincentive to publicise personal political views on the web. As observed by Zittel (2009) for the setting up of candidates' personal websites, such a generational effect is likely to show for the adoption of VAAs as well, and for other campaigning technological innovations in the future. Note that since Luxembourg implemented its first VAA six years later than Switzerland, we would expect the age category of a candidate to be less of a strong determinant of VAA adoption in Luxembourg than in Switzerland.

H4: Younger candidates are more likely to participate in a VAA

When concentrating on multi-member constituencies only, in Switzerland each candidate faces on average 10 challengers within and across parties, with 6.5 in Luxembourg. In the latter country we find a clear dividing line between the two large (magnitude of 23 and 21) constituencies and the two small ones (9 and 7), whereas in Switzerland the number of multi-member constituencies is 20 and their magnitude varies from 34 to 2. More importantly, the number of candidates fielded by each party in a given constituency can also vary widely. This is not the case in Luxembourg where 7 parties presented full lists (corresponding to the number of MPs to elect) in all constituencies and an eighth party presented lists in only 2 of those, making the number of competitors per seat only vary between 7 and 8 across constituencies. Overall, in 80 per cent of the Swiss constituencies this rate is equal or larger than in any constituency in Luxembourg. Given these differences in the context of competition faced by an average candidate, we would expect variables pertaining to the perceived probability of being elected to perform differently in the two contexts. More specifically, since an incumbent's probability of re-election is on average much smaller in Switzerland than in Luxembourg, the strength or even the direction of the relationship of the incumbency variable could differ in the two contexts.

The logistic regressions performed allow us to study the propensity of candidates to participate in *smartvote*. More than 2,800 candidates in Switzerland ran for the 200 seats in the National Council in 2003, whereas in Luxembourg there were 452 candidates for 60 seats in the Chamber of Deputies in 2009. On the occasion of the first implementation of *smartvote* in both countries, about 50 per cent of candidates running for elections decided to participate and entered their policy profile. Note that owing to potential gender differences in the uses of the internet for political information and for the evident under-representation of female candidates in elections, we control for gender in all of our analyses.

Results

Table 11.2 displays results of three models ran on the 2003 Swiss and 2009 Luxembourg first experiences with VAAs. Hypothesis 1 is verified in Luxembourg by the fact that model 2 candidates holding a high-level political mandate (minister, MP or MEP) were actually less likely to participate in *smartvote* (but the effect is not significant) than those who do not, whereas those who hold a local mandate only were twice as likely to use it than those who either had a more visible political mandate or none at all in model 3. This clearly follows our argument regarding the perceived chances of being elected influencing the decision to wage a personalised campaign. Results for Switzerland, however, contradict Hypothesis 1 as incumbent MPs were much more likely (with a substantive and significant effect) to use the VAA than other candidates. We alluded earlier to the fact that competition for parliamentary seats is fiercer in Switzerland than in Luxembourg. In such a context, a much wider pool of candidates have no real expectations (nor even motivations, as a fair number of candidates are known as 'list-fillers' who only accept the invitation made by their party to be part of a list in order to present full plates) of being elected and are therefore less likely to invest time and effort in their campaign, whereas incumbents perceive a lower probability of re-election than in environments where they face less inter- and intra-party competition. Therefore this result does not fundamentally alter our expectation that the subjective probability of being elected has an impact on the decision of candidates to use new technologies to increase their personal visibility in electoral campaigns.

All models also show results in line with Hypothesis 2, in that the direction of the effects for the C:P index reflecting intra-party competition and its squared term both have the expected sign. The propensity of candidates to use *smartvote* therefore rises with intra-party competition up to a point where this index reflects the situation of parties holding a single seat in a large constituency, for which we expected – as in the case of parties that did not hold any seat in a constituency – a partisan rather than a personalised campaign to be favoured. These effects reflecting the strategic context in which candidates are embedded are significant in Switzerland, further confirming the importance of the level of competition in this context, as well as in Luxembourg in model 2 when the first version of the incumbency (high-level mandates) variable is used.

The direction of the variable reflecting the position of candidates' parties regarding democratic participation is positive as expected by Hypothesis 3 but only significant in Luxembourg. This could be due to the greater weight of strategic motivations in Switzerland, but may also account for the fact that the operationalisation of the respective positions of parties was here inferred from the average position of their candidates present on the VAA. This could cause bias given that these candidates would probably be those among their parties who would be more open to further democratic participation. However, as this would arguably be the same for all parties, that these positions matched national expert expectations, and that we restricted the dataset to parties large enough to have a known opinion on these issues, this risk is somewhat limited. In any case, the effect of this variable in model 1 is weak and non-significant whilst it is large and significant in Luxembourg.

Finally, comparing models 1 and 2 of Table 11.2 reveals a common pattern with regard to the age of candidates that verifies Hypothesis 4. Younger ones were clearly more likely to participate in *smartvote*, with an effect that is already significant

Table 11.2: Binary logistic regression models explaining SV usage by candidates – (exp(B)), robust standard errors by clustering on constituencies in parentheses

	Model 1: Switzerland	Model 2: Luxembourg	Model 3: Luxembourg
Age (ref: 18–29)			
30–39	1.004	1.231	1.104
	(0.330)	(0.351)	(0.315)
40–49	0.994	0.781	0.690
	(0.298)	(0.318)	(0.288)
50–59	0.726	0.591**	0.490***
	(0.166)	(0.155)	(0.136)
60 +	0.247***	0.591***	0.565***
	(0.054)	(0.106)	(0.118)
Sex (ref: female)	1.001	1.701***	1.638***
	(0.163)	(0.207)	(0.215)
Incumbency (ref: challenger)	2.002***	0.860	
	(0.505)	(0.125)	
Local mandate (ref: no local mandate)			2.012***
			(0.201)
C:P index	1.036**	1.079*	1.020
	(0.019)	(0.047)	(0.041)
C:P index squared	0.999***	0.996**	0.999
	(0.000)	(0.002)	(0.002)
Democratic participation	1.144	1.701***	1.715***
	(0.287)	(0.166)	(0.193)
Pseudo-R^2 (Nagelkerke)	0.11	0.05	0.07
N included	2,001	420	420

Notes: in Luxembourg 'incumbency' refers to either being incumbent MP, incumbent MEP or incumbent government minister; in Switzerland the variable only includes incumbent members of the National Council. In Switzerland the democratic participation value for a party is obtained by averaging the scores of the candidates of this party on five *smartvote* statements and the dataset is restricted to parties that fielded at least 200 candidates (which overall gained about 95 percent of the seats in 2003). In Luxembourg the score is computed for the official position of the party on five similar *smartvote* statements and the dataset is restricted to the parties that presented lists in all four constituencies (the only 'party' lacking was a newcomer that did not and refuse to participate to *smartvote*; it failed to win any seat in 2009 and disintegrated soon after the elections).

when comparing candidates below 30 and those above 50 in Luxembourg. In Switzerland the effect only becomes significant for the comparison with those aged 60 and more, but the substantive effect is much larger, leaving our expectation regarding the differential power of the age variable in the two contexts studied with mixed results. Gender, which was controlled for in each model, however, shows distinct results across country experiences, having no significant effect and a slight tendency towards more feminine participation in Switzerland and a clear and significant positive male effect in Luxembourg.

Discussion

This chapter explored the resemblances and differences between VAAs and Web 2.0 applications used by candidates in contemporary electoral campaigns. A number of hypotheses were generated to account for VAA adoption as electoral technological innovation and were tested in an exploratory empirical analysis.

In our analysis we introduced some theoretically relevant party-level variables (position on democratic participation and size in the constituency through the C:P index) and controlled to some extent for the lack of independence between candidates within constituencies through robust standard errors. Multilevel models could further estimate distinct relationships between the factors highlighted in the present chapter and integrate further characteristics at the level of the party (for instance, the degree of party centralisation, that would supposedly decrease the likelihood of personalised campaigns) or the constituency (for instance, the proportion of highly educated citizens among the voting population) the candidate is a member of. However, several explorative analyses indicate that their aptitude to increase the explicative values of our models is limited at best.[15] Indeed, our models include factors that suppose a rational behaviour of candidates based on strategic or civic motivations in a given electoral context but do not include a large number of other factors that could explain candidates' adoption of new electoral applications. Alternative factors for explaining its non-usage could be that candidates were not aware of its existence, that they reject a priori any internet application, or that they consider VAAs as a simple toy with no impact. On the opposite side, alternative factors for explaining its adoption could be that candidates are electronic 'geeks' or, simply, that they found the instrument interesting or 'fun' to use independently of any civic, strategic or contextual motivations. The analysis of the effects of these specific attitudes would require complementing our analysis with data derived from VAA-related questions included in a candidate survey. Such an analysis could, however, not be conducted for our study since no candidate survey was conducted in Switzerland in 2003, while for Luxembourg

---

15. Explorative models indicate that the relationships stand when taking the constituency as a level-2 variable in generalised linear models with a logit link and a random intercept. An empty model also showed that, as could be expected, the variance between constituencies is much greater in Switzerland (up to 32 per cent of the variance to be explained at the level of the individual candidate) than in Luxembourg (only 2 per cent of the variance).

the candidate electoral survey did not include a sufficient number of candidates who did not use *smartvote*. Further research on the determinants of VAA adoption as an instance of electoral campaign technological innovation is in order, and will be carried on, concentrating on candidates using such instruments for the first time in later implementations in Switzerland and Luxembourg, as well as in any other country where a candidate-centred tool was generated and in which candidate survey material relating to the election is available.

Chapter Twelve

Using VAA-Generated Data for Mapping Partisan Supporters in the Ideological Space

Fernando Mendez and Jonathan Wheatley

This chapter examines whether VAA-generated data can be used to provide meaningful insights on the policy positions of party supporters in the ideological space. Typically, scholars of party politics have relied on expert surveys or the analysis of manifestos for estimating the ideological positions of parties. In other cases surveys of party activists have been used to the same end. Rarely are mass survey respondents' policy positions used to map parties. In this chapter we examine whether VAA-generated data could be used as a complementary strategy for mapping political parties in the ideological space.

It should be pointed out at the outset that the aim of a VAA is to help voters decide which party/candidate most closely matches their policy preferences and that, therefore, the primary logic of a VAA is that of an application to benefit the voter, rather than a survey tool. However, VAA-generated data can also serve as a useful survey tool to examine 'old' questions in political science and it is this potential that this chapter seeks to explore. In this sense, our interests depart somewhat from the more VAA-centric literature, which focuses largely on aspects directly related to VAA design and effects (for a review, *see* Cedroni and Garzia 2010, Triga *et al.* 2012). So far, limited published work exists that has exploited VAA-generated data in relation to some of the traditional concerns of political science. One area in which such data could be revealing is in relation to the literature on mapping political parties. To investigate the feasibility of our claim we first provide a short overview of the mapping literature and its principal techniques before moving on to examine the nature of VAA-generated datasets, and some of the problems associated with their reliability. In the empirical analysis section we present our approach for extracting latent political dimensions from VAA data and techniques for constructing ideological scales. The findings, in terms of policy dimensions extracted and estimates of the ideological positions of partisan supporters, are then presented and discussed further in the concluding section.

Party mapping

Political parties are central to the operation of democracy and this has been reflected in the attention devoted to them in the political science literature. What concerns us in this paper is a particular sub-field of the party literature that focuses on mapping the policy positions of political parties and their supporters. The aim of scholars working in this field is to estimate the positions of parties with respect to certain policy dimensions, and they have employed two dominant strategies to this effect: the use of expert surveys and the analysis of manifestos (for a review, *see* Volkens 2007). A third approach, which has been used rather rarely, is to use mass surveys. An early example of this approach is that of Sani and Sartori (1983), who used mass survey data to measure party polarisation based on the self-defined location of party supporters. More recently, Leimgruber *et al.* (2010) have used election survey data to compare the policy orientations and degree of ideological polarisation of party voters with candidates in Switzerland. Our point of departure will be based on this third approach, but we will draw from opinion data generated from VAAs. It is predicated on the belief that political parties are defined not only by party elites and manifestos but also by party supporters at grassroots level, or, to use V.O. Key's classic term, 'the party-in-the-electorate' (Key 1964).

In terms of which policy dimensions are used to define the positions of political parties, the core focus has usually been on the traditional left–right scale. However, the notions of left and right are ambiguous and have been used to accommodate a wide variety of issues. With the exception of one case (*see* discussion below) in this chapter we use the terms 'left' and 'right' to refer to economic ideologies, with the left representing a socialist ideology and the right embodying a free market, capitalist ideology. For purposes of clarity, we will refer to this dimension as 'the economic dimension', with left and right representing the two opposite poles.

Having identified one economic dimension of political competition, it is clear that many issues fall outside this dimension, most notably so-called 'cultural' issues such as those relating to lifestyle choices, law and order, immigration and national identity. For Kriesi *et al.* (2006) this dimension – especially insofar as it relates to immigration and EU integration – has gained increasing salience in Europe recently as the process of globalisation has created 'winners' and 'losers' in society. This 'cultural dimension' of political competition has variously been described as a clash between libertarian and authoritarian values (Kitschelt 1994), between a libertarian-universalistic and a traditionalist-communitarian worldview (Bornschier 2010), or between green/alternative/libertarian (GAL) values and TAN values, representing traditionalism/authority/nationalism (Marks *et al.* 2006).

Overall, we would suggest that in most polities at least two dimensions of political competition are relevant: one economic and one cultural. However, at the same time we will remain open to the possibility that either one or both of these dimensions may be irrelevant in certain contexts, that they may combine to form a single dimension, or even that other dimensions may be relevant. Unlike VAA designers that impose pre-defined dimensions when launching a VAA, the inductive approach of this chapter allows us to generate relevant dimensions from the datasets collected.

VAA-generated data

To briefly recap on the discussion thus far, our approach could best be considered as a demand-side perspective, since the focus is on the mass opinions of party supporters. This can be contrasted with the supply-side type of analysis used in traditional approaches to party mapping, which focus on the supply of party positions as measured by manifestos or expert placements. In order to conduct our demand-side analysis of the political space we shall draw on seven datasets generated by VAAs deployed between May 2011 and February 2013 by the *Preference Matcher* research consortium.[1] To maximise potential variance across the cases we have chosen to group the VAA datasets in terms of three types of elections: presidential, national parliamentary and regional. For each type of election we have selected two countries. Note that even in the case of presidential elections, we are not mapping the positions of the presidential candidates but rather identifying partisan supporters from the data to map their parties. The following cases are included: national parliamentary elections in Greece (held on 6 May 2012) and Romania (held on 9 December 2012); regional elections in the United Kingdom and Spain (held in Scotland on 5 May 2011, in Galicia on 21 October 2012 and in Catalunya on 25 November 2012); and presidential elections in Cyprus and Ecuador, both held on 17 February 2013.

In all cases the VAA was operational for approximately three weeks prior to the election and included a set of thirty policy statements that were designed to reflect the most salient political issues. Respondents were provided with answer categories on a five-point scale: 'completely agree', 'agree', 'neither agree nor disagree', 'disagree', 'completely disagree'. A 'no opinion' option was also included as a response category and treated as a missing value in the analysis. In all cases the research team partnered with election studies experts from the countries involved in drawing up the policy questionnaire, as well as for coding the parties or candidates. In the analysis presented in the subsequent section we shall restrict the number of political parties mapped to those parties that obtained more than three per cent of the vote share in the relevant election.

As with any VAA experiment, not all dataset entries can be considered 'valid' for analysing the questions dealt with in this chapter. Having cleaned the datasets of potentially rogue entries we proceeded to try and identify party supporters from within each dataset (on data cleaning, *see* the chapter by Andreadis in this volume). How this was done was crucial to our research objective, that of mapping the parties. Here the problem is that the VAA is marketed as – and indeed its purported function is – a tool that is used by voters who have not yet decided how to vote. Surely, therefore, it cannot purport to tell us anything about the policy orientations of party supporters? However, the reality is that voters fill in a VAA for a wide variety of reasons, often because they have a general interest in politics and elections, or even out of sheer curiosity. For this reason, all the VAAs that

---

1.   For more information on datasets and VAA experiences see the Preference Matcher website at http://www.preferencematcher.org.

form the focus of this paper contain within them supplementary questions that distinguish between 'floating voters' and more committed 'party supporters'.

For these supplementary questions respondents were asked to provide additional details, such as age, sex, education, party affiliation and voting intention. For party affiliation, the option 'none' was always available. Those that a) expressed a particular party affiliation, and b) intended to vote for the same party or the coalition to which that party belonged were flagged as party supporters and were subsequently used in the party mapping process. In Cyprus where only presidential elections were held, condition (b) was replaced by the condition that respondents voted for their preferred party in parliamentary elections held twenty-one months previously. This reduced subset of respondents was then used in the party mapping process. The numbers of party supporters fulfilling both conditions are given in Table 12.1 (all tables included in this chapter can be accessed from an online Appendix).[2]

Analysis and results

In terms of analysis, the first step was to derive the most pertinent policy dimensions from the responses of the VAA users to the policy issue statements. To do this, we first generate a matrix of polychoric correlations on the user response data (after cleaning). We then perform exploratory factor analysis (principal axis in the R programming language) using the matrix as input. This method of dimension reduction is particularly appropriate for ordinal data. The number of dimensions extracted is based on the eigenvalues associated with each factor. In order to decide how many factors to extract we use the Cattell scree test, which plots the eigenvalues of each component on a graph and identifies a break-point, or 'elbow', where the curve flattens out. We retain those factors that appear above the 'elbow' in the graph (Costello and Osborne 2005). After the number of factors to extract is identified, we use a varimax rotation to best identify groups of items that measure more or less the same latent dimension.

The next step is to create a scale that effectively 'measures' the position of each respondent along the dimensions extracted. We use a version of Mokken scale analysis to identify latent variables or scales from amongst those items that load strongly (with factor loadings of greater than 0.4 or less than -0.4) onto one or other of the dimensions identified by factor analysis. For a scale to constitute a Mokken scale, all items that belong to it must a) conform to the monotone homogeneity model, b) register a positive normalised covariance H_{ij} with all other items and c) register a normalised covariance $H_i > 0.3$ for all H_i with respect to the rest scores.[3]

---

2. http://www.preferencematcher.org/wp-content/uploads/2012/09/Tables.pdf.

3. For more on the assumptions of the monotone homogeneity model, *see* Sijtsma and Verweij (1992) and Van der Ark *et al.* (2007). The analysis was carried out and coefficients calculated using the package mokken in the R programming language. Specifically, the function coefH was used to calculate the coefficients while the function check.monotonicity was used to test mono-tone homogeneity. For check.monotonicity, the minimum size of violations reported was set at

Once a dimension and its corresponding Mokken scale has been identified by means of the two above-mentioned methods, the next task is to compute the position of each respondent with respect to each scale. We do this by summing respondents' responses to the individual items that load onto each Mokken scale and reversing the polarity of each item when necessary (i.e. if the factor loadings derived from the factor analysis are negative). We then normalise the scores to vary between 0 and 1. Party supporters are then identified and the mean positions of each group of party supporters along each scale are calculated.

Altogether, three dimensions were extracted from the Scotland dataset, one dimension was extracted from the Galicia dataset and two dimensions were extracted from all the others. This corresponds to the number of factors that are located above the 'elbow' in the corresponding scree plots. The factor loadings and Mokken scales (including values for the coefficients H_i and the overall scalability coefficients H) for each of the thirty policy items across the cases are presented in the online Appendix.[4] The dimensions are listed in the tables as dim 1, dim 2 and (if necessary) dim 3 in the order that they were extracted. Strong loadings (>0.4 or <-0.4) are highlighted in bold, as they indicate that a particular issue statement is especially important with respect to a given dimension, while weak loadings (-0.1–0.1) are omitted. Items that belong to more than one Mokken scale are considered ambiguous and excluded from the relevant scales.

In Scotland, Cyprus, Greece, Romania and Ecuador an economic (left–right) dimension and a cultural dimension emerged as independent dimensions, while in the two Spanish cases economic and cultural issues all loaded onto a single overarching dimension. In Scotland and Catalunya, a separate 'regional autonomy' dimension could be identified. In Galicia, issues of regional autonomy also loaded onto the first (and only) dimension. In all cases in which an economic dimension emerged as a separate dimension, it embodied issues that mainly related to the role of the state in society and pitted those in favour of a greater regulatory role of the state (economic left-wingers) against those who advocated free-market solutions (economic right-wingers). In Ecuador and Romania issues involving the protection of the national economy from global capitalism also formed a part of this dimension, with (unsurprisingly) the economic left tending to favour such protection. The content of the cultural dimension was much more varied; in Scotland issues involving law and order and immigration predominated; in Greece, an issue relating to defence also loaded onto this dimension; in Cyprus the vexed question of the future status of Cyprus was included; while in Ecuador moral issues such as religion, homosexuality and abortion prevailed. Finally, in Romania, this dimension consisted exclusively of issues that involved rights for

---

0.03, while the minimum size of a rest score group was set a 10 per cent of the total sample. The maximum number of significant violations allowed for each Item was 40, although in none of our cases did the number exceed 20.

4.   The loadings given may differ slightly from the loadings indicated in two journal articles that draw from the same datasets (Wheatley 2012; Wheatley *et al.* 2012). This is because a slightly different method is used to extract them (one that is based on the R platform, rather than STATA).

national minorities. Overall, the cultural dimension separated those with a socially liberal and cosmopolitan standpoint from those with a conservative, authoritarian and/or (majority) nationalist standpoint. Finally, in Scotland and Catalunya, the regional autonomy dimension pitted those in favour of greater autonomy for their territories against those who resisted more autonomy.

In both Spanish cases the overarching dimension that incorporated both economic and cultural issues separated economically left-wing social libertarians from economically right-wing social authoritarians. In Galicia, where issues involving greater autonomy or independence of the region also load onto this dimension, pro-independence sentiments are associated with the left and anti-independence views with the right.

Once the relevant scales had been identified, each user was assigned a value with respect to each scale in the manner described above, and the positions of party supporters were mapped (*see* Figures 12.1–12.7). Only those parties a) for which at least 100 supporters could be identified from our sample, and b) won at least 3 per cent in the corresponding elections, were included in the analysis.[5] In the maps (except Figure 12.3) the black squares represent the mean position of each party's supporters on each scale, while the associated contour lines each enclose 50 per cent of the relevant party's supporters. The abbreviations given for each party are provided in Appendix 12.1. In the case of Galicia (Figure 12.3), where there is only a single scale, a density map of each party's supporters with respect to that scale is provided instead. In Greece, Romania, Cyprus and Ecuador the x-axis represents a scale based on the divide between economic left and economic right, while the y-axis represents a cultural dimension dominated by a different mix of national, lifestyle and security issues (*see* Figures 12.2, 12.5, 12.6 and 12.7). For Scotland, a third scale (z), representing Scottish autonomy/independence, is added to the economic and cultural scales, in conformity with the three-dimensional structure of the Scottish political space, and three maps are therefore included (x versus y, x versus z and y versus z, *see* Figure 12.1). Finally, in Catalunya an overarching left–right scale that pits left-liberals against right-conservatives co-exists with an 'autonomy' axis (Figure 12.4). In all maps, the economic left (whether or not it is also imbued with cultural values) is located on the left side of the maps, while (unsurprisingly) the economic right is located on the right. If the cultural dimension is an independent dimension, culturally conservative or nationalist orientations are placed at the top of the maps, while socially progressive or cosmopolitan views are placed at the bottom. Finally, in Scotland and Catalunya, a pro-independence position is placed at the top, while an anti-independence position is located at the bottom.

The party positions as reflected by party supporters reveal a fairly consistent picture, albeit one with marked differences across the cases in terms of relevant dimensions extracted, polarisation of party supporters, and ideological consistency

---

5. In Ecuador, we were forced to exclude two parties that were able to overcome the 3% barrier (the Partido Sociedad Patriótica and the Partido Roldosista Ecuatoriano) as there were less than 100 supporters in our sample. In all other cases all relevant parties were mapped.

Figure 12.1a: Scotland (1)

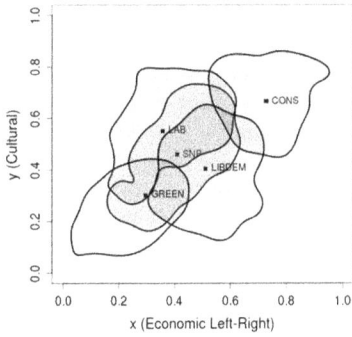

Figure 12.1b: Scotland (2)

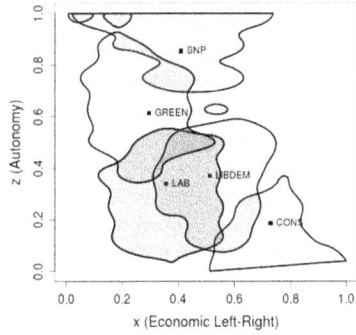

Figure 12.1c: Scotland (3)

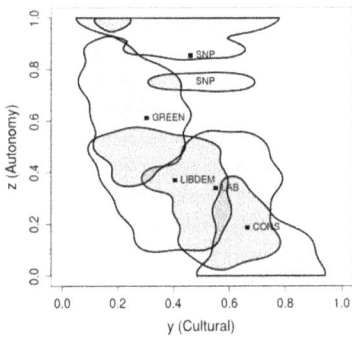

Figure 12.2: Greece

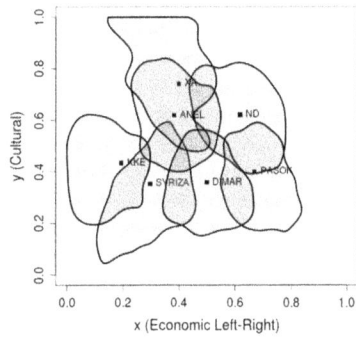

Figure 12.3: Galicia

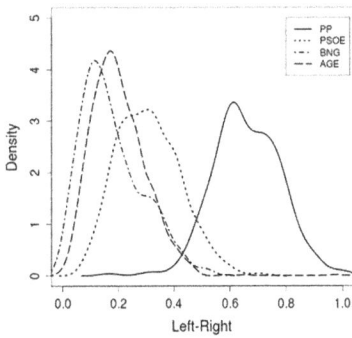

Figure 12.4: Catalunya

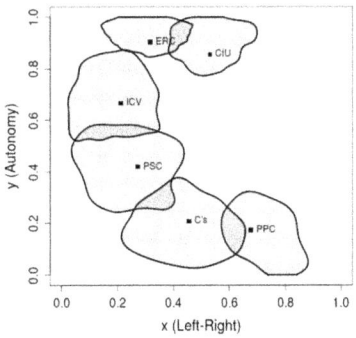

Figure 12.5: Romania

Figure 12.6: Cyprus

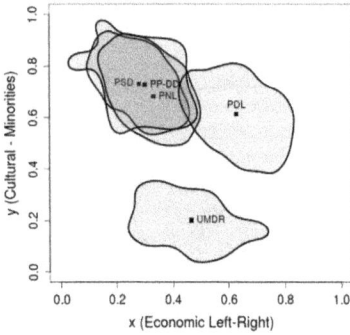

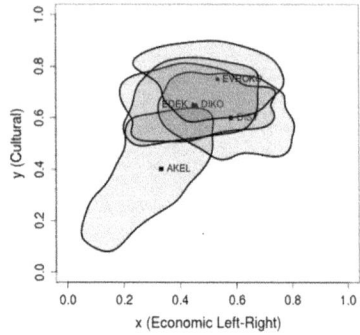

Figure 12.7: Ecuador

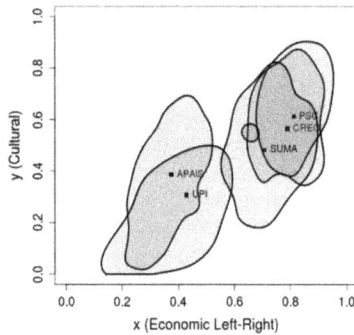

of supporters, as revealed by the area enclosed by each contour. It would of course be much more revealing to look at the rich nuances across the party positioning within each of the seven party systems analysed. Unfortunately, space constraints do not permit us to engage in such an analysis. Instead, we can point to some of the more macroscopic tendencies revealed by the findings.

Looking at the polarisation of the political space, in most of the cases the parties occupy fairly distinct policy 'niches' as represented by the mean party position. In both Greece (Figure 12.2) and Catalunya (Figure 12.4) there is a distinct spread across both dimensions of the political spectrum. In Catalunya, there is a particularly strong polarisation of parties along the 'autonomy' axis, and the rather small areas defined by the contour lines suggest that party supporters have fairly distinctive policy preferences. Party supporters in Galicia (Figure 12.3) are also quite strongly polarised with respect to the single left/pro-autonomy versus right/centralist axis. In Romania (Figure 12.5) three distinct ideological poles can be identified amongst party supporters: one on the economic left opposing minority rights; one on the economic right and only slightly more liberal in terms of minority rights; and one more or less in the centre in economic terms and in favour of minority rights (supporters of the mainly ethnic-Hungarian UDMR). In Scotland (Figure 12.1) the existence of three ideological dimensions paradoxically reduces polarisation as party supporters that take a relatively extreme position on one of the scales often take a moderate position with respect to at least one of the others. In both Cyprus (Figure 12.6) and Ecuador (Figure 12.7) there is a strong overlap in the positions of the supporters of the different parties, particularly in the case of centre-right parties.

In general the findings present a fairly consistent portrait of the ideological policy space of party supporters in the cases analysed. What they show is that although many 'floating voters' may fill in VAAs, it is nonetheless possible to identify party supporters from the datasets generated. Furthermore, it is possible to extract meaningful insights into the dimensionality of the political space. Based on the nature of the political space it is then possible to estimate the ideological positions of partisan supporters using our demand-side approach. Evidently, such an exercise can only present a snapshot at a particular temporal juncture. But as VAA experiments are further deployed – and perhaps some common standards emerge – it may be possible to map changes over time and gain additional theoretical insights into the linkages between party elites and their social constituencies.

A number of objections can be raised questioning the validity of the findings. One issue that arises with the use of a VAA as a data-gathering device is that of sample representativeness. Typically, VAAs are accessed by a self-selected sample of relatively well-educated (and disproportionately young or middle-aged) voters and cannot be considered to be a representative sample of the electorate. Can we, therefore, make reliable inferences about the population at large from data provided by such a non-representative sample? Evidence to date suggests that we can; an earlier analysis of the Scotland dataset suggests that the two-step method of exploratory factor analysis followed by Mokken scale analysis proves robust insofar as the scales remain more or less unaltered when the method is repeated on samples that are randomly selected to approximate the voting preferences of the population at large (Wheatley et al. 2012).[6]

The issue of representativeness could also be used to question the validity of party mapping on the grounds that the party supporters who use these applications may not be representative of rank-and-file party voters. Those who use such online tools are better educated and more politically aware than the norm. However, if our aim is to study the issue positions of parties – as defined by their grassroots, rather than their elites – it is perhaps even preferable to draw from the views

---

6.   The dataset on which the earlier study draws (n=12,053) is slightly smaller that the dataset used in this paper (n=14,864), because it excludes all those users that do not answer questions about their age, gender, vote intention and party identification.

of politically interested and well-informed citizens. Indeed, traditional methods for mapping parties (such as expert surveys, surveys of party elites or manifesto analysis) are not representative, nor are they supposed to be. The method described in this paper is simply a new and innovative technique for party mapping based on the views of well-informed party supporters.

A final point relating to the validity of the findings concerns the way issue statements are selected. Specifically, they are elaborated by local experts who may have chosen them on the basis of their preconceived ideas about the underlying policy dimensions. Thus, the dimensions we identify may tell us less about the political orientations of users and more about the assumptions of the question-naire designer. On the other hand, while it is true that experts may have chosen some statements based on their own notions of, say, a left–right or a conservative–liberal system of values, it was not the choice of statements that predetermined whether economic and cultural issues would collapse into a single over arching dimension (as in the Spanish cases) or would form two independent dimensions (as in the other cases). Instead these differing patterns emerged from analysis of the data and, presumably, reflected real differences in how the political space is constructed. Nevertheless, we cannot exclude the possibility that the way the questionnaire is designed and, specifically, the extent to which it includes the issues most relevant to citizens may have some bearing on what – and how many – dimensions are extracted.

Conclusion and discussion

Our main aim in this chapter was to show how VAA-generated data can be used as a complementary strategy for the purposes of party mapping. Our basic claim is that an appropriately designed VAA and cleaned dataset can indeed provide meaningful insights on party ideological positions. The results obtained appear to be largely intuitive in terms of the dimensions identified in the scholarly literature. In this regard, the mapping of party supporters on the basis of VAA-generated data could provide direct and meaningful insights to ongoing research in the field of party mapping. Furthermore, it can do this from the perspective of what we have called the demand side. At the same time, the implications of this type of analysis can also feed right back into VAA-centric concerns, such as those related to design issues. For instance, one very obvious conclusion from our mapping exercise directly relates to the various visualisations employed by VAA sites. A typical graph used in VAAs is a two-dimensional plot (e.g. left–right versus liberal–conservative). This is because in our VAA experiments we assume most items to load onto two pre-imposed dimensions. However, in this analysis we see that this assumption is not always justified and there may be one, two or even three relevant dimensions. This suggests that much greater attention should be paid to multiple-dimension mapping by VAA designers.

Overall, this chapter has shown how data generated from VAAs can be exploited in the study of one of the traditional fields of political science, that of party politics and, specifically, the ideological positioning of party supporters. While the data cannot be equated directly with data from a representative survey, it can shed light on how the ideological space is constructed and on the orientations of a particular (i.e. relatively young and well-educated) subset of party supporters. The fact that the data obtained is not representative of the population as a whole should not be ignored. On the other hand, if care is taken to avoid making over-ambitious claims and to be open about the limitations of what these data can tell us, we can draw from the insights that they provide to help us gain a better understanding of one of the most interesting phenomena of political behaviour.

Appendix 12.1

Abbreviations of parties

Scotland

CONS	Scottish Conservative Party
GREEN	Scottish Green Party
LAB	Scottish Labour Party
LIBDEM	Scottish Liberal Democrats
SNP	Scottish National Party

Greece

ANEL	Anexartitoi Ellines (Independent Greeks)
DIMAR	Dimokratiki Aristera (Democratic Left)
KKE	Kommounistikó Kómma Elládas (Communist Party of Greece)
ND	Néa Dimokratía (New Democracy)
PASOK	Panellinio Sosialistiko Kinima (Panhellenic Socialist Movement)
SYRIZA	Synaspismós Rizospastikís Aristerás (Coalition of the Radical Left)
XA	Chrysi Avgi (Golden Dawn)

Galicia

AGE	Alternativa Galega de Esquerda (Galician Left Alternative)
BNG	Bloque Nacionalista Galego (Galician Nationalist Bloc)
PP	Partido Popular (People's Party)
PSOE	Partido dos Socialistas de Galicia (Socialiist party of Galicia)

Catalunya

Cs	Ciutadans – Partido de la Ciudadanía (Citizens – Party of the Citizenry)
CiU	Convergència i Unió (Convergence and Union)
ERC	Esquerra Republicana de Catalunya—Catalunya Sí, Republican (Left of Catalunya—Catalunya Yes)
ICV	Iniciativa per Catalunya Verds – Esquerra Unida i Alternativa, (Initiative for Catalunya Greens – United and Alternative Left)
PPC	Partit Popular Català (People's Party of Catalunya)
PSC	Partit dels Socialistes de Catalunya (Party of Socialists of Catalunya)

Romania

PDL	Partidul Liberal Democrat (Democratic Liberal Party)
PNL	Partidul Naμional Liberal (National Liberal Party)
PP-DD	Partidul Poporului – Dan Diaconescu (People's Party – Dan Diaconescu)
PSD	Partidul Social Democrat (Social Democratic Party)
UDMR	Uniunea Democrată Maghiară din România (Hungarian Democratic Union of Romania)

Cyprus

AKEL	Anorthotikon Komma Ergazomenou Laou (Progressive Party of Working People)
DIKO	Dimokratikon Komma (Democratic Party)
DISY	Dimokratikos Sinagermos (Democratic Rally)
EDEK	Kinima Sosialdimokraton (Movement for Social Democracy)
EVROKO	Evropaiko Komma (European Party)

Ecuador

APAIS	Movimiento Alianza PAIS (PAIS Alliance Movement)
CREO	Creando Oportunidades (Creating Opportunities)
PSC	Partido Social Cristiano (Social Christian Party)
UPI	Alianza Unidad Plurinacional de las Izquierdas (Plurinational Unity of the Lefts)
SUMA	Sociedad Unida Más Acción (SUMA Movement)

Chapter Thirteen

Matching Voters with Parties in Supranational Elections: The Case of the *EU Profiler*

Maria Laura Sudulich, Diego Garzia, Alexander H. Trechsel and Kristjan Vassil

The last decade has witnessed the dramatic spread of Voting Advice Applications across European countries and voters. Countries like Belgium, the Netherlands and Switzerland have pioneered the use of VAAs in the run up to general elections. Nowadays, it is hard to find a single European country in which no VAA is in use prior to general elections. In the 'pioneering' countries, VAAs for local elections have been made available too (*see* Ladner is this volume).

Until the European election of June 2009, however, no platform of this sort had ever engaged with the task of providing fundamental information on parties' stands to European voters in the context of EP elections.[1] The *EU Profiler* (available online at http://www.euprofiler.eu) launched by the European University Institute (EUI) in conjunction with the Dutch *Kieskompas* and the Swiss *smartvote* for the first time allowed citizens across Europe to position themselves on the basis of thirty issue statements and simultaneously to avail themselves of information on the positions of political elites across the entire European Union. A well-informed electorate is crucial for the democratic mechanism to work. In such a notoriously information-scarce context as the EP elections, the role of information on what political elites stand for is therefore particularly important. Empirical evidence has consistently pointed at a widespread lack of information on political actors and more in general on EU institutions – although recent studies indicate an over-time increase in volume (De Vreese 2003; De Vreese *et al.* 2006; Schuck *et al.* 2011). Moreover, research has indicated that information on EU-related matters and more specifically on EP elections tend to be uneven across countries (De Vreese *et al.* 2006). In such a scenario, supranational VAAs can play an especially important role because of their ability to offer the same level of information across countries.

---

1. Before the European election of 2004, and again in 2009, the *EU-Votematch* (available online at: http://www.votematch.eu) was launched by the Network of European Citizenship Education (NECE) – a group encompassing agencies and NGOs in the field of citizenship education from twenty-five different European countries (cf. Marschall and Garzia in this volume). One notes, however, that this application did not illustrate to users their degree of match with actual political parties but only with 'nominal' transnational party groups present in the European Parliament.

The *EU Profiler* project provided voters with easily accessible information on positions of parties running at the 7th European Parliament election, and did so by offering the exact same amount of information to voters across all of Europe. The *EU Profiler* – launched six weeks before the June 7 EP election – was the first supranational VAA that simultaneously collected data on 274 parties in the 27 member countries of the European Union, as well as in Croatia, Turkey and Switzerland. Parties were positioned on the basis of their stands on 28 issues statements (common to all countries) and 2 country-specific issues. A large team of scholars at the EUI selected the 28 issues statements in common, whereas country specialists chose the 2 remaining issues. Other than its role in informing the public and allowing citizens to have a clearer idea of where parties stood in relation to themselves, this VAA also had an important impact for the scientific community interested in the representative linkage between European elites and citizens. The heterogeneity in terms of scales, metrics and computational techniques for combining multidimensional distances into a unique score is enormous among VAAs, and so are the differences in the number and nature of issue dimensions in use (*see* Mendez and Wheatley in this volume). Therefore, comparisons among voters and parties located in different countries are challenging endeavours that *de facto* limit comparative research in the field. Such a lacuna for a long time represented a strong limitation to the use of VAA data in a comparative perspective. However, the *EU Profiler* successfully managed to fill the gap by providing the first platform able to place parties and voters in 30 different countries.

In this chapter, we seek to describe such a project and its features in relation to national as well as sub-national VAAs, in order to evaluate the extent to which supranational VAAs can complement existing platforms and advance the field. The chapter proceeds as follows: we begin by exploring the peculiar nature of a VAA in the context of European Parliament elections. We proceed by describing the *EU Profiler*, and then critically evaluate challenges and opportunities arising from it. We conclude by reflecting upon paths for future applications.

Voting Advice Applications in the context of European Parliament elections

While the number of VAAs has exponentially grown in recent years, the *EU Profiler* represented by then the sole pan-European VAA and the only case of a voting advice platform thought and designed for European Parliament elections. Given the particular nature of these elections, we ought to consider a number or elements that determine the environment affecting EP-elections-tailored VAAs.

EP elections have been famously labelled 'second order elections' (Reif and Schmitt 1980) as their results do not determine the formation of governments or executive bodies. Scholars have consistently pointed out a number of characteristics of EP elections as their defining elements: lower turnout compared to national elections, tendency of national government parties to under perform, and high incidence of success for small parties (Franklin and Hobolt 2011; Marsh 1998). Furthermore, EP elections are confronted with the 'democratic deficit' of

EU institutions, whose design and modes of political representation are primarily national, rather than European in nature (Anderson and Ellassen 1996; Coultrap 1999; Karl *et al.* 2003; Marsh and Norris 1997). Research and theoretical accounts of the sources of the EU's democratic deficit argue that the media is failing to act as a legitimacy-building intermediary between the EU and its citizens – pointing to the low levels of interest displayed towards EU affairs in national media coverage (Anderson and Ellassen 1996; De Vreese 2003) and the non-emergence of a European-level media system or 'public sphere' (Scharpf 1999; Schlesinger 1999). The internet represents a unique case in its capacity to offer limitless, easily reachable information to anyone with access to it. Compared to traditional media, it exponentially multiplies opportunities to gather information on any issue an individual may be interested in. Therefore, the design and implementation of a pan-European VAA such as the *EU Profiler* is particularly important. If VAAs can play a successful role in informing citizens (Wall *et al.* 2009), mobilising them and increasing their propensity to engage with politics at large (Garzia 2010; Ladner and Pianzola 2010), then EP-targeted VAAs are potentially even more crucial at doing so than VAAs designed for national elections.

If we accept Zaller's claim that contextual information is vital to translate people's predispositions into support for a candidate, party or policy (Zaller 1992), then the potential for pan-European VAAs to act as facilitators of such a process is patent. VAAs provide users with information on political actors and policies that allow voters to also clarify their own stands and act accordingly. To the extent that information availability and campaign intensity play a role in determining vote choice, VAAs help reduce uncertainty voters may have with regard to their own preferences or about political elites' positions. Given that voters tend to make their judgment on how to vote at EP elections on the basis of party cues and national-level considerations, pan-European VAAs help clarify what parties' positions with regard to European matters are as well as providing an overview of the supranational political space. This is valuable information that voters are rarely exposed to; pan-European VAAs such as the *EU Profiler* can indeed provide a snapshot of the political party landscape at the European level. The *EU Profiler* – as we will describe in more detail below – presented European citizens with the possibility of placing themselves in a common political space, where not only could they evaluate their proximity to national parties, but also to parties running in EP elections in other member states. This pioneering feature of the *EU Profiler* is magnified by the fact that party positions had been recorded and estimated all at the same time. The *EU Profiler* team successfully aggregated information on party stances and policy positions for over 270 parties all over Europe. As it stands, the *EU Profiler* represented the largest container of information on elites' positions ever made (freely) available to citizens. Therefore, the informative function performed by the *EU Profiler* was extensive, to say the least. Indeed, a survey of *EU Profiler* users found that more than half of respondents considered their experience with the VAA useful (Bright *et al.* 2014).

The *EU Profiler*: Resources and challenges for political research

The project was of primary importance in providing a space where voters could simultaneously learn about party positions and concurrently about their own placement in relation to elites. As with every VAA, the makers of the *EU Profiler* aimed primarily at helping voters make a well-informed decision. Therefore, it represented a tangible contribution from the academic community towards the European public. Nevertheless, it also provided specialists with an unprecedented rich source of scholarly valuable data. Indeed, the *EU Profiler* was innovative and unique in providing an opportunity for simultaneous and coordinated comparative research into party positions across different political systems in a single electoral context.[2]

Parties were given the same opportunity to react to the issue statements and provide their self-placement. The *EU Profiler* team identified and contacted parties running for the 2009 EP elections, inviting them to fill in an online questionnaire and motivating their choices by supplying supporting material (for an extensive description of the procedure for the party self-placement option and the reaction from the party side, *see* Trechsel and Mair 2011). Almost 38 per cent of parties contacted by the *EU Profiler* team filled in the questionnaire. Where parties declined the invitation, a team of specialists, composed of PhD students, researchers and professors in social sciences, and selected on the basis of country of expertise, proceeded to code parties' positions. Expert coding was also preferred to party self-placement when parties provided farfetched positions and/or failed to offer supporting material to motivate their choices. Moreover, experts were asked to specify what documentation they had used in order to place parties. They were invited to use eight types of sources hierarchically ordered (plus an 'other' category). By means of an online platform, expert coders recorded and documented their choices by providing references to party manifestos, party programmatic documents and official statements of party leaders, MPs and MEPs. In order to ensure the highest possible level of reliability among coders, cross-checks were organised within each team, while country team-leaders ran additional checks before finalising the process of party placement. It is worth noting that while most of the interaction among coders took place within national teams, the online platform designed to facilitate the coding procedures also provided space for discussion among coders from different country teams. The final output of such a coding effort represents, to date, the largest dataset on European party positions, comprising a total of 8,220 party positions on 30 issues for 274 parties.

---

2. There are several challenges involved in the conceptualisation and implementation of a supranational VAA (for a review, *see* Lowerse and Otjes 2012), especially when it comes to the design of a common questionnaire able to discriminate not only across countries but also within a given country. In most countries the *EU Profiler* statements divided the parties running in the elections, offering users alternatives across a wide range of positions. Some national constituencies, however, contained a more limited political offer. In Malta, for instance, every political party running in the 2009 EP 2009 elections strongly opposed the idea that euthanasia should be legalised; and in Denmark, every party strongly agreed with the reduction of subsidies to the EU's farmers.

The dataset, including supporting material and coding documentation, is freely available to scholars and to the public at large.[3]

Clearly, the coding effort of the *EU Profiler* team was extensive and it achieved not only a high degree of reliability but it also managed to assess party positions beyond traditional manifesto coding (Trechsel and Mair 2011). While most content analytical projects, such as the Comparative Manifesto Project (CMP) or the PIREDEU (Providing an Infrastructure for Research on Electoral Democracy in the European Union) Manifesto Project, limit the sources for extracting party positions to party manifestos, the *EU Profiler* made use of a larger array of sources. Election manifestos for the 2009 EP election were regarded as the most relevant source, but the rationale behind *EU Profiler* coding provided greater flexibility insofar as it allowed coders to use other types of documents, in case the election manifestos in question did not suffice. This becomes especially relevant when some parties, particularly smaller ones, postpone the release of their election manifestos making it unfeasible to include them in the VAA. In some instances, the *EU Profiler* team found that parties were unable to respond to some of the issue statements altogether or failed validating their selected stance with reliable documentation. Small niche parties were particularly prone to forming their positions during the election campaign or *vis-à-vis* the questions posed by the *EU Profiler*. In such cases it is pivotal to any VAA to ensure that party positions are not only reliably coded, but also proved by valid source documents. *EU Profiler* ensured this by relaxing the assumption that all party positions need to be found in party manifestos compiled for this particular election. Instead, older manifestos, party programs, media texts, broadcasts, etc. were used for coding party positions. If still not found and included in the VAA, nonetheless a VAA faces a challenge of explaining to its audience why parties are treated on unequal grounds – the bulk of parties are required to provide source documents and others are not. Yet, leaving out some of the small parties in particular electoral contexts might make little sense to local voters. Thus, issues that are perhaps less salient for national VAAs become considerably more accentuated for a supranational VAA.

Overall, the *EU Profiler* approach to coding party positions was unique in allowing for a dynamic interaction between parties and experts. The *EU Profiler* team interacted with parties when inconsistencies emerged and provided each and every party with the final positions estimated by experts. As such, while the logic behind extracting party positions from party documents is the same for the CMP, the PIREDEU Manifesto Project and the *EU Profiler*, the latter relied on a wider range of sources, it engaged directly and dynamically with parties and it provided a large degree of transparency by making coding and references to support documentation available to the public.

Over 2.5 million unique users visited the website during the six weeks prior to the June 2009 elections, with 919,422 complete voting advices having been

---

3.   The *EU Profiler* dataset is available for download at http://dvn.eudo.eu/dvn/dv/euprofiler.

generated. Users could react to each and every issue statement by stating their level of agreement on a standard five-point scale – 'completely agree'; 'tend to agree'; 'neutral'; 'tend to disagree'; 'completely disagree'; plus a 'no opinion' option. They could also assign saliency to issues by indicating to which extent they regarded each issue as 'personally important to them'.

A standard compass graphically depicting the position of users in relation to parties provided the matching between parties and users' positions (*see* Figure 13.1). Users could compare their own positions not only with national parties, but also with parties from other countries as well as with regional parties (e.g. Swiss parties could be disaggregated into German, French and Italian; UK parties could be presented in disaggregated form by region: Scotland, Wales and Northern Ireland). Such a possibility is unprecedented in the realm of VAAs but also more broadly in research that aims at assessing the linkage between parties and voters. Overall, comparative research has suffered enormously from the lack of comparable data. Van der Brug and van Spanje (2009) explore the issue of party representativeness by matching two different expert surveys (Benoit and Laver 2006; Hooghe *et al.* 2010) with voters' positions from the European Social Survey (ESS), and acknowledge the complexity of matching positions extracted by different surveys. The same goes for Rohrschneider and Whitefield (2012) who also use the EES in combination with an original expert survey. In this respect, the *EU Profiler*-generated data allows the addressing of these questions from a new angle by assessing representatives and represented according to a homogenous scale. The phrasing of key questions that determine elites and voters' placement is in fact fundamental in ensuring the validity of any attempt at combining parties and voters' attitudes and positions. Most notably, the *EU Profiler* represents a unique case of identical phrasing of issue statements presented to voters and elites in thirty countries at the same time.

Some scholars have pointed out the new challenges and opportunities for VAA developers inherent in the actual option for intra-Union migrants to cast their votes in EP elections in the receiving country (Dziewulska and Ostrowska 2012). In this sense, the possibility for users to compare their position with parties from more than one political system stands as one of the distinctive features of the *EU Profiler* in relation to real-world transnational dynamics. And even while a wide majority of European voters is blinded to expressing their own preferences in their country of residence, parties running outside their constituency (or their state) could nonetheless provide a better match to their position. Indeed, the developers of the *EU Profiler* accounted for such a possibility and allowed users to match their preference with any party competing in the EP election, therefore producing a list of best- to worst-matching parties across the entire continent (*see* Figure 13.2).

Bright *et al.*'s (2014) analysis of *EU Profiler*-generated data provides evidence that the vast majority of users are potential 'party migrants' insofar as their degree of closeness to the partisan offer would be drastically increased were they able to vote for a party outside their national district. They also find that there is noteworthy active demand among citizens for a transnational voting space of this kind and that this demand is correlated with the perception that a transnational

Figure 13.1: The two-dimensional visualisation of the outcome

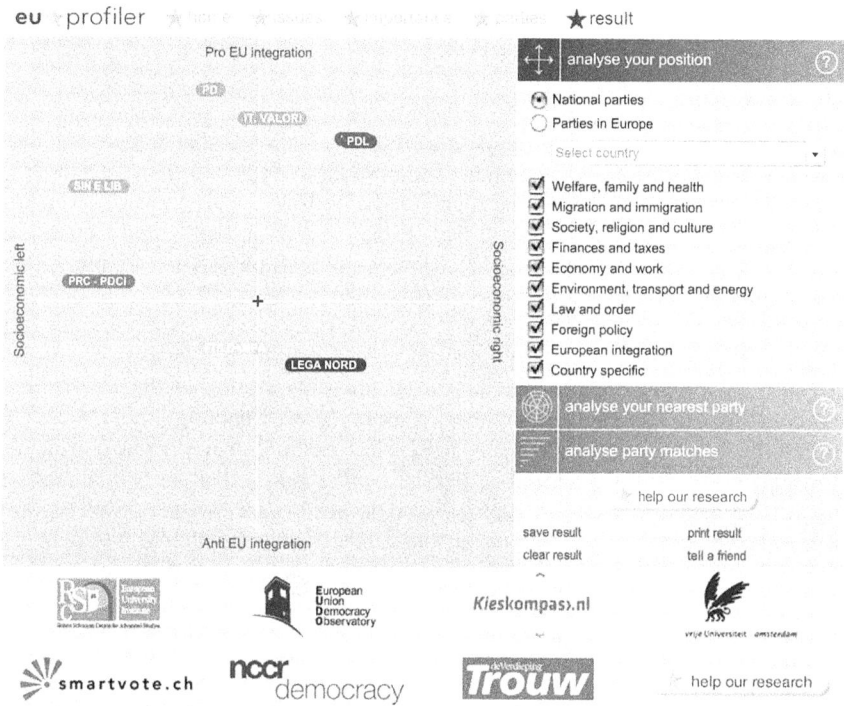

Figure 13.2: Measuring the representative deficit in a national (above) and a transnational (below) voting district

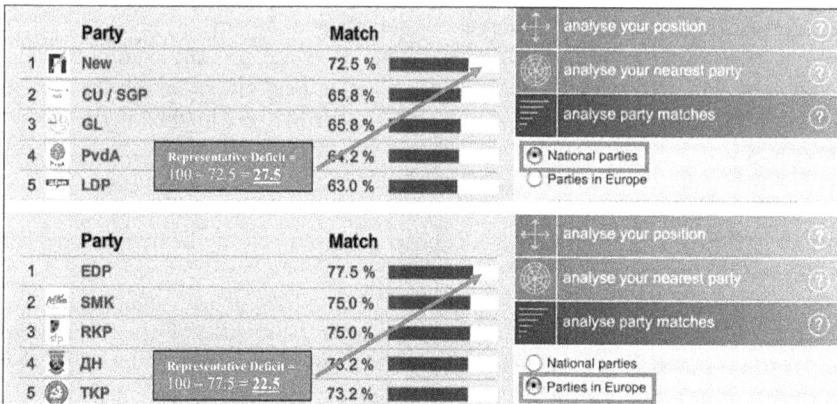

See http://press.ecpr.eu/resources.asp for full colour figures.

voting space could improve their quality of representation. Such study stands only as an example of how *EU Profiler*-generated data can insightfully contribute to the field of empirical democratic theory (Anderson and Fossen in this volume; for a review, *see* Garzia and Marschall 2012).

Conclusions

There are challenges and caveats intrinsic to any VAA that intends to deal with European Parliament elections. The popular attention to these elections is weak while at the same time the media dedicate little coverage to such events. European campaigns experience lower levels of intensity compared to national elections (Bellucci *et al.* 2010, 2012). Moreover, levels of turnouts are low across the continent, indicating that these elections per se are not mobilising citizens. Therefore, environmental conditions are not particularly favourable for the success of VAAs, although their functions would be of utmost importance in such a context. Despite the unfavorable setting, the 2009 edition of the *EU Profiler* successfully attracted a large number of users. More crucially, it contributed to filling the information void typical of EP elections and proved to be a valuable instrument at citizens' disposal. The *EU Profiler* allowed users to match their own policy positions with those of political parties both within their own country of residence and abroad. Importantly, these functions were offered online to the entire European citizenry as well as to countries candidate to EU membership. Not only could voters use the VAA to inform their vote choice, but also non-voters could avail themselves of this information. Users could also decide what weight to give to issue statements proposed on the platform and revise their position in the wake of their own interest scale. Finally, they could easily locate the parties ideologically closest to themselves thanks to a graphical visualisation. As such, the *EU Profiler* 2009 played an essential role in informing the electorate, and it pioneered the implementation of Voting Advice Applications in EP elections.

If the contribution offered to the public was essential, given the scarce media coverage of the electoral appointment, the scholarly contribution of the *EU Profiler* can be regarded as equally important. The team behind the platform succeeded in collecting the largest simultaneous record of political elites' positions in Europe to date. The data-collection procedure and coding exercise were thorough and extensive, despite time constraints. The assessment and self-assessment of party positions was performed according to a method that perfectly mirrored the procedure in use for voters' self-positioning. A dynamic element of involvement connected the academic team to political parties in the effort of accurately presenting party positions to voters. Data recorded on the supply side are, by all means, comparable with those pertaining to the demand side. Data collected by the project are freely available to scholars and, more generally, to anyone wishing to consult them. Certainly, the endeavour was complex, and as with every innovative project there was no prior experience of a pan-European VAA to build on. However, the project successfully managed to deliver both a scholarly contribution and a contribution to informing the European public, which provides a crucial benchmark for future efforts of this sort. European Parliament elections remain, after all, the context that most needs Voting Advice Applications.

Chapter Fourteen

Does the Electoral System Influence the Political Positions of Parties and Candidates? Answers from VAA-Research

Andreas Ladner

Voting Advice Applications (VAAs) not only provide voters with information about parties and candidates running for elections, they also gather a huge amount of information about their users and the parties and candidates they are supposed to vote for.[1] This information can be of utmost interest for political scientists.

In this chapter we shall – on the basis of VAA data – address a question which has been debated for quite some time: What is the impact of the electoral system on the positioning of parties and candidates in the course of electoral campaigns? Do majority systems really encourage parties to cluster around the centre of the political space whereas proportional systems (PR) foster greater ideological divergence, or are there other variables which might account for the ideological distance between the different parties? The theoretical arguments for these questions go back to Downs' (1957) theory of the median voter and Duverger's (1954) law, which claims that majority voting promotes two-party systems. More recent work, however, brings forward some quite contradictory empirical findings (Dow 2001, 2010; Ezrow 2008; Curini and Hino 2012).

The Swiss political system and the data from the Swiss VAA *smartvote* offer an excellent opportunity to contribute empirical evidence to this debate. The elections for the two chambers of the national parliament take place the same day, in the same constituencies but under two distinct electoral systems, with PR for one and majority voting for the other chamber. As for the data, it is the specific use of the VAA which outreaches the data from electoral studies in general. The nearly 3,600 candidates running for the two houses not only have very strong incentives to participate, which leads to more comprehensive data than traditional candidate surveys provide, but they also do it with the voters they want to address in mind, which reveals their strategic intentions to attract the voters they think they need to get elected. Since the users (voters) of *smartvote* reveal their political positions on the basis of the same questions, we are able to measure the distance between the candidates and different groups of voters directly. It is thus the quality and the quantity of the data and the instrumental use of the VAA by the candidates which lead to a promising research setting to answer the question outlined above.

---

1. There are, of course, also data protection issues at stake here. Such issues are not addressed in this paper.

I shall start this chapter by presenting the theoretical considerations behind the questions addressed and the empirical findings so far. Then I will introduce the context of analysis and present the findings. The chapter ends with a conclusion and a roadmap for further research.

Theoretical considerations

Studying the impact of electoral systems on distribution and preservation of power, on parties and political representation, on conflict resolution and political stability belongs to the core interests of a political scientist. It is generally believed that electoral systems matter and this serves as a proof that political institutions – which can be engineered by people – produce specific, more or less adequate outcomes. The electoral system in this perspective is seen as an independent variable and not as a consequence of pre-existing cultural or political circumstances. The impact of the electoral systems in our field of research operates in a twofold manner: directly, on the political positions of parties and candidates, and indirectly, through the number of parties, which itself has an influence on the positions of parties and candidates (*see* Figure 14.1).

The arguments behind such a conceptualisation go back to authors like Duverger and Downs. According to Duverger's law, a majority vote in one ballot is conducive to a two-party system; whereas proportional representation is conducive to a multiparty system. A majority vote on two ballots, finally, is conducive to a multiparty system, inclined toward forming coalitions (Duverger 1954). Whereas for Downs (1957) it is basically the median voter mechanism motivating parties in a two-party system to opt for a position in the centre of the political spectrum where the crucial voter needed to get more than 50 per cent of the votes is likely to be found. As for the more recent literature, the different positions are nicely summarised by Ezrow (2008: 482 ff.).

The conventional – ideal-type-like – understanding in the spatial modelling study by Cox (1990) claims that proportional electoral rules exert centrifugal incentives that motivate parties to present non-centrist policy programs. Parties have weaker incentives to maximise votes in a proportional system (Dow 2001) than they do in a majority system, where disproportionality is high and the winner takes it all. It is in the latter systems where parties have to cluster around the centre in order to win, whereas in the former they are freer to bring forward their true policy beliefs and still get a proportional share of the seats. Therefore, more extreme party positions are more likely to occur in PR.

As for the indirect effect, Cox (1990) concludes that the greater the number of competitors in a political system, the stronger the expectations that some of these parties will present non-centrist positions. Merrill and Adams (2002) argue very similarly that the vote-seeking politicians' centrifugal incentives grow stronger when the number of parties increases. Since the number of parties (for a measurement, *see* Taagepera and Shugart 1989) is presumably higher in PR systems, it is again PR constituencies being more often confronted with party extremism.

Figure 14.1: Direct and indirect effects of the electoral system on the political positions of parties/candidates

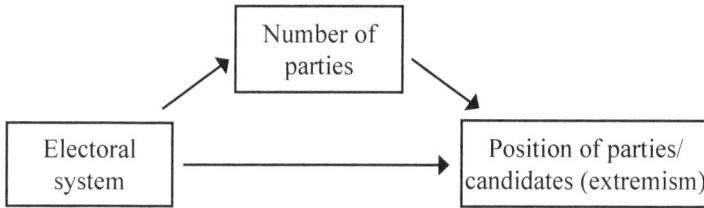

There are, however, also contributions which question the ideal-type way of arguing. Interesting to remember here is the work of Sartori (1976), which makes – at least theoretically – for highly fragmented party systems (i.e. with a high effective number of parties) a distinction between segmented multipartism and a polarised multipartism, which means that there must also be party systems with more than two (or three) parties where party competition is clustered around the centre. In a similar vein, Green-Pedersen (2004: 326) insists that if there is a strong centre party the chances of finding a centripetal party competition are as high as in a two-party system. Finally, it was Hans Daalder (1984) who had already claimed that it is more reasonable to believe that in systems with three or more parties (if there is at least one party having a position between the others) there might be centrifugal and centripetal tendencies in party competition. It might, for example, be the case that maximising votes is less important than being included in a coalition. Especially for smaller parties, a centrist position can thus become attractive (Schofield *et al.* 1999). There have also been attempts to introduce strategic incentives related to party activists. Some party activists – holding more extreme positions – provide campaign resources such as money and time (Miller and Schofield 2003). Another argument stresses the strategic implications of 'valence' dimensions of party evaluation, i.e. dimensions related to voters' impression of party elites' competence, honesty or charisma (Stokes 1963). Valence-disadvantaged parties have electoral incentives to differentiate themselves on policy grounds because if they present centrist policies that are similar to those advocated by valence-advantaged parties they will have no chances to be successful (Schofield and Sened 2005).

In a nutshell, there are strong arguments that PR fosters party extremism either directly or indirectly through more parties, but there are also arguments that PR can go hand in hand with more moderate party positions. Parties are more than catch-all (Kirchheimer 1965) or electoral parties (Panebianco 1988). They have a past and they belong to ideological families, which has an impact on their marge de manœuvre when it comes to defining their political positions.

And finally, parties, in order to be successful, have to respond to the needs of the electorate, which might also change over time. Here, the questions are: Are voters really clustered around the centre of the political spectrum and do they vote for parties and candidates having exactly the same political positions as they have (proximity voting)? Or do they vote strategically and opt for candidates with more extreme positions if they are on the same side of a political dimension as they are (directional voting; *see* Rabinowitz and Macdonald 1989)?

Empirical findings so far

The empirical evidence regarding the impact of PR on party extremism is ambiguous. Dow (2001), by analysing the spatial dispersion among parties and candidates in the majoritarian electoral systems in Canada and France and the highly proportional systems in the Netherlands and Israel, finds that parties and candidates in the majoritarian systems are located closer to the centre of the distribution of voters. He comes to the same conclusion nearly a decade later by looking at thirty-one electoral democracies: proportional systems support greater ideological dispersion and party extremism (Dow (2010).

But there are also contrary positions. Curini and Hino (2012) conclude that hypotheses derived from electoral systems and from the number of parties find little empirical support when it comes to explaining party system polarisation. They discuss other variables such as expectations of coalition formation and the role the elections play, for example, in relation to the presidential elections. And Ezrow (2008) finds no evidence at all that average party-policy extremism increases under proportional representation, nor that policy extremism increases in countries that feature large numbers of parties.

Methodological considerations

Although the question to answer seems quite simple and straightforward, there are a few methodological problems to be solved. A first concern is the measurement of the dependent variable. Is it sufficient to analyse party extremism on the left–right dimension or should we rather look at a multidimensional political space (*see* Ezrow 2008: 495)? And how do we establish the political positions of parties and candidates? Do we rely on expert judgments and on party manifestoes, or do we let the parties/candidates position themselves?

Despite the attractiveness of comparative studies on an international level, there are also some problems when it comes to the selection of countries (*see* also, Dow 2010: 360), and there might be important differences as far as the (political) culture is concerned. It is quite often countries with an Anglo-Saxon background which have an electoral system favouring two-party systems. The process of coalition-building or related presidential elections might be additional variables to control for.

And finally, and perhaps more intriguing, is the fact that party competition can change over time. The polarisation of a party system may vary without any changes in the electoral system or a significant increase in the number of parties. This calls for a control of the longitudinal dimension as well.

Using subnational units (constituencies) – as we shall do on the pages that follow – can offer a more laboratory-like situation to test the influence of the electoral system in a comparative manner, reducing the variance of the electoral systems to a necessary minimum and controlling for inter-country differences.

Research context and hypotheses

The elections for the Swiss National Parliament provide an excellent opportunity to analyse the impact of the electoral system on the positioning of parties and candidates, especially since the Swiss VAA *smartvote* covers these elections comprehensively.

The Swiss parliament has two chambers which have exactly the same competences (symmetric) but are elected differently:

- The National Council (the People's Chamber) consists of 200 members. The number of seats of the cantons varies according to their population: the canton of Zurich, for example, has 34 seats, and the canton of Glarus only 1.[2] The electoral system is proportional representation (PR) with open lists. The voters have the possibility to customise their ballot paper by taking candidates from different parties either by using an empty list or by discarding candidates from a party list ('panaschieren'), additionally they can express their preferences for specific candidates by writing down their names twice instead of once ('kumulieren').

- The Council of States (Chamber of Cantons) has 46 cantonal representatives (2 from each of the 20 cantons and 1 from each of the 6 half-cantons).[3] The elections for the Council of States in general take place the same day as the elections of the National Council. In an overwhelming majority of the cantons the electoral system used is a majority system.[4]

Since the constituencies are the cantons, the Swiss elections to the National Parliament consist of about 50 rather independent elections taking place the same weekend, half of them under PR and half of them under majority rule. There have been

---

2. The strongest party in the National Council (after the 2011 elections) is the Swiss People's Party (SVP) with 54 seats (26.6 per cent of the vote), followed by the Social Democrats (SP) with 46 seats (18.7 per cent of the vote), the Liberal Party (FDP.Die Liberalen) with 30 seats (15.1 per cent of the vote) and the Christian Democrats with 28 seats (12.3 per cent of the votes).

3. The strongest parties in the Council of States are, after the 2011 elections, the Christian Democrats (CVP) with 13 seats, followed by the Radical Democrats (FDP.Die Liberalen) and the Social Democrats (SP) with 11 seats and the Swiss People's Party (SVP) with 5 seats.

4. Only the two cantons Neuchâtel and Jura use a PR system, and in the half-canton of Appenzell-Innerrhoden they elect their representative at the Landsgemeinde (assembly).

   Although the majority systems takes place in two ballots (absolute majority in the first round, relative majority in the second) it is not usually expected to have a second ballot. The candidates rather go for a win in the first round, and coalition-building for a possible second round is unlikely to influence their positioning. In 2007, for example, there were second ballots in five cantons only. The 2011 elections, with thirteen cantons going for a second ballot for the Council of States, was rather an exception due to an increasing number of candidates from the Swiss People's Party (SVP).

in the course of the elections in 2011 roughly 140 candidates running for the Council of States and clearly more than 3,400 candidates running for the National Council.

The Swiss VAA *smartvote* is – in accordance with the electoral systems applied – candidate based. This means that every candidate has its own political profile and the users not only see which party is closest to their political preferences but they also get a list of candidates with the candidates closest to their positions at the top. The candidates reveal their political profile by answering the same questions (issues) as the users will do at a later stage. They are more or less free to position themselves according to their personal preferences and strategic considerations. The parties, of course, try to influence their candidates, especially for the most important questions, but it is the candidates themselves who hand in their answers.

The way the candidates present themselves and the political profile they have is not unimportant. *smartvote* is very popular and quite influential. More than 80 per cent of the roughly 3,600 candidates running for both houses reveal their political profile on the website. About 15 per cent of the voters consult the web-site before voting, and it can be shown that *smartvote* has an influence on electoral turnout (Ladner and Pianzola 2010) and on the electoral decisions of the users (Ladner *et al.* 2010: 113 ff.; Pianzola 2013).

Using the research setting and the *smartvote* data described above, the following hypotheses can be tested:

- Majority voting fosters centrism: candidates running for the Council of States tend to move closer to the median voter and will have more moderate positions.

- Centrism is more pronounced in the case of extreme parties. The profiles of candidates from parties at the far ends of the political spectrum (the Social Democrats and Swiss People's Party) running for the Council of States are more likely to be different from the profiles of their fellow candidates from the same party running for the National Council.

Our research setting and the *smartvote* data, however, also bear some methodological problems we have to keep in mind. Some candidates (seventy-nine candidates in 2011) are running for both houses. The Council of States, however, is more prestigious so we expect that this will influence the way the candidates present themselves politically. But there are also candidates from smaller parties who do not have a chance to get elected in majority elections. They simply use their candidature for the Council of States to attract more attention and gain more votes for the National Council. The data about the candidates is quite reliable since it covers an overwhelming majority of the candidates. The data about the users, however, needs special attention. As it has been shown (*see* for example, Ladner 2012: 101 f.; Ladner and Fivaz 2012: 186 f.), it is far from representative. It is the better-educated supporters of left-wing parties which are overrepresented. Therefore, this data has to be weighted.

Empirical results

We start our analysis with the 2007 elections for which we have for the first time comprehensive data concerning the political positions of candidates and voters/ *smartvote* users on the left–right dimension. Figure 14.2 shows the median position of all voters (1)[5] and the position of all candidates (2) taken together. The median position of all candidates is slightly to the right of the voters, which is easy to understand since there are more right-wing parties than left-wing parties running for the elections. There is no difference to be found between candidates for the National Council and the Council of States.

As for the four most important parties, the Social Democrats (SP, 3), the Christian Democrats (CVP, 4), the Liberal Party (FDP.Die Liberalen, 5) and the Swiss People's Party (SVP, 6), the position of the candidates for the Council of States, elected under majority rules, should, according to our hypothesis, be closer to the position of the voters than the position of the candidates for the National Council. This is only the case for the Social Democrats. The differences between the two groups of candidates for all parties are rather small. Taken all together, our hypotheses do not seem to be confirmed; especially for the very right-wing Swiss People's Party, the candidates for the Council of States do not try to attract more moderate voters from the centre of the political spectrum.

For the 2007 elections the left–right dimension has been constructed by aggregating a specific number of issues which are usually used to differentiate between left and right positions. In the 2011 national elections, *smartvote* built up the political space empirically by means of a correspondence analysis.[6] We also add another possible element we have to take care of. One of the reasons the candidates for the Council of States did not all put forward more moderate issue positions might be that the electoral market is segmented. Since each canton has two seats to elect under majority rules, it may well be that there is an electoral competition for a seat on each side of the political spectrum. This would mean that the competition is no longer around the median voter of all voters but rather around the median voters of the right and the left half of the voters.[7]

Figure 14.3 therefore shows additionally the quartiles for the voter's position on the left–right dimensions (1). Nevertheless, with one exception the results contradict our hypotheses even more clearly. The results of the candidates for the two chambers of parliament now show more differences, with the candidates for the Council of States moving to the right of the median voter (2). This reflects the more right-wing positions of the candidates for the Council of States in all four

---

5. The position of the *smartvote* users which is biased towards the left has been weighted with the election results of the parties making the users vote like the electorate did.

6. For a description of the method used, *see*: http://www.smartvote.ch/downloads/methodology_smartmap_de_CH.pdf (24.6.2013).

7. This idea is supported by results from the Swiss Electoral Studies (Selects). If we look at the electorate in the elections of 2007 and 2011, there is no normal but rather a bipolar distribution of voters on the left-right dimension to be found. This is also the case when we look at the users of *smartvote*.

Figure 14.2: Left–right positions of the candidates for the Council of States and the candidates for the National Council (2007)

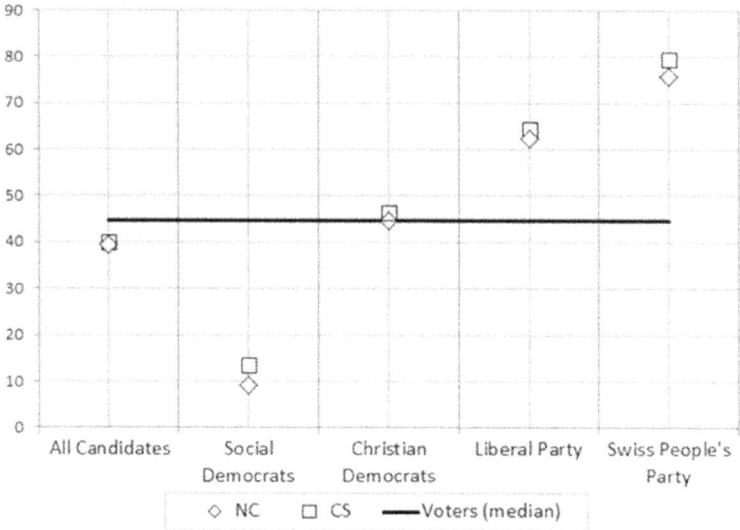

N: voters 12771; N NC/CS: All candidates 2635/54; Social Democrats 388/6; Christian Democrats 314/18; Liberal Party 402/14; Swiss People's Party 334/9

Figure 14.3: Left–right positions of the candidates for the Council of States and the candidates for the National Council (2011)

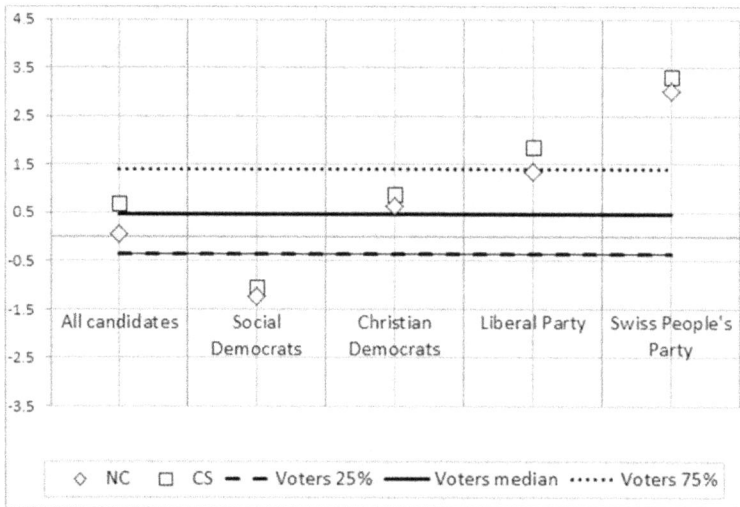

N voters 6276; N NC/CS: All candidates 2922/138; Social Democrats 406/23; Christian Democrats 338/21; Liberal Party 404/24; Swiss People's Party 290/20

See http://press.ecpr.eu/resources.asp for full colour figures.

big parties compared to their fellow candidates for the National Council. For the Social Democrats (3), again, this can be seen as a move towards the median voter in general or at least towards the median voter of the left fifty per cent of the voters if we apply the idea of a segmented competition. For the Christian Democrats (4) the move to the right of their candidates for the Council of States can now be seen as a move towards the median voter of the right 50 per cent of the voters, whereas for the Liberals (5) and for the Swiss People's Party (6) there is no sign of rational behaviour in terms of bringing forward more moderate positions to approach the median voter of all voters or the median voter of the right half of the voters.

Thus, our first results do not corroborate our hypotheses. There seems to be no clear incentives in majority elections to move towards the centre, not even for the more extreme parties, at least not for the one on the right side of the political spectrum: the Swiss People's Party.

There are different explanations of why our hypotheses are not supported by our empirical findings:

- First of all, and very simply: Including all cantons and candidates allows us to describe the situation for the whole country. There might however be an important number of uncontrolled variables which dilute the results. Electoral laws have different effects according to the number of seats the candidates are running for, the party systems and the strength of the parties differ from one canton to another, and there might also be different reasons why and how candidates run their electoral campaigns.
- And second: The left–right dimension might not be precise enough – as for example mentioned by Ezrow (2008: 481) – to analyse party competition and electoral strategies. Since issue voting seems to become more and more important it might be that electoral populism concentrates on issues which are not easily captured by the left–right dimension.

For the remaining part of the paper we shall try to take care of these possibilities in order to rescue our hypotheses or to strengthen our results.

Cantons with real PR elections for the National Council and real candidates for the Council of States only

As a matter of fact, the size difference between the cantons is quite important. This does not influence their representation in the Council of States where every canton is represented with two seats. In the National Council, however, the representation of cantons depends on their number of inhabitants. Only seven cantons (Zurich, Bern, Vaud, Aargau, St. Gallen, Genève and Luzern) have more than ten seats. Some of the cantons have only one or two seats. For the latter, the parties and candidates find themselves in a situation which is very similar to majority elections. They need support from voters who usually vote for other parties to get elected. Only in cantons with a higher number of seats are the hurdles low enough to theoretically allow for a more independent positioning and extremism.

If we concentrate on the bigger cantons only and look at the same time at the larger parties we almost automatically solve another problem we may encounter with our data. Some candidates for the Council of States are also running for the National Council. They very well know that they have little chance of winning enough votes to be successful in a majority vote but they use this campaign to gain additional visibility for the National Council. Among the twenty-eight candidates for the Council of States in our sample, there are perhaps two or three who rather concentrate on the National Council and who have to be excluded from our sample.[8]

Figure 14.4 shows the positions of the candidates for the two chambers on the left–right dimension in the cantons with more than ten seats and for candidates with a real chance to get elected in the Council of States only. The results are, apart from the Christian Democrats, even worse than those in Figures 14.2 and 14.3. It is not only the candidates of the Swiss People's Party and the Liberal Party who do not move in the direction the median voter theory predicts – this time it is also the candidates of the Social Democrats who obviously move in the wrong direction compared to their colleagues running for the National Council. Or, to formulate it differently, the candidates for the National Council do not seem to take advantage of the PR system to bring forward more pronounced political positions.

This negative result – unfortunately – is also confirmed when we go down to the level of individual cantons. Even in the case of the Social Democrats, which follow best the predictions of our hypotheses, there are exceptions where the candidate for the Council of States is further left than the median positions of their fellow candidates for the National Council.[9] Sometimes it works for the Christian Democrats and very rarely for the Liberals,[10] but it hardly ever works for the Swiss People's Party.

Can we rescue our hypotheses by taking up Ezrow's (2008) remark that the left–right dimension might not be able to capture party competition adequately?

Differences on eight policy dimensions

Following the argument that the left–right dimension is not precise enough to capture the differences between the parties, we shall extend our analysis to a larger number of dimensions. *smartvote* offers eight policy dimensions (built on the grounds of a selected number of questions from the *smartvote* questionnaire) which are also used to present the political profile of the parties, the candidates and the voters.[11]

---

8. This applies to three representatives of the Christian Democrats (Schmid AG, Hany ZH and Barthassat GE), for which one might think that they did not expect to get elected in the Council of States.

9. This is, for example, the case of Paul Rechsteiner (SG) who is positioned further left than his colleagues running for the National Council.

10. Mr Gutzweiler (ZH) is positioned further right than his colleagues for the National Council but Ms Egerszegi (AG) is positioned closer to the centre than her colleagues running for the National Council.

11. For the construction of these dimensions, *see*: http://www.smartvote.ch/downloads/methodology_smartspider_de_CH.pdf.

Figure 14.4: Left–right positions of the candidates for the Council of States and the candidates for the National Council (2011) – only cantons with real PR elections and candidates with a real chance to win the elections for the Council of States

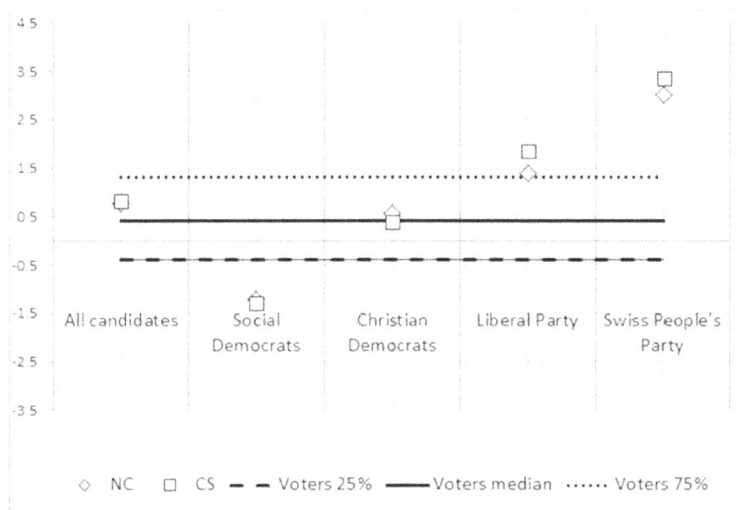

N voters 4509; N NC/CS: All candidates 899/28; Social Democrats 270/7; Christian Democrats 200/5; Liberal Party 263/8; Swiss People's Party 166/5.

See http://press.ecpr.eu/resources.asp for full colour figures.

Using the data from 2011 the results are unambiguous but unfortunately again not in the direction of our hypotheses (*see* Figure 14.5). There is not much difference between the candidates running for the National Council, who are elected in a PR system, and the candidates running for the Council of States, who are elected in a majority system. Not even the candidates from more extreme parties (Swiss People's Party and Social Democrats) seem to have stronger incentives to move towards the voters when they compete in majority system elections. The candidates for the Council of States are on the majority of the dimensions plotted even further away from the median position of the voters than their fellow party candidates for the National Council.

Even if we look at policy dimensions which are of crucial importance in electoral campaigns (in Switzerland), such as immigration, and offer themselves particularly well for populist vote-seeking and vote gains, such as law and order, the welfare state and independence in regard to the European Union and international integration, there are no clear signs that candidates for the Council of States move away from their party line towards positions where the bulk of voters is located.

Figure 14.5: Parties: Candidates in PR, and majority voting and median voter (2011)

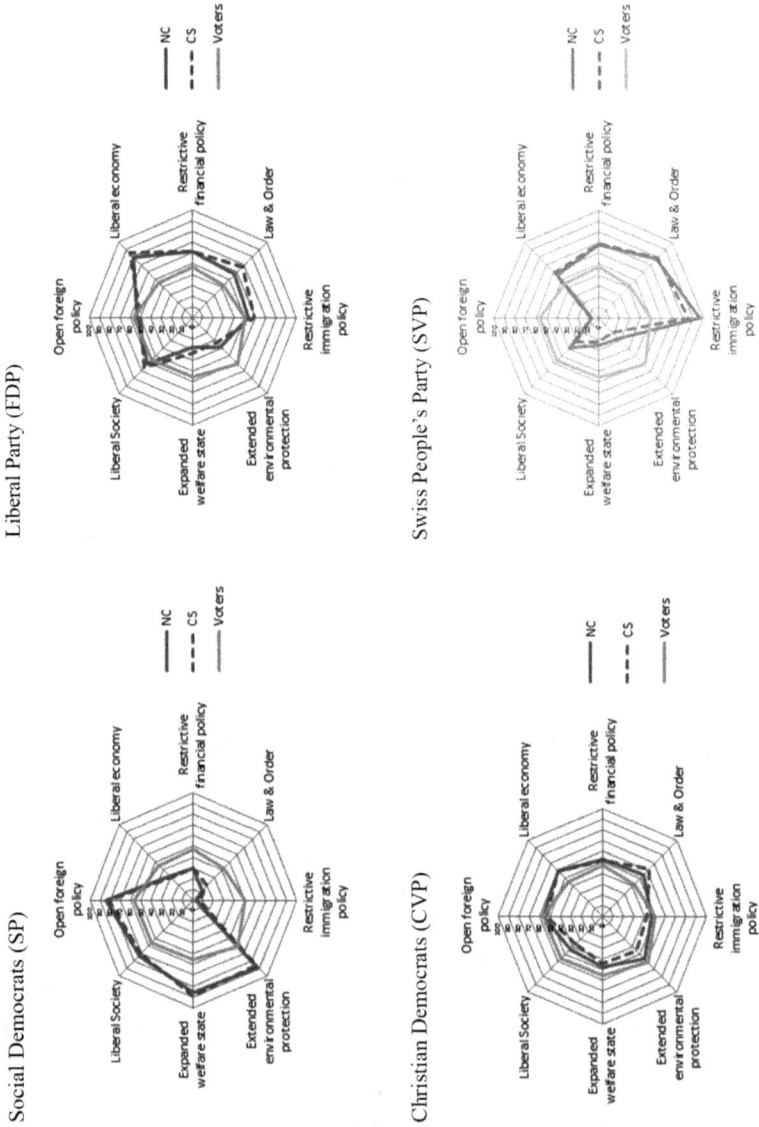

Social Democrats (SP)

Liberal Party (FDP)

Christian Democrats (CVP)

Swiss People's Party (SVP)

See http://press.ecpr.eu/resources.asp for full colour figures.

Conclusion and discussion

Our findings support the results of Ezrow (2008) rather than the results of Dow (2010). Our analyses, which were made possible through data collected by the Swiss VAA *smartvote*, convincingly show that at least in the Swiss case and for the elections of the two houses of the National Parliament there are no reasons to believe that PR increases policy extremism or that majority voting leads to more moderate issue positions. Neither is it the case that the candidates of more extremist parties have stronger incentives to adapt their positions in the direction of the median voter if they have to attract a higher percentage of the electorate to get elected. In the case of the Swiss People's Party (SVP), the contrary even seems to be the case. The drift to the right of their candidates does not astonish observers of Swiss politics, since in the 2011 elections for the Council of States, the Swiss People's Party tried in vain to increase its low share of the seats by presenting their most prestigious exponents coming from the very right wing of the party. This again clearly shows that the simple claim that majority elections lead to more moderate political positions cannot be maintained. There are also other motives influencing the positioning of parties and candidates.

The candidates do not seem to be free or willing to change their policy positions if they have to reach a bigger part of the electorate. Is it loyalty with their party which keeps them on track? Of course, being asked they will pretend to have a political program they stick to and they will not change their positions for electoral reasons. This might even be partly true. However, it doesn't make much sense to run for elections with no chance of getting elected. Perhaps there are valence factors of the candidates (prestige, charisma) which play a more important role. Some candidates get elected regardless of their political positions. Or is it the fact of being an incumbent which allows or forces them to stick to their program?

There are two other possible explanations, following different tracks and asking for more research; one is rather technical, the other concerns the voters. It would be interesting to investigate to what extent the openness of ballot lists in the Swiss PR system combines PR with majority-system effects. Candidates running for the National Council compete not only against other parties but also against members of their own party since not all candidates of the list get elected but only those with the highest number of votes. This means that candidates for the National Council can also have incentives to bring forward more moderate positions, especially if they look for votes from other parties which are closer to the centre. And as far as the voters are concerned, the question is to what extent they vote for candidates which have exactly the same issue positions as they have. If they vote strategically themselves (Lachat and Selb 2010), they might also opt for more extreme candidates in the elections for the Council of States.

As for the particularities of the VAA data we used to address this question, we are quite confident on the side of the candidates. Since they know that their answers matter to maximise votes they position themselves strategically rather than reproducing the official party line only, which is exactly what we want to look at. The quality of the data on the side of the users is more questionable.

Since it is still a specific part of the voters using VAAs, we had to weight the data. Although the weighted positions of the candidates from the different parties seem quite plausible, we are not dealing with a representative sample. Here there is more research to be done. Once we have the possibility to control for the selection bias for those using VAAs, the millions of users will provide new and unexpected insights into electoral behaviour.

Chapter Fifteen

Keeping Promises: Voting Advice Applications and Political Representation

Jan Fivaz, Tom Louwerse and Daniel Schwarz

Introduction

This chapter deals with a simple question: To what extent does the post-electoral legislative behaviour of Members of Parliament (MPs) correspond to their pre-electoral campaign pledges?

Among voters it is a popular belief that politicians take liberties with the truth, that they often tell lies to get elected and that they are not especially eager to keep their pre-electoral promises once elected. Such a behavioural pattern would raise severe challenges for a well-functioning democracy. It would foster an increasing alienation and abstention of citizens from parties and politics in general. But first and foremost it would undermine a cornerstone of modern representative democracies: political trust and effective control mechanisms of voters over politicians (Andeweg and Thomassen 2005).

According to the concept of promissory representation (Mansbridge 2003), voters are mainly forward-looking and use elections to steer future policy outcomes. This process of prospective voting (Powell 2000) includes the expectation that MPs act according to their pre-electoral promises. If voters cannot rely on this linkage to translate their preferences into policies, the foundation of representative democracy is undermined.

Thus, it is not surprising that the reliability of pre-electoral promises has been central to numerous studies (for a brief overview, *see* the following section). With this chapter we intend to add an additional perspective by using data from Voting Advice Applications (VAAs). Our analysis compares pre-electoral policy positions captured by VAAs with post-electoral parliamentary voting. Our starting point forms the study by Schwarz *et al.* (2010), which we have subsequently extended and refined. Whereas Schwarz *et al.* solely focussed on pledge fulfilment in Switzerland we add the Netherlands as a second country. Both countries have in common some general characteristics like multiparty systems/governments and the extensive use of VAAs by parties and voters. But the two cases also differ in important respects, most notably regarding the electoral system, executive–legislative relations, and the degree of party discipline.

The party mandate

Political scientists often assert that congruence between the opinions and attitudes of voters and what actually happens in parliament and in government is an important measure of the quality of democratic representation (Schattschneider 1942; Powell 2000). According to the (party) mandate model, the presentation of pre-electoral programmes from which voters can choose presents an important condition for the proper functioning of a promissory system of representation (Mansbridge 2003; Thomassen 1994). The degree to which parties and individual MPs fulfil their election mandates, then, is an important criterion for judging the quality of the system of representation.

The existing work on the (party) mandate can be divided into three approaches: the pledge approach, the saliency approach and the spatial approach (Royed 1996; Louwerse 2011b). Our approach is most similar to the pledge approach, which compares specific pre-electoral pledges in party manifestos or public speeches with governmental policy actions after the election (for an overview, *see* Petry and Collette 2009). Contrary to the oft-heard complaint that 'parties do not do what they promise', most of the studies in the field find a decent level of pledge fulfilment. The level of pledge fulfilment by government parties ranges from about 80 per cent for single-party governments in Britain (Rallings 1987; Rose 1980; Royed 1996), to about 50 per cent in the Irish coalition governments, with other coalition, minority cabinet or presidential systems somewhere in between (Mansergh and Thomson 2007).

The limitation of the pledge approach is that it looks at the mandate in terms of pledge that are actually made, making it vulnerable to selective pledge-making by parties and changes in the political agenda (Louwerse 2011b). By taking parties' positions in VAAs as an indicator of their pre-electoral policy stance, we are able to mitigate these problems. After all, VAAs force parties to indicate their policy position on all of the most relevant policy issues in an election. Our analysis therefore does not depend on the selection of issues parties choose to include in their manifestos.

Most studies of party mandate fulfilment have traditionally focused on the party mandate for government: how pre-electoral commitments relate to government policy. The studies ignore the parliamentary or representative mandate (Louwerse 2011b). This effectively limits these studies to the mandate of government parties. We should not expect that opposition parties are able to translate their election pledge into government policies. On the contrary, if there is real choice between competing 'mandates' at election time, opposition parties should be unable to fulfil their pledges after the elections (Mansergh and Thomson 2007). This leaves the question, however, how opposition parties act in parliament: to what degree does their (voting) behaviour relate to their pre-electoral commitments? This question is especially relevant to the functioning of representative democracy in more consensual political systems, in which the distinction between electoral winners and losers is vaguer.

Moreover, existing studies have not looked extensively at how different mechanisms of law-making in legislative–executive relations impact on mandate fulfilment: how does what happens in parliament affect pledge fulfilment? Especially in political systems where individual politicians have a relatively strong position *vis-à-vis* their party and a personal electoral mandate, individual-level factors (incumbency, disagreement with party, district magnitude) as well as characteristics of the parliamentary vote (published or secret voting) have been shown to be relevant in explaining pledge fulfilment (Schwarz *et al.* 2010). Therefore, we compare candidates' or parties' VAA positions with their voting behaviour in parliament.

Comparing the Netherlands and Switzerland

MPs, parties and VAAs do not act in a political vacuum but within a framework of formal and informal rules defined by political institutions and the prevailing political culture. Before we present our research design we name the key characteristics of the two countries included in our study.

The Netherlands

The Netherlands is characterised as a typical example of a consensus democracy (Lijphart 2012). We are studying voting behaviour in the directly elected first chamber ('Tweede Kamer') of its bicameral legislature, which is generally regarded as the most important chamber. The electoral system for the first chamber uses the proportional d'Hondt largest average method in (effectively) a single national district of 150 members with a very low 'natural' electoral threshold (0.67 per cent). The Gallagher Index for the 2006 national election was just .9, which is very low in comparative terms (ParlGov 2012).

It should come as no surprise that the highly proportional electoral system is accompanied by a relatively high number of political parties. Since the implementation of proportional representation in 1917, no party has achieved a majority in parliament. The effective number of parties in terms of seats was 5.5 in the 2006 election, which is a typical value for the last two decades (ParlGov, 2012). The fragmentation of parliament has made coalition government the norm. In recent years it has been necessary to include at least three parties to secure a parliamentary majority. In every election since 2002 there has been a (partial) change in the government composition. In 2006 the outgoing government of CDA, VVD and D66 was replaced by a coalition of CDA, PvdA and Christian Union.

Probably as a result of the large number of parties as well as the system of coalition government, parliamentary parties act in a very unitary way (Andeweg and Thomassen 2011). Most votes are by show of hands, recorded by party rather than by individual. Moreover, voting behaviour is substantially affected by voting along government–opposition lines (Otjes 2011).

The Netherlands was the first country to introduce VAAs, with a paper version appearing in 1989 and an online version in 1998. Since then, usage numbers have increased to about one-third of the electorate in 2010 (Louwerse and Rosema 2013). *StemWijzer* was the first VAA to be developed and it is still the most popular tool. *Kieskompas* was launched in 2006 in a bid to provide more insight into the 'political landscape.' Contrary to their Swiss counterpart, both Dutch VAAs provide a national advice (not regional) for parties (not candidates).

Switzerland

The Swiss legislature consists of two symmetric, but non-congruent chambers (Lijphart 2012: 199): the National Council ('Nationalrat') and the Council of States ('Ständerat'). Only the National Council keeps roll-call records, therefore we solely focus on this chamber in our analysis. The National Council consists of 200 members and is elected by a proportional system in 26 electoral districts (the Swiss cantons). Every canton is guaranteed one seat. Additional seats are assigned in proportion to population figures. Thus, the number of seats per district ranges from 1 to 34, and subsequently the electoral threshold also differs strongly across electoral districts. The Gallagher Index for the 2011 national election was 3.6, which is four times higher compared to the Netherlands but still low compared to other countries (ParlGov 2012).

The electoral system is not only fragmented into numerous electoral districts, it also combines party- and candidate-centred features. One way of voting in Switzerland is to cast a party list. Alternatively, voters can compose their own ballot. They receive as many votes as there are seats in the electoral district and by vote splitting they can vote for candidates from different parties. Additionally, voters can support their favourite candidates by giving them two votes instead of one (so-called cumulative voting).

Similar to the Netherlands, the proportional electoral system leads to a high number of parties. The effective number of parties in terms of seats in the 2011 elections was 5.6 (ParlGov 2012).

Due to the political fragmentation and decentralised structure of the country, candidates are selected by cantonal party sections, which enjoy considerable autonomy from the national level. It is thus not unusual if policy positions between candidates of the same party differ, and national party leaders lack the power to prevent it.

The Swiss government is formed by a multi-party coalition. From 1959 to 2007 the four largest parties (CVP, FDP, SP and SVP) formed the government according to the so-called 'magic formula'. Since 2007 a fifth party is included. This government coalition combines more than 80 per cent of all MPs. In contrast to coalitions in other countries, there is no binding coalition agreement. The government is elected by parliament for a fixed four-year term (no possibility for a non-confidence vote or call for early elections). The effect is twofold: first, government parties can double-cross as government and opposition depending on the specific issue at stake. The shared responsibility for governmental actions leads to no responsibility in specific issues. Second, the need for government parties to enforce a strong discipline in parliament is lowered. Compared to 'genuine' parliamentary systems, party discipline is somewhat weaker.

Switzerland was among the first countries where VAAs were operative. The Swiss VAA *smartvote* reflects the complexity and the particularities of the Swiss electoral system in its design. In contrast to most VAAs in other countries, not the parties but the candidates directly are invited to answer the *smartvote* questionnaire. Subsequently, *smartvote* offers a voting advice for parties (lists) as well as for individual candidates. Voters appreciate the service: in 2011 about 15 per cent of the voters used *smartvote*.

Data and research design

The paper's main focus is to explain incongruence between the pledges made during election campaigns and the later voting behaviour in parliament. The large institutional differences between our two cases entail that incongruence in the case of Switzerland is measured at the level of individual MPs and in the Dutch case at party level. This is why we conduct two separate case studies instead of one combined model. The research designs share the research question, the operationalisation of the dependent variable, as well as a common core of explanatory variables.

Both case studies use VAA data. In Switzerland, this is the 2003 and 2007 versions of *smartvote* (www.smartvote.ch), while for the Netherlands the data base is formed by the two VAAs *Stemwijzer* (www.stemwijzer.nl) and *Kieskompas* (www.kieskompas.nl) in 2006. The chapter compares the answers given in the VAA surveys with (virtually) identical parliamentary votes: thirty-four in Switzerland and forty-nine for the Netherlands (*see* full list in Appendix 15.1). For the Dutch case, there were multiple cases in which we found multiple matching votes to a single VAA statement. In these cases, we took the modal voting behaviour into account and we calculated average values for the explanatory variables on the level of the parliamentary vote.

Contrary to previous studies we rely on VAA questionnaires rather than party manifesto data to identify pre-electoral pledges. This implies two restrictions: first, there is a distinction between explicit campaign pledges provided by party manifestos and the more general positions on a number of policy issues revealed by VAAs. Unlike manifestos, VAA questions are not drafted by parties but contain a whole range of issues which parties avoid on different grounds (because the topic is too hot or because they don't really care). However, parties and candidates answering VAA surveys reveal their general political values and positions – which should be approximately the same after the election, no matter if they attached a pledge to it or not. Thus, we think that VAA data is very suitable to serve the needs of our study.

A second restriction is the possibility that candidates and parties answer a VAA questionnaire strategically in order to present themselves in the most favourable manner. This could be especially true for countries with an extensive use of VAAs by voters, which subsequently could increase the instrumental use of VAAs for successful electoral campaigns. For both the Netherlands and Switzerland there is evidence indicating strategic behaviour of this kind. In the Netherlands, parties have openly admitted this practice and it has subsequently been broadly discussed in the media (Ladner and Fivaz 2012). In Switzerland, as well, it is no secret that some parties provide their candidates with guidelines for answering the VAA questionnaire (Ladner *et al.* 2010).

However, receiving guidelines and following them are two different stories. Based on a comprehensive survey among Swiss candidates, Ladner *et al.* (2008: 108–109) could show that only 10 per cent of the candidates followed the instructions to a considerable extent, and a further 45 per cent did so at least partially regarding a few specific questions. From a representational point of view, strategic answers in a VAA questionnaire are only problematic if the post-electoral behaviour deviates from the pre-electoral policy positions, and this is exactly what we will analyse.

The dependent variable is a binary congruence measure for every matching pair of VAA item and parliamentary vote: it is 1 if the voting behaviour matches the VAA answer (positional congruence), otherwise it is 0 (positional incongruence). Since answer options in the VAA surveys and in parliamentary votes are not the same, we match (full) agreement in a VAA to a yes-vote and (full) disagreement to a no-vote. Neutral VAA positions as well as abstention or absenteeism in legislative votes are treated as missing values (for details, *see* Appendix 15.1).

Hypotheses and explanatory variables

Common explanatory variables

Strength of political preference: MPs or parties that reveal strong preferences in the VAA survey are less likely to change their mind during parliamentary debates. Strong preference means that a straight yes/no answer ('strongly agree/ disagree') was given to an item, while the weak 'agree/disagree' option is taken as an indicator of weak preference structure.[1]

Positional centrality (or policy extremism) of a party: Parties at both ends on the common left–right scale are more extreme in their standpoints (which is basically why they are located there), more ideology-driven and less willing to compromise with others. In contrast, parties more to the centre of the political system usually hold less stubborn views and thus are welcome partners in centre left or centre-right coalitions (Netherlands), or in legislative alliances (Switzerland). We hypothesise that the more extreme (the less central) the party position is, the higher its positional congruence. For the Dutch case, we use the distance of individual parties' positions from the centre on the left–right scale, as measured by the Chapel Hill Expert Survey (2010). In the Swiss case, we use the average party success rates in parliamentary votes to measure the positional centrality of a party.

---

1. As the Dutch *Stemwijzer* uses a three-point answer scale, we cannot measure the strength of the preferences from that VAA.

Table 15.1: Number of MPs and MP votes by party (Swiss case)

	Number of MPs	Number of MP votes	Average number of votes per MP
CVP	38	736	19.4
FDP	44	704	16.0
GPS	27	474	17.6
SP	62	1,301	21.0
SVP	61	1,243	20.3
Other parties	22	342	15.5
Total	254	4,800	18.9

Table 15.2: Number of VAA statements and number of votes by party (Dutch case)

	Number of VAA statements	Number of votes
CDA	45	116
ChristenUnie	44	112
D66	42	106
GroenLinks	48	123
PvdA	45	115
PvdD*	19	50
PVV	48	128
SGP	48	126
SP	45	123
VVD	49	129
Total	-	1,128

Note: This excludes statements for which parties provided 'neutral' or 'neither' answers.

* = PvdD not included in *Kieskompas*.

Party core issues/issue saliency: The salience approach postulates that party manifestos mainly highlight issues that are relevant and important to the party in question (Budge and Hofferbert 1990; Klingemann *et al.* 1994), whereas VAA questionnaires are composed of the full range of political areas. We assume that election pledges concerning issues, which are particularly important to an MP or a party, are more often respected than presumably irrelevant issues. We are using expert survey estimates of party issue saliency from the Chapel Hill Expert Survey 2010.[2] The survey uses a scale ranging from 0 to 10. For the Dutch case, the

---

2.   We are using the 2010 edition, because this includes more relevant policy dimensions.

relevant saliency scales have been matched to the issue categories used in the two VAAs. We were able to find acceptable matches for all but three of the VAA categories (education, democratic reform, and culture and media). In the Swiss case we first matched the issue areas from the Chapel Hill Survey directly to the thirty-four selected items (*see* Appendix). In a second step, issues were defined salient for a party if the average expert score in the Chapel Hill Survey reached six or above on the ten-point scale.[3]

Time span between VAA survey and legislative vote: Political contexts can and do change over time. Pre-election positions are sometimes overtaken by events, which should lead responsible MPs to change their mind, be it for the benefit of their voters or for the common good.

Swiss-specific variables

As an alternative to the positional-centrality/policy-extremism variable, we employ *party dummies* in order to estimate the effect of individual parties on the dependent variable (reference category = CVP). The inclusion of party dummies requires dropping party random-effects levels.

Relevance of the vote: Not every vote is equally significant within the legislative process. Some votes may have a direct law-making effect (e.g. votes on amendments to government bills) while other votes merely charge the administration to consider some measures (parliamentary motions). Out of the thirty-four selected items, twenty-six are government bills or parliamentary initiatives with high law-making relevance, and eight are parliamentary motions of low relevance.[4]

Positional incongruence with party group majority: Positional congruence by an MP is more likely if the party group takes the same stance on the issue. If an MP finds out after the election that the majority of their fellow party members take another position there should be an increased propensity that they will eventually conform to the majority position (peer pressure). This variable is binary, analogically defined to the dependent variable.[5]

District magnitude: Voting theory suggests that the electoral connection is closer in small districts because a lower number of MPs makes it easier to keep track of their legislative behaviour (Bowler and Farrel 1993; Carey and Shugart 1995; Cox 1997). We therefore expect that pre-election positions are more likely to be

---

3.   We used this threshold approach to circumvent implausibility in the expert judgments

4.   As a large majority of the votes in the Dutch case concern motions, we only include this variable for the Swiss case.

5.   If there was no majority in the party group (e.g. if a tie occurred), any VAA answer was rated in line with the party group majority. MPs not a member of a group are treated as missing values.

disregarded in larger districts. Because district magnitude is not expected to show a linear effect, we use two dummy variables which capture the smallest districts with up to four seats and the largest ones with fifteen or more seats (reference category = medium-sized districts).

Incumbency: The effect of incumbency on pledge fulfilment is theoretically ambiguous: incumbents know how the land lies. Unlike freshmen, they are more consolidated in their political positions. But incumbents also have gained self-confidence from the fact that they have been constantly re-elected, which could weaken the chain of delegation and broaden political leeway (Shugart *et al.* 2005; Tavits 2009).

Moreover, we control for the year of the vote, language (French- and Italian-speaking minorities), as well as MPs' age and sex.

Dutch-specific variables

Government participation: In parliamentary systems like the Netherlands it is mainly up to the government coalition to fulfil their pledges. They are under tougher observation by the media than the opposition parties whose hands are tied and often struggle to get their core issues on the legislative agenda. However, the responsibility of government entails higher political flexibility too: coalition negotiations as well as a changing external environment after the government has been formed almost inevitably lead to the abandoning of election pledges (Mansergh and Thomson 2007: 320). It thus seems easier for the opposition than for the government to stick adamantly to their pre-election positions in their parliamentary (voting) behaviour.[6]

We control for party size (it might be easier for smaller, more cohesive parties to stick to their pre-electoral commitments), VAA source (*Kieskompas* or *StemWijzer*) and match certainty. The latter captures the quality of the match between the VAA statement and the parliamentary vote.[7]

Research method

Given the clustered structure of the data, we will run a number of mixed-effects (multilevel) regression models to explain positional (in)congruence in Switzerland

---

6. Because legislative decision-making in Switzerland is not driven by the distinction between government and opposition parties (*see* e.g. Schwarz *et al.* 2011), we do not include this variable in the Swiss case.

7. This is captured on a scale from 0 = not a good match at all, to 100 = (near-) perfect match. In practice, we only matched statements and proposals with a value of 50 (adequate match, but a somewhat different issue), 60 (adequate match), 70 (appropriate match, but issue is slightly different or a sub-issue), 80 (good match, although wording might be stronger/weaker), 90 (very good match) or 100 (near- perfect match). This is not used in the Swiss case because the selection process only took into account issues representing good or very good matches.

and the Netherlands. While all models come with the same binary structure of the dependent variable, the statistical details of the models will vary according to the country under consideration (different definition of model levels and composition of covariates).[8]

In the Swiss case the hierarchical data structure features four levels: individual MP, electoral district (canton), national party, and the single vote/issue. These levels are not perfectly nested; the model specification thus has to deal with cross-classification (e.g. national parties appear in different cantons and every MP gives their opinion on a number of different votes). The cross-classification structure is simplified by the fact that 'empty model' estimations containing only random effects indicated that the contribution to the explained variance by the level of cantons is extremely small (results not reported here). We therefore dropped cross-classifications involving parties and cantons, but leave those between votes/issues and MPs/parties.

In the Dutch case all data was recorded on the party level, therefore the individual and district level do not come into play. We took into account the party level as well as the issue category level.

Explaining positional (in)congruence

Empirical analysis of the Dutch case

We expected government participation to be of paramount importance in the voting behaviour of Dutch parliamentary parties. The difference between government and opposition parties is indeed marked: on average, opposition parties voted in a congruent way in about 82 per cent of cases, while government parties did so in only 51 per cent of the cases (*see* Table 15.3). This effect is in line with our expectations and indeed with earlier analyses of Dutch parliamentary behaviour (Louwerse 2011a, 2012).

The main driver of the government parties' behaviour seems to be the fact that they reject opposition parties' proposals even if they agree with the general message. For example, government party CDA positioned itself in favour of extending nuclear energy before the elections. In parliament, however, it rejected motions from the right-wing opposition, which asked for more nuclear power. At the same time, it also rejected motions from the left-wing opposition demanding a moratorium on new nuclear power plants. Instead, it seemed to prefer to leave the matter entirely up to the government.

A multivariate analysis of the Dutch data confirms the importance of government participation. We ran five different models, the first of which is an 'empty model' including only random effects and an intercept. In model 2, which includes all

---

8.   We used the 'glmer' function for generalised linear mixed-effects regression in R's 'lme4' package.

Table 15.3: Government participation and congruent behaviour

	Congruent behaviour	N
Government parties	51.0%	134
Opposition parties	81.6%	299
All parties	72.2%	433

Note: Difference of means test: $t(207.26) = 6.1703$, $p < .01$.

explanatory variables, we find a strong effect for the variable government party. The odds ratio is 0.14, signalling that the odds of government parties voting in line with their VAA position is 6 to 7 times lower than the odds of opposition parties. This strong effect remains also if we control for party size and policy extremism. These factors do not have an effect on congruence once we control for government participation.

Issue saliency is the second explanation for which we find support. Parties vote more in line with their pre-electoral position on issues that they find more important. The odds ratio is 1.32, which means that for an increase of one point on the saliency scale (ranging from 0 to 10), the odds of voting congruently increase moderately. This finding stands in contrast to Thomson's findings (2001), who observed that issue saliency, as measured by the Comparative Manifestos Project, did not affect the degree to which manifesto pledges were implemented by the government. Note, however, that we not only use a different operationalisation of issue saliency (expert survey *vs.* document analysis), but also that our measurement of pledge fulfilment is different: whereas Thomson studied pledge fulfilment by governments, we are looking at congruent parliamentary voting behaviour.

Because issue saliency is not observed for all cases, we also estimated models without saliency (model 3), and without saliency but with the same cases as in model 2 (model 4). This does not affect our findings in substantively important ways, although the significance of some effects changes somewhat between specifications. Model 5 includes the effect of preference strength, which can only be observed for the *Kieskompas* statements. Preference strength does not seem to have an effect on the probability of congruent voting behaviour, nor does its inclusion change any of the other coefficients significantly.

In all models, the certainty of the match between VAA statement and parliamentary proposal, as estimated by the coder, did seem to have a small effect on congruence levels. If the match was more exact, the probability of congruent voting behaviour was higher. On the one hand this implies that we must be careful in matching votes with VAA proposals, because, depending on the exact wording of a proposal, parties might take different positions. On the other hand, it also tells us something about changes in the political agenda: parties' voting behaviour is

Table 15.4: Logit predictions for positional congruence between pre- and post-election sphere. Two-level cross-classification models (parties, issue categories).

	Model 1	Model 2	Model 3	Model 4	Model 5
(Intercept)	1.06***	-1.75	0.60	-0.29	-3.95†
	(0.28)	(1.26)	(0.91)	(1.10)	(2.28)
Government party		-1.90***	-1.88***	-2.20***	-2.32**
		(0.51)	(0.44)	(0.54)	(0.89)
Party size		0.00	0.02	0.02	0.00
		(0.01)	(0.01)	(0.01)	(0.02)
Policy extremism		-0.01	-0.08	-0.05	-0.02
		(0.18)	(0.15)	(0.18)	(0.32)
Saliency		0.24*			0.36†
		(0.10)			(0.21)
VAA = *StemWijzer*		-0.37	-0.46†	-0.42	
		(0.28)	(0.24)	(0.27)	
Time-span to vote		-0.01	-0.01	-0.01	0.00
		(0.01)	(0.01)	(0.01)	(0.02)
Match certainty		0.03*	0.02†	0.03*	0.05*
		(0.01)	(0.01)	(0.01)	(0.02)
Preference strength					0.61
					(0.49)
Log Likelihood	-241.52	-187.54	-230.57	-190.32	-84.65
Num. obs.	433	373	433	373	196
Num. groups: Category	12	9	12	9	9
Num. groups: Party	10	10	10	10	9
Variance: Category (Int.)	0.07	0.28	0.15	0.23	0.61
Variance: Party (Intercept)	0.58	0.00	0.00	0.04	0.00

***$p < 0.001$, **$p < 0.01$, *$p < 0.05$, †$p < 0.1$ (standard errors in brackets)

Table 15.5: Congruence of MP positions (averages by party)

	Congruent behaviour	N
CVP	75.8%	736
FDP	80.3%	704
GPS	93.7%	474
SP	93.4%	1,301
SVP	86.6%	1,243
Other (small parties)	82.9%	342
All MPs	86.3%	4,800

likely to become less predictable if the exact proposals that are voted on are very different from the proposals that were central during the election campaign.

All in all, the Dutch case provides strong evidence for both the influence of policy and office on pledge fulfilment. Government parties are less likely to vote in a congruent way, while parties are more likely to vote congruently on issues that they find important.

Empirical analysis of the Swiss case

Table 15.5 lists the average positional congruence of Swiss MPs by party. Overall, congruent behaviour is 86.3 per cent, which means that legislative voting is in agreement with VAA statements in almost 9 out of 10 cases. However, the figures vary a lot across parties. As a general pattern, the larger the political distance from the political centre of the party system, the higher the congruence rates. The highest congruence with over 93 per cent can be found among members of the Greens and the Social-Democrats, while members of the Christian-Democrats and Liberals come up with relatively low congruence of 80 per cent or less.

Ideological and organisational aspects of parties seemingly account for some variation in positional congruence. For an in-depth study of the possible driving factors we ran four statistical models to predict positional congruence between VAA positions and voting behaviour in parliament (Table 15.6). The first one is an 'empty' model with only random effects included. In the second model additionally a number of socio-demographic control variables are included. Models 3 and 4 carry all fixed effects; they only differ in the way they capture the party effects (random level *vs.* dummy fixed effects).

The estimations in the 'full' models 3 and 4 largely confirm the results in Schwarz *et al.* (2010): by far the most important factor to explain positional incongruence between VAA answers and parliamentary voting is incongruence between an MP's VAA answer and the later majority position in their legislative party group. The logit coefficient close to -4 indicates that the odds of a positional change are about 500 times higher if the VAA position does not match the majority position in the party group.

Other highly significant factors in our models include party centrality (MPs from pivotal parties in the political centre are more likely to change their mind) and the newly introduced preference strength measure (stronger preferences produce higher positional congruence). Weakly significant are small electoral districts (MPs from small cantons with no more than four parliamentary seats show higher positional congruence).

To sum up, positional (in)congruence in the Swiss case is attributable to a very small number of factors: the situation in the own-party group after the election, the strength of own preferences in the VAA survey, ideological/structural aspects of the own party, and the smallness of the own electoral district.

Table 15.6: Logit predictions for positional congruence between pre- and post-election sphere. Three-level cross-classification models (MPs, parties, issues).

	Model 1	Model 2	Model 3	Model 4
(Intercept)	1.86***	1.76***	2.98***	2.11***
	(0.22)	(0.35)	(0.57)	(0.58)
Minority language (F/I)		-0.05	0.00	-0.03
		(0.10)	(0.14)	(0.15)
Age		0.00	-0.00	0.00
		(0.01)	(0.01)	(0.01)
Sex: male		-0.01	-0.05	0.03
		(0.11)	(0.15)	(0.16)
Year of vote			0.04	0.04
			(0.06)	(0.06)
Time span to vote			-0.01	-0.01
			(0.01)	(0.01)
Incumbent			0.20	0.20
			(0.14)	(0.15)
Relevance of vote			0.02	0.02
			(0.24)	(0.24)
District ≤ 4			0.51†	0.51†
			(0.26)	(0.26)
District ≥ 15			-0.10	-0.13
			(0.14)	(0.14)
Preference strength			1.26***	1.26***
			(0.13)	(0.13)
Disagreement with party group			-3.98***	-3.96***
			(0.13)	(0.13)
Core issue			0.10	0.12
			(0.10)	(0.11)
Party centrality			-0.18**	
			(0.06)	
Party FDP				0.04
				(0.21)
Party GPS				0.71*
				(0.31)
Party SP				0.66**
				(0.23)

	Model 1	Model 2	Model 3	Model 4
Party SVP				0.15
				(0.20)
Party small				-0.07
				(0.28)
Log Likelihood	-1782	-1782	-966	-962
Num. obs.	4800	4800	4744	4744
Num. groups: MP	254	254	250	250
Num. groups: Party	14	14	12	
Num. groups: Issue	34	34	34	34
Variance: MP (Intercept)	0.00	0.00	0.07	0.06
Variance: Party (Intercept)	0.37	0.37	0.00	
Variance: Issue (Intercept)	0.34	0.34	0.19	0.17

Notes: ***p < 0.001, **p < 0.01, *p < 0.05, †p < 0.1 (Standard errors in brackets)

Conclusions

While the Swiss and Dutch political systems are both characterised as consensual (Lijphart 2012), the way in which the party mandate works differs to a great extent. In the Swiss candidate-centred electoral system the congruence between pre-electoral policy positions of candidates and their parliamentary voting behaviour is best explained by looking at disagreement with the party group, preference strength, government participation and party centrality. Those who disagree with the party before the election are much more likely to change their position, as are those with weaker preferences. At the party level, smaller effects can be found: members of centre parties and government parties are more likely to display congruence between their pre-electoral and post-electoral positions. These effects are, however, considerably smaller than explanations that relate to an individual candidate's position on a specific statement.

In the Dutch case, we could not observe the individual-level factors that affect congruence in behaviour in the Swiss case. Parties rather than candidates are positioned on VAA statements, and parliamentary voting usually is (de facto) performed and recorded by party. Government participation is the most important explanation of positional congruence: government parties are much more likely to take a different position in a vote than opposition parties. While government parties need to abandon some of their pre-electoral commitments during the coalition negotiations, opposition parties are free to stick to their pledges (Holzhacker 2002). Although one might expect opposition parties to oppose basically everything the government does, the relatively strong powers of the

Dutch opposition parties provide them with the opportunity to forward their own agenda in parliament (Döring 1995; Louwerse 2012). A lot of what is voted on in parliament concerns motions from the opposition. Most of these are rejected, but at least it allows opposition parties to signal to their voters that they acted upon their electoral pledges. Other factors that affect congruence are the saliency of the political issue as well as the 'quality' of the match between the pre-electoral statement and the parliamentary votes.

It seems that MPs are in both cases deeply affected by the specific characteristics of the specific political and electoral systems: in the Netherlands the role as a government-respectively oppositional party is the most important aspect, whereas in Switzerland government participation can be neglected (since this factor is rather weakly founded in theory). The finding that the most important factor is the average (majority) position of the own party is in line with our institutional expectations: during electoral campaigns the relatively weak position of parties and the candidate-centred voting system set clear incentives for candidates to stress their individual profile and to simultaneously seek personal and party votes. But after the elections, MPs belonging to the same party have to work together and find, as far as possible, common positions in order to play an effective role in parliament and send coherent signals to the electorate. Thus, MPs have an incentive to give up at least some of their outlier positions and take over the positions of their fellows – particularly if issues are concerned to which they indicated weaker preferences in the VAA.

The two countries yet have some aspects in common. First of all, the results confirm the observation from the previous study by Schwarz *et al.* (2010) that despite the often-heard public belief in dishonest politicians, MPs are rather reliable with regard to their pre-electoral policy positions. Previous studies using different sources of data and different approaches have drawn similar conclusions (Mansergh and Thomson 2007; Louwerse 2012). Moreover, in both systems congruence is most affected by the demands of effective implementation of the party mandate. The Swiss system provides incentives for MPs to act in unity in parliament to be able to implement the party policy agenda. In the Dutch system, party unity almost seems taken for granted (Andeweg and Thomassen 2011). Here, the need to form government coalitions based on an elaborate coalition agreement requires government parties to abandon some of their pre-electoral commitments. Moreover, in both systems the degree of 'importance' of a statement also impacts upon the probability of congruent voting behaviour. In Switzerland, MPs are less likely to vote congruently if their preferences are weaker, while the analysis for the Netherlands demonstrated the impact of issue saliency on congruence. While these are arguably somewhat different indicators, they both refer to how central an issue seems to be to an individual candidate (Switzerland) or a party (Netherlands). This constitutes a new finding, since earlier studies, which used a different operationalisation of issue saliency (Thomson 2001; Louwerse 2011a), did not find such an effect. Essentially, our findings are 'good news' for mandate theory: Swiss and Dutch parties and MPs stick to their pre-electoral positions and even more so on the issues that matter most to them.

Our analysis also provides some insight concerning the informational reliability contained in VAAs. The question whether VAAs are a reliable source indicating how parties will behave after the election is of crucial importance for VAAs. Both in Switzerland and the Netherlands the ratio of kept promises is relatively high, which suggests that VAAs generally provide a good indication of how parties will act upon those issues after elections. Two points of caution are, however, appropriate here. First, we have looked at how parliaments vote on bills, amendments and motions. Of course, congruent voting is in many cases a long way from actually implementing a specific policy. If parties or MPs are on the losing side of a parliamentary vote, they might keep their parliamentary mandate by voting in a manner that is congruent with their VAA position, but actual policy is unaffected. Second, our analysis shows that there is a high degree of congruence for VAA statements with a related parliament vote. Quite a few VAA statements are, however, not part of the legislative agenda, either because the agenda changes, party position changes, or because the policy statement in the VAA was stated in a very broad manner. What we thus do not know from our analysis is whether the selection of VAA statements provides an accurate prediction of the totality of voting behaviour in parliament after the elections. This would be a very relevant topic for further research.

In general, we could show the potential of VAA data outside the box of VAA research. VAA data comprise a useful alternative to party manifesto and survey data to capture party positions and electoral promises. However, there are important differences. Compared to party manifestos, VAA data is only an indirect measure of electoral promises. Important is also the fact that the structure of manifesto data (e.g. the selection of the covered issues) is defined by the parties, whereas VAAs force the parties to position themselves on issues which parties or candidates might find irrelevant.

For future research we see two major directions. First, in our analysis we identified electoral promises based on very specific VAA statements. Alternatively, using all VAA statements belonging to a certain policy area, one could also define more general and latent kinds of electoral promises (e.g. 'a position clearly in favour of environmental protection'). This would allow measuring of the level of kept promises on the grounds of entire policy areas and not on the grounds of very specific and often technical single issues, which would probably move the analysis closer to how voters see and interpret politics. Second, while our analysis of two quite different systems leads us to expect that positional congruence is not limited to just these two countries, an earlier study by Skop (2010) found that the ratio of promises kept in the Czech republic is significantly lower than the ratios we found. It would be interesting to analyse in more detail Skop's hypothesis that the lower ratio in Eastern European countries can be explained by the fact that they are young democracies. Future work that includes a larger number of countries with even more diverse democratic backgrounds would thus be very welcome.

Appendix 15.1

Operationalisation of the dependent variable (congruence between VAA answer and legislative behaviour)

	Legislative behaviour	
	Yes	No
smartvote (SWI)		
Fully agree	1	0
Weakly agree	1	0
Weakly disagree	0	1
Fully disagree	0	1
StemWijzer (NL)		
Agree	1	0
Neither	-	-
Disagree	0	1
Kieskompas (NL)		
Fully agree	1	0
Agree	1	0
Neutral	-	-
Disagree	0	1
Fully disagree	0	1

Appendix 15.2

Distribution in the dependent variable (percentages in brackets)

	Legislative behaviour		
	Yes	No	Total
smartvote (SWI)			
Fully agree	1,701 (35.9)	163 (3.4)	1,864 (39.3)
Weakly agree	394 (8.3)	226 (4.8)	620 (13.1)
Weakly disagree	146 (3.1)	337 (7.1)	483 (10.2)
Fully disagree	116 (2.4)	1,655 (34.9)	1,771 (37.4)
Total	2,357 (49.7)	2,381 (50.3)	4,738 (100)
StemWijzer (NL)			
Agree	67 (33.5)	34 (17.0)	101 (50.5)
Neither	3 (1.5)	0 (0.0)	3 (1.5)
Disagree	24 (12.0)	72 (36.0)	96 (48.0)
Total	106 (47.0)	94 (53.0)	200 (100)
Kieskompas (NL)			
Fully agree	41 (15.7)	8 (3.1)	49 (18.8)
Agree	40 (15.3)	33 (12.6)	73 (27.9)
Neutral	7 (2.7)	18 (6.9)	25 (9.6)
Disagree	14 (5.4)	64 (24.5)	78 (29.9)
Fully disagree	3 (1.1)	33 (12.6)	36 (13.7)
Total	105 (40.2)	156 (59.8)	261 (100)

Chapter Sixteen

Voting Advice Applications and Political Theory: Citizenship, Participation and Representation[1]

Joel Anderson and Thomas Fossen

Introduction

Voting Advice Applications (VAAs) are interactive online tools designed to assist voters by improving the basis on which they decide how to vote. In recent years, they have been widely adopted, (*see* Marschall, Chapter Seven in this volume) but their design is the subject of ongoing and often heated criticism (*see* the various chapters by van Camp *et al.*, Gemenis and van Ham, and Mendez in this volume). Most of these debates focus on whether VAAs accurately measure the standpoints of political parties and the preferences of users and on whether they report valid results while avoiding political bias. It is generally assumed that if their methodology is sound, then VAAs can be seen as strengthening the democratic process. But as we argue in this chapter, the setup of VAAs raises basic questions of normative democratic theory as well. Insofar as VAAs are supposed to improve the functioning of the democratic process, it must be clarified in what sense they aim to make a contribution, before it even makes sense to discuss their effectiveness at doing so.

VAAs are often intended to enhance the democratic process by one or all of the following: (1) informing voters about the policy standpoints of political parties (or individual candidates), (2) increasing voter turnout, and (3) ensuring that the composition of parliaments more accurately reflects the political attitudes of the electorate. In the next three sections, we discuss three central bones of contention in current democratic theory that are crucial to these ways in which VAAs typically take themselves to contribute to strengthening the democratic process:

1. Questions about citizen competence: What forms of competence do citizens need to have, and to what extent, for a democracy to function properly?

1. Work on this article was funded by a grant from the Netherlands Organisation for Scientific Research (NWO) for project #311–99–014, 'Voting Advice Applications and the Politics of Citizen Competence'. Anderson further acknowledges the support of a fellowship at the Netherlands Institute of Advanced Study, and Fossen acknowledges support from another NWO-project, 'Between Deliberation and Agonism: Rethinking Conflict and its Relation to Law in Political Philosophy'. Authorship of this chapter is equally shared.

2. Questions about political participation: What forms and extent of participation are vital to democracy?

3. Questions about democratic representation: How should the relation between the elected and the electorate be understood?

For each issue we aim to show, first, how the design and setup of mainstream VAAs are tacitly structured by a specific conception of the democratic aim at issue and, second, what some alternative positions on these questions are within contemporary political theory. In the final section, we will discuss some of the implications of this analysis for the responsibilities of VAA developers, and particularly for the procedural neutrality to which they are typically committed. Our conclusion will be that once these issues are identified, developers of VAAs should either argue in favour of their views on democratic competence, participation and representation, or they should rethink the design of VAAs in ways that move beyond their current assumptions, or both.

VAAs and citizen competence

The most prominent claim about how VAAs strengthen democracies is that they address long standing concerns with voter ignorance. The literature on voter ignorance and citizen incompetence makes clear that the majority of citizens have low levels of political knowledge, reason irrationally about the best means to realise their ends, and exhibit widespread, predictable biases in their preferences for candidates, parties and standpoints (Delli Carpini and Keeter 1996; Caplan 2008; Brennan 2011). Some of this is contested, of course, in particular whether ignorance about matters of geography or history is really such a threat to a well-functioning democracy (Lupia 2006) and whether certain cues can serve as reliable heuristics (Goren 2012). But there are also ample grounds for doubting that voters know what they are choosing when they cast a ballot for a candidate or party (Somin 2006), and it certainly seems problematic for voters to choose on the basis of mistaken beliefs about the political positions of candidates and/or parties, for it means that the ballots cast may have little to do with what voters actually find to be important.

As we have argued elsewhere (Fossen and Anderson, forthcoming), this ignorance about where the parties (or candidates) stand is the form of citizen incompetence that VAAs aim, above all, to address. More precisely, they aim to help close a 'competence gap' (Anderson 2009) between how well informed voters actually are, and how well informed they would need to be for the electoral process to function properly.[2] To the extent to which one views democratic

---

2. Since we are here making exclusively a formal point about the VAA design needing to address this point, we can refrain from taking a substantive position on what would count as the 'proper function'. It is worth adding that normative issues could include concerns with the comparative size of the competence gaps among citizens and the resulting threats to political equality. (We would like to thank Stefan Marschall for raising this issue with us.)

electoral systems as premised on voters knowing what they are voting for, the potential for a problematic competence gap looms large, especially when sorting out the positions of parties and candidates turns out to be a demanding task, as is often the case in multiparty parliamentary systems. Voters need to be able to sift through lengthy party programs and sort out the claims and counterclaims made about what parties' positions really are, even as the parties do their best to obscure the differences, so as to appeal to as many voters as possible. Thus, even assuming wide-spread access to information and high levels of literacy, the level of political knowledge presupposed by this conception of a democratic electoral system can exceed what most citizens have (or take the time to develop). On the assumption that there are significant competence gaps here, VAAs aim to close such competence gaps by leveraging voters' limited knowledge and time (Garzia 2010).

To the extent to which voters are ignorant of parties' actual positions, the democratic contribution of current VAAs would seem uncontroversial. And yet the exclusive focus on this aspect of citizen incompetence – ignorance about party positions – reveals an implicit commitment to issue voting as a normative principle. The typical setup of current VAAs, centred around a set of statements on policy issues, assumes that competent voting is a matter of finding the party whose stand on current issues best fits with one's political preferences. This 'matching model' of VAAs assumes that citizens lack accurate knowledge of the policy programs of political parties (or candidates), even though they have fairly clear and stable policy preferences on which they are expected to base their vote. But there are strong currents within political theory that challenge this model. To illustrate how contentious this conception of competent voting actually is, consider the following three challenges to it in current political theory.

First, consider the analysis developed within the family of political theories referred to as agonism. The defining characteristic of agonistic political theory is its refusal to equate 'democracy' with existing electoral practice, emphasising democracy's dynamic character and the contestability of a given implementation of democratic ideals (Mouffe 2000; Honig 2007; Tully 2008; for an overview, *see* Fossen 2008). While current VAAs help voters to orient themselves within a given electoral landscape, agonistic theorists would argue that this treats the status quo of mainstream discourse as a given and depoliticises the selection of issues on the public agenda. From this perspective, the greater concern is that citizens lack the critical attitude and insights that would allow them to resist the myriad and powerful ways in which policy options, 'key issues' and the political landscape itself get packaged (Fossen and Anderson, forthcoming). But once one considers the agonistic position that citizen incompetence is more a matter of an over-readiness to accept the current political offering as given and an lack of imagination in seeing beyond the present horizon, it becomes clear that current VAAs have made a politically significant choice to the extent to which they focus exclusively on ignorance about the policy positions of parties.

A second, parallel point is made by political theorists who see the primary crisis of citizen incompetence not as ignorance about party positions but rather a failure of voters to form well-considered political positions in the first place. The matching model of VAAs treats the political preferences of citizens as givens, as authoritative inputs into the process of selecting the party and candidate for whom to vote. In recent years, however, a wide range of political theorists and political psychologists have argued that voters not only lack adequate information but also make frequent errors in interpreting the information they have (Somin 2006). Moreover, although it is sometimes claimed that voters' errors end up cancelling each other out and are thus unproblematic, evidence is mounting that citizens are in fact systematically biased in their reasoning about probabilities (Caplan 2008; Kahneman 2011), in selectively filtering out information that challenges existing beliefs (Rosenberg 2007), and in falling prey to how issues are framed (Kelly 2012). Especially within deliberative democratic theory, theorists have contested the very idea that any automatic authority should be given to the political preference that people simply happen to have. They argue instead that democratic politics is best understood in terms of trying to work out the best way of resolving social problems and political challenges (e.g. Bohman and Rehg 1997; Gutmann and Thompson 1996; Habermas 1996; Goodin 2008). On this view, voting competently is not a matter of successfully choosing the option that advances one's political inclinations or material interests, but rather a matter of participating in a problem-solving civic process, oriented towards a common good – a process that may well transform one's political preferences. Individual preferences are a suitable guide to policy- and law-making only if they are well considered, which means they take the perspective of others into view. This is a fundamentally different point of departure than is presupposed in matching VAAs, which are built on the premise that users respond to the VAAs' statements on the basis of positions that they had taken (or were unsure of) before starting to use the tool.[3]

From the standpoint of deliberative democratic theory, however, there is no reason to assume that political opinions should be left unchanged. After all, deliberative democratic theorists typically argue that the democratic process is primarily about transforming preferences, rather than aggregating them (though they often admit that a moment of counting the votes is indispensable in mass democracies). Here again, then, VAAs take a position on how to strengthen democracy that is much more contested than they acknowledge.

A third and perhaps even more fundamental presupposition of current VAAs is thematised in recent work in political theory on the relationship between the 'epistemic' aspirations of a conception of democracy and the scope of the citizen competence it presupposes. As Jamie Kelly has recently argued (2012), building on related work by David Estlund (2008), various theories of democracy differ in terms of the extent to which they see the democratic electoral process as

---

3. This is particularly true for those VAAs that aspire to serve as measurement tools, as a form of polling. Setting this goal commits designers of VAAs to minimising the extent to which users' individual stand on the issues changes as a result of using the tool, since as a matter of measurement, that would reflect a corruption of the data. Arguably, however, this could be a reason not to approach VAAs as measurement tools.

justified on epistemic grounds or non-epistemic grounds. Epistemic approaches see the point of democratic politics as lying in its distinctive contribution to better justified, more warranted legislation (and other collective undertakings). Non-epistemic approaches, by contrast, understand the point of democratic elections in terms of ensuring stability or avoiding procedural unfairness. Corresponding to the positions along this epistemic/non-epistemic continuum, Kelly points out (2012, Ch. 2), these approaches vary in the level of competence that is expected of citizens. Much less citizen competence is presupposed in conceptions of democracy that view elections primarily as stability-generating public rituals in which power alternates between elites, as in elitist theories of democracy (e.g. Schumpeter 1942; Best and Higley 2010). Once the democratic electoral process is justified on the basis of its contribution to the adoption of better laws, policies and governments, then the whole point of elections depends on it being plausible to assume that voters have a relatively high level of citizen competence needed for reliably discerning what votes will actually lead to better results. Accordingly, conceptions of citizen competence – and thus of the mandate for VAAs – differ not only with regard to type of ability and knowledge involved, but also the extent to which it is urgently needed. It may well be appropriately prudent for VAAs to focus on more limited improvements to citizen competence, but this is not obvious, and should not be treated as such. As is so often the case, concerns with feasibility amount, in point of fact, to taking a controversial political standpoint.

In each of these three regards, fundamental questions are being asked, within political theory, about how we ought to think about citizen competence, the ways in which voters fall short of these standards, and the relative urgency of measures to raise citizen competence. These are discussions with significant implications for the potential contribution of VAAs within the democratic electoral process and for the future design of VAAs.

VAAs and political participation

A second and related way in which VAAs are seen as strengthening democracies lies in their potential to address another persistent concern among political commentators: low or declining political participation. VAAs are presented as lowering the cost of political participation by making the whole process more convenient (Garzia 2010). Key information is collected in an easily accessible form, the decision-making process is streamlined, and some have even suggested allowing valid ballots that could be printed from the VAA (or submitted electronically) (Ladner *et al.* 2010: 120–121). In addition, VAAs have been presented as an antidote to voter disengagement. Stefan Marschall (2008) has argued, for example, that VAAs can increase voter turnout by heightening users' awareness of differences between parties and thus of how much is at stake in the election. For those who don't vote because the parties all seem to be the same, VAAs can provide an additional motivation by sharpening the perceived differences. Here again, however, these claims about how promoting participation strengthens democracy are the topic of lively debates in contemporary political theory, debates that make clear that particular ways of setting up VAAs presuppose understandings of political participation that are contested.

Consider, first, the assumption that increasing voter turnout itself strengthens democracy. It seems obvious that, other things being equal, higher turnout increases the democratic credentials of elections, since it means that more people express their preferences, and therefore the outcome can more closely reflect the will of the people. Recently, however, a number of political philosophers have been asking hard questions about the assumed desirability of high voter turnout. In *The Ethics of Voting*, Jason Brennan (2011) has argued that citizens who vote without understanding the issues are engaging in a form of recklessness, since they are acting without knowing whether their voting behaviour will cause harm to others (by helping ineffective, ill-willed, or irrational politicians into power). For Brennan and others (Caplan 2008, Friedman 2006), then, raising voter turnout does not necessarily improve the democratic process – not unless the quality of the democratic process is simply assumed to be a matter of more preferences being aggregated. As we saw in the previous section, there is a strong tradition in political theory according to which improvements to the democratic process are measured in terms of whether the resulting governments and laws are better – more just, more effective, more legitimate, or more inclusive. In line with this, one could argue that the only turnout that strengthens democracy is the turnout of competent citizens who vote responsibly, in the sense of voting in a way that they 'justifiably perceive to contribute to the common good' (Brennan 2011: Ch. 5, p.133). We are not claiming here that Brennan's view is correct, but rather signaling a concern that has arisen in the political theory literature and challenges one of the central justifications of VAAs. And it may well be that the voters who vote as a result of completing a VAA are also significantly better informed, in which case Brennan's objections would be rendered moot. But it is not yet clear what psychological mechanisms would link the two, and we are not aware of any empirical studies that demonstrate that completing a VAA raises the probability of individual users both casting a vote and being better informed. The risk that VAA-usage will increase incompetent (or overconfident) voting may well be worth taking, but it is precisely the point of these critics that this gamble should not be taken on the basis of wishful thinking but on a sober assessment of the evidence.

A second challenge to the focus on voter turnout is taken up by theorists who argue that casting a ballot is not the only, nor perhaps even the most significant, form of democratic participation, as has been argued emphatically by advocates of participatory democracy (Pateman 1970, 2012; Barber 1984); the individual act of casting a ballot is an extremely limited form of participation. It is a private act, carried out in isolation, and it gives citizens no opportunity to shape the content of what is being decided. It is far removed from the dynamic contexts of a town hall meeting or a workers' council, in which participants can see themselves as jointly and transparently determining the conditions of their cooperation. As Pateman has recently put the point:

In a privatized social and political context in the twenty-first century, consumer-citizens need to be extra vigilant and to monitor providers; they require information, to be consulted, and occasionally to debate with their fellow consumer-citizens about the services they are offered. In contrast, the conception of citizenship embodied in participatory democratic theory is that citizens are not at all like consumers. Citizens have the right to public provision, the right to participate in decision-making about their collective life and to live within authority structures that make such participation possible. However, this alternative view of democracy is now being overshadowed. (Pateman 2012: 15)

From this perspective, the concern is that the overwhelming focus on increasing voter turnout serves to undermine recognition of the importance of these other forms of participation. To the extent that this is the case, the potential success of VAAs in strengthening electoral turnout might have the paradoxical effect of weakening other forms of participation by creating the mistaken impression that concerns about diminished political participation have been adequately addressed. On the other hand, however, one might see increased electoral participation as a step on the way to a deeper sense of political mobilisation (Marschall 2008). As psychological claims about what motivates citizens to become active, informed participants, these arguments clearly deserve further empirical study. And at the theoretical level, more work needs to be done to explain the normative significance of increased turnout.

VAAs and democratic representation

Another sense in which VAAs can be thought to strengthen democracy is by increasing the extent to which elected representatives mirror or are congruent with the views of the electorate (Golder and Stramski 2010). Implicit in the construction of VAAs is the widespread assumption that we have a well-functioning system of representative government just in cases where the legislative actions taken by elected representatives match the positions of their constituents. This is reflected in the exclusive emphasis in many VAAs on matching users' policy preferences with the policy-plans of candidates or parties: representatives are supposed to mirror the will of voters. Yet here again, the proper understanding of the relation between the elected and their constituency is a longstanding subject of debate in political theory, with VAAs tacitly assuming one side in the debate.

The central debate here turns on a classical, if somewhat crude (Rehfeld 2009), distinction between seeing representatives as 'trustees' who are to act according to their best judgment as to the common good, and seeing them as 'delegates' who are to act on the wishes of their constituents (Pitkin 1967). In these terms, if one adopts a delegate model of democratic representation, then it is rational to favour electoral designs that select representatives whose positions regarding the legislative agenda are closely aligned with the positions of voters. And this fits well with what many VAAs aim to do, by matching voters and parties or candidates according to their policy preferences (rather than, say, their preferences for political ideology, group identification, or leadership style). Indeed, the emphasis on issues is something VAAs frequently mentioned as a way of encouraging voters to engage with matters of substance, rather than distracting candidate images and soundbites (de Graaf 2010; Nuytemans *et al.* 2010). This issue-oriented understanding of political substance suggests that developers are committed to a delegate rather than trustee conception of representation. Users are supposed to choose policies; the tool finds those candidate-representatives who mirror those preferences most closely.

Although VAAs seem to take it for granted, this delegate model of representation is contested by many political theorists. If, for example, one affirms a view of representation as trusteeship, which allows elected representatives more discretion, considerations other than policy preferences can and should count for voters at the ballot box. In selecting good trustees, it matters less whether they pursue specific policies that their constituents endorse and more whether they can maintain the people's trust (Manin 1997; Mansbridge 2003). From that perspective, it becomes crucial to promote electoral procedures (and VAAs) that focus on other aspects, such as candidates' leadership competence, expertise, or commitment to values and principles. Current matching VAAs seem compatible with a trustee conception to a limited extent insofar as one takes policy positions as indicative of underlying ideological commitments, but other pertinent aspects are typically left out. Moreover, questions arise about the degree to which VAAs capture the relevant ideological dimensions and whether user responses really reflect underlying values and principles.

Recent developments in the debate about democratic representation have further complicated the picture of representation as a principal–agent relation between the electorate and the elected (whether as trustees or delegates) (Dovi 2011; Urbinaty and Warren 2008). Some theorists argue that establishing fair representation of marginalised groups and maintaining their trust calls for special forms of group representation (Williams 1998; Mansbridge 1999). Others have argued for acknowledgment that representatives have a constitutive role in shaping and articulating the interests and preferences of those being represented (Disch 2011; Saward 2010). Saward, for instance, argues that political representation in general, and democratic representation more specifically, should be understood in terms of the ongoing activity of making and contesting 'representative claims'. In his view, the elected representative is a special case of formally recognised representative, but by no means the only form – representative claims (claims to speak on behalf of some constituency) can be legitimately made and backed up by a variety of political actors (Rehfeld 2006). The upshot of the recent debate has been to significantly broaden the notion of representation, as well as to challenge the opposition between direct and representative democracy, since any form of democratic rule involves some form of representative claim (Näsström 2006).

These theoretical developments reveal the complexity of political representation, but surprisingly little work has been done to show how these conceptual developments feed back into and enhance our understanding of democratic elections, and consequently more work is needed to assess their implications for VAAs. What is clear, however, is that it would be a highly controversial assumption to claim that democratic representation is simply a matter of mirroring voters' policy preferences.

Conclusion: Contested neutrality and justifying VAAs

We have argued that current VAAs are premised on assumptions about what strengthens democracies, assumptions that may seem obvious but that are, in fact, hotly contested in political theory. In highlighting the competing conceptions of citizen competence, political participation, and democratic representation, we have not made any claims about which conception is more appropriate. Our point is rather that none of these conceptions can simply be assumed, without justification, as a standard for evaluating VAAs. In this closing section we will discuss some of the implications of our analysis, with particular attention to the responsibilities of developers.

As more and more voters rely on VAAs, the developers of VAAs incur significant responsibilities to demonstrate that they can be trusted, that they do not mislead or manipulate users, that they do not have conflicts of interest, that they adhere to methodological best practices, and so on. In this vein, Ladner *et al.* (2010) have argued for the importance of standards of quality and transparency in VAAs. Their discussion focuses on the dangers of insufficient scientific quality, as well as bias and intentional manipulation.

> Because VAAs can be more than toys, political scientists should not stay away from them. It is their responsibility too that such tools are set up as transparently as possible on the grounds of scientific knowledge about political issues and the political space. In order to prevent possible distortions these tools have to be researched continuously. In this respect, scientists could be held accountable. (Ladner *et al.* 2010: 117)

While we endorse their point that there is no uniquely correct way of setting up a VAA and their call for best practices in VAA development, there is also a danger of assuming that methodological rigour and scientific expertise guarantee legitimacy.

Designers of VAAs frequently position themselves as playing a neutral role in mediating between voters and political parties or candidates. This neutrality is thought to be demonstrated by their claims to political expertise. On this understanding, VAA developers do not themselves take a political stance but merely help citizens to orient themselves in the landscape as they (developers) find it. Accordingly, what is taken to be decisive for the justification of VAA designs is their ability to provide a neutral mapping of the political landscape that provides a place for everyone, such that the subjective preferences of users can be mapped onto what is presented as an objective depiction of the political landscape. This focus on proceduralist neutrality explains why debates over the methodological rigour and accurate measurement of VAAs are so heated – and so important. At the same time, in our discussion of what VAAs presuppose regarding citizen competence, political participation and democratic representation, we have seen several ways in which non-partisanship between parties in an election is not the same as neutrality. Indeed, an overly scientific conceptualisation of VAAs carries the danger of obscuring those presuppositions (Fossen and Van den Brink, 2014, n.d.; Fossen and Anderson forthcoming). Even when developers of a VAA successfully avoid favouring a particular party (which itself is no minor accomplishment), they still take sides – implicitly or not – on questions about citizen competence, political participation and democratic representation. As we have seen, for some political theorists the improvements to the democratic process that are needed are decidedly radical: not (merely) knowledge about party positions, but about the issues and the alternatives; not (merely) higher levels of voter turnout, but deeper and stronger forms of political participation; not (merely) a higher level of issue-based congruence between the electorate and the legislature, but a rethinking of democratic representation and of the role of political leaders.

The upshot of this is that, to the extent to which the design of a VAA is justified on the basis of its contribution to strengthening democracy, it unavoidably takes a political stance regarding the understanding of democracy thereby presupposed. It is part of the responsibility of designers of VAAs to be open and transparent about these issues. For all we know, the presuppositions of current matching models – in terms of a social choice theory of democracy; a minimalistic, voting-centred conception of political participation; and a delegate model of democratic representation – might be vindicated. But, certainly for the foreseeable future, these assumptions about the ideals of democracy will continue to be contested.

The Lausanne Declaration on Voting Advice Applications[1]

Preamble

Elections are a central element of democracy. They legitimise the allocation and the use of political power. Elections have to be organised in a true and fair manner, allowing citizens to make their decisions based on their free will. Citizens have to be informed about the available electoral choices they have.

Being convinced that Voting Advice Applications (VAAs) provide valuable information about candidates and parties running for elections, support citizens in the decision-making process in the course of elections, and allow for electoral choices which are closer to the political position of the voters, and considering that VAAs have become increasingly popular and potentially influential in the electoral process, we abstain from suggesting an ideal form of a VAA, but rather recommend certain standards and minimal requirements that should be respected by all the makers of VAAs.

General Standards

   1.1   In order to contribute sustainably to the good functioning of democracy, VAAs should be open, transparent, impartial and methodologically sound.

Organisation and Management of VAAs

   2.1   All institutions, organisations, associations, groups, private companies and individuals financially supporting a VAA have to be made visible. Funding has to be made transparent.

   2.2   All intentions and purposes associated with these tools have to be revealed by the makers of VAAs.

---

1.   The aim of this declaration is to serve as a starting point for the debate on the professional and ethical aspects of making VAAs. It owes its name from a workshop held in Lausanne in May 2013 at which all contributors of this book took part and where such issues were debated. It is based on a draft version presented by Andreas Ladner at the ECPR General Conference in Bordeaux in September 2013. For helpful comments to the first version we owe a debt of gratitude to Stefaan Walgrave. The sole responsibility for the Lausanne declaration rests with the editors of this volume.

Access and Selectiveness

3.1 A VAA should be freely accessible to all citizens.

3.2 A VAA should aim at the inclusion of as many parties/candidates that are on the ballot as possible. The criteria for the exclusion of parties and candidates should be publicly available and justified.

3.3 Parties and candidates should not be excluded from the tool for ideological reasons.

Usability

4.1 VAAs should be designed in a simple and intuitively understandable manner.

4.2 VAA makers ought to carefully watch that the design does not favour a party/candidate in a systematic manner.

Functioning

5.1 VAAs are based on the assumption that users' proximity to parties and candidates can be measured by their degree of accordance on political issue positions. Ideally, VAAs make this presumption visible.

5.2 The issue statements included in a VAA should be relevant and reveal the different dimensions of competition in the political system for which the VAA is designed. If applicable, voters should be able to express their issue salience by weighting or deciding on which issues they want to be compared to parties and candidates.

5.3 Party and candidate positions on the statements can be coded on the basis of expert opinions, of documents and party manifestos, and of self-placements. The method used to position parties and candidates should be made known to the users of the VAA.

5.4 Following the principle of transparency, the algorithm matching users to parties and candidates should be documented and clearly explained to users.

5.5 The results can be presented to users in the form of rankings, maps, spiders and graphs. Visualisations should be valid and instructive. Guidelines for understanding the results should be provided to the users.

Bibliography

Aarts, K. and van der Kolk, H. (2007) 'The parliamentary election in the Netherlands, 22 November 2006', *Electoral Studies*, 26: 797–837.

Abold, R. (2008) '1000 Mini Election Campaigns: The Utilization of Private Weblogs in the Run-up to the 2005 German Election', in D. M. Farrell and R. Schmitt-Beck (eds) *Non-Party Actors in Electoral Politics: The Role of Interest Groups and Independent Citizens in Contemporary Election Campaigns*, Baden-Baden: Nomos, pp. 209–235.

Abric, J.-C. (1994) 'Les représentations sociales: aspects théoriques', in J.-C. Abric (ed.) *Pratiques sociales et représentations*, Paris: Presses Universitaires de France, pp. 11–35.

Adams, J. (1999) 'Policy divergence in multiparty probabilistic spatial voting', *Public Choice*, 100: 103–22.

Ahuvia, A. (2008) 'Traditional, Interpretive, and Reception Based Content Analyses: Improving the Ability of Content Analysis to Address Issues of Pragmatic and Theoretical Concern', in R. P. Franzosi (ed.) *Content Analysis: What is Content Analysis? Defining the Methodological Playing Field*, London: Sage Benchmarks in Social Research Methods, pp. 185–209.

Alvarez, M. R. and Nagler, J. (2004) 'Party system compactness: consequences and measures', *Political Analysis*, 12 (1): 46–62.

Alvarez, M. R., Levin, I., Trechsel, A. H. and Vassil, K. (2014). Voting Advice Applications: How Useful? For Whom?, *Journal of Information Technology & Politics*, 11: 82–101.

Alvarez, M. R., Levin, I., Mair, P. and Trechsel, A. H. (2014) 'Party preferences in the digital age: the impact of voting advice applications', *Party Politics*, 20 (2): 227–236.

Anderson, C. J. (1995) *Blaming the Government: Citizens and the Economy in Five European Democracies*, Armonk, NY: ME Sharpe.

Anderson, J. (2009) 'Autonomielücken als soziale Pathologie: Ideologiekritik jenseits des Paternalismus', in R. Forst, M. Hartmann, R. Jaeggi and M. Saar (eds) *Sozialphilosophie und Kritik*, Frankfurt: Suhrkamp, pp. 433–453 [English: bit.ly/1acEvDy].

Anderson, S. S. and K. A. Ellassen (eds) (1996) *The European Union: How Democratic is it?*, London: Sage.

Andeweg, R. B. and Thomassen, J. J. A. (2005) 'Modes of political representation: toward a new typology', *Legislative Studies Quarterly*, 30 (4): 507–528.

—— (2011) 'Pathways to party unity: sanctions, loyalty, homogeneity and division of labour in the Dutch parliament', *Party Politics*, 17 (5): 655–672.

Andreadis, I. (2012) 'To Clean or not to Clean? Improving the Quality of VAA Data', paper presented at the *XXIInd World Congress of Political Science*, Madrid, Spain, 8–12 July, http://www.polres.gr/en/sites/default/files/IPSA-2012.pdf.

—   (2013a) Who Responds to Website Visitor Satisfaction Surveys? *General Online Research Conference GOR 13*, DHBW Mannheim, Germany, 4–6 March, http://www.polres.gr/en/sites/default/files/GOR2013.pdf.

—   (2013b) 'Voting Advice Applications: A Successful Nexus Between Informatics and Political Science', paper presented at *BCI '13*, Thessaloniki, Greece, 19–21 September, http://www.polres.gr/en/sites/default/files/BCI-2013.pdf.

Armstrong, J. S. (2006) 'How to make better forecasts and decisions: avoid face-to-face meetings', *Foresight: The International Journal of Applied Forecasting*, 5: 3–8.

Asp, K. (1983) 'The struggle for the agenda', *Communication Research*, 10: 333–355.

Baka, A., Figgou, L. and Triga, V. (2012) 'Neither agree, nor disagree: a critical analysis of the middle answer category in voting advice applications', *International Journal of Electronic Governance (Special Issue: Voting Advice Applications and the State of the Art: Theory, Practice and Comparative Insights)*, 5 (3/4): 244–263.

Bakker, R., de Vries, *et al.* (2012) 'Measuring party positions in Europe: The Chapel Hill Expert Survey trend file, 1999–2010', *Party Politics*, DOI: 10.1177/1354068812462931.

Barber, B. R. (1984) *Strong Democracy: Participatory Politics for a New Age*, Berkeley: University of California Press.

Bartels, L. (2006) 'Three Virtues of Panel Data for the Analysis of Campaign Effects', in H. E. Brady and R. Johnston (eds) *Capturing Campaign Effects*, Ann Arbor: University of Michigan Press, pp. 78–112.

Bassili, J. N. (1993) 'Response latency versus certainty as indexes of the strength of voting intentions in a CATI survey', *Public Opinion Quarterly*, 57 (1): 54–61.

Bassili, J. N. and Fletcher, J. F. (1991) 'Response-time measurement in survey research a method for CATI and a new look at nonattitudes', *Public Opinion Quarterly*, 55 (3): 331–346.

Bassili, J. N. and Scott, B. S. (1996) 'Response latency and question problems', *Public Opinion Quarterly*, 60 (3): 390–399.

Bellucci, P., Garzia, D. and Rubal, M. (2010) 'Campagna elettorale e popolarità dei governi nelle elezioni europee', *Comunicazione Politica*. 1/2010: 17–36.

—   (2012) 'Importa Europa en las Elecciones Europeas? Un modelo explicativo de las elecciones del 2009 al Parlamento Europeo', *Revista Española de Investigaciones Sociológicas*, 137 (1): 25–42.

Benoit, K. and Laver, M. (2006) *Party policy in modern democracies,* London: Routledge.

—   (2012) 'The dimensionality of political space: epistemological and methodological considerations', *European Union Politics*, 13 (2): 194–218.

Best, H. and Higley, J. (eds) (2010) *Democratic Elitism: New Theoretical and Comparative Perspectives*, Leiden: Brill.

Billiet, J. (2006) 'De gestandaardiseerde vragenlijst', in J. Billiet and H. Waege (eds) *Een samenleving onderzocht: Methoden van sociaal-wetenschappelijk onderzoek*, Antwerp: De Boeck, pp. 223–284.

Blais, A., and Bodet, M. A. (2006) 'Does Proportional Representation Foster Closer Congruence Between Citizens and Policy Makers?', *Comparative Political Studies*, 39 (10): 1243–1262.

Bohman, J. and Rehg, W. (1997) *Deliberative Democracy: Essays on Reason and Politics*, Cambridge, MA: MIT Press.

Bolger, F. and Wright, G. (1992) 'Reliability and validity in expert judgment', in G. Wright and F. Bolger (eds) *Expertise and Decision Support*, New York: Plenum, pp. 47–76.

Boogers, M. and Voerman, G. (2003) 'Surfing citizens and floating voters: results of an online survey of visitors to political web sites during the Dutch 2002 General Elections', *Information Polity*, 8 (1–2): 17–27.

Bornschier, S. (2010) *Cleavage Politics and the Populist Right: The New Cultural Conflict in Western Europe*, Philadelphia: Temple University Press.

Bowler, S. and Farrel, D. (1993) 'Legislator shirking and voter monitoring: impacts of European Parliament electoral systems upon legislator–voter relationships', *Journal of Common Market Studies*, 32 (1): 45–69.

Brady, H., Johnston, R. and Sides, J. (2006) 'The Study of Political Campaigns', in H. Brady and R. Johnston (eds) *Capturing Campaign Effects*, Ann Arbor: University of Michigan Press, pp. 1–29.

Brandenburg, H. (2002) 'Who follows whom? The impact of parties on media agenda formation in the 1997 British General Election campaign', *Harvard International Journal of Press/Politics*, 7: 34–54.

Brennan, J. (2011) *The Ethics of Voting*, Princeton: Princeton University Press.

Bressanelli, E. (2013) 'Competitive and coherent? Profiling the Europarties in the 2009 European Parliament elections', *European Integration*, 35 (6): 653–668.

Breuer, F. (2010) 'The EU Profiler: A new way for voters to meet parties and to understand European elections', in W. Gagatek (ed.) *The 2009 Elections to the European Parliament – Country Reports*, Florence: European University Institute, pp. 27–31.

Bright, J., Garzia, D. *et al.* (2014) 'Transnationalising Europe's Voting Space', *EUI Working Papers*, RSCAS 2014/02, Florence: European University Institute.

Budge, I. (2000) 'Expert opinions of party policy positions: Uses and limitations in political research', *European Journal of Political Research*, 37: 103–113.

Budge, I. and Hofferbert, R. (1990) 'Mandates and policy outputs: U.S. party platforms and federal expenditures', *American Political Science Review*, 84 (1): 111–131.

Campbell, A., Converse, P. E. *et al.* (1960) The American Voter, Chicago: University of Chicago Press.

Caplan, B. (2008) *The Myth of the Rational Voter: Why Democracies Choose Bad Policies*, Princeton: Princeton University Press.

Carey, J. and Shugart, M. (1995) 'Incentives to cultivate a personal vote: a rank ordering of electoral formulas', *Electoral Studies*, 14 (4): 417–439.

Çarkoğlu, A., Vitiello, T. and Moral, M. (2012) 'Voting Advice Applications in practice: answers to some key questions from Turkey', *International Journal of Electronic Governance* (Special Issue: *Voting Advice Applications and the State of the Art: Theory, Practice and Comparative Insights*), 5 (3/4): 298–317.

Carlson, T. and Strandberg, K. (2005) 'The 2004 European parliament election on the web: Finnish actor strategies and voter responses', *Information Polity*, 10 (3): 189–204.

Carmines, E. G. and Huckfeldt, R. (1996) 'Political Behavior: An Overview', in Goodin, R. E. and H. D. Klingemann (eds) *A New Handbook of Political Science*, New York: Oxford University Press, pp. 223–254.

Carmines, E. G. and Stimson, J. (1980) 'The two faces of issue voting', *American Political Science Review*, 74: 78–91.

Carrubba, C. and Timpone, R. J. (2005) 'Explaining vote switching across first- and second-order elections: evidence From Europe', *Comparative Political Studies*, 38 (3): 260–281.

Carver, R. P. (1992) 'Reading rate: theory, research, and practical implications', *Journal of Reading*, 36 (2): 84–95.

Castles, F. G. and Mair, P. (1984) 'Left–right political scales: Some "expert" judgments', *European Journal of Political Research*, 12: 73–88.

Cedroni, L. (2010) 'Voting Advice Applications in Europe: a comparison', in L. Cedroni and D. Garzia (eds) *Voting Advice Applications in Europe: The State of the Art*, Napoli: Civis, pp. 247–257.

Cedroni, L. and Garzia, D. (eds) (2010) *Voting Advice Applications in Europe: The State of the Art*, Napoli: Civis.

Chiburis, R. C., Das, J. and Lokshin, M. (2012) 'A practical comparison of the bivariate probit and linear IV estimators', *Economics Letters*, 117 (3): 762–766.

Christian, L. M., Parsons, N. L. and Dillman, D. A. (2009) 'Designing scalar questions for web surveys', *Sociological Methods & Research*, 37 (3): 393–425.

Condor, S. and Gibson, S. (2007) '"Everybody's Entitled to their own Opinion": ideological dilemmas of liberal individualism and active citizenship', *Journal of Community and Applied Social Psychology*, 14: 115–140.

Costello, A. B. and Osborne, J. W. (2005) 'Best practices in exploratory factor analysis: four recommendations for getting the most from your analysis', *Practical Assessment, Research & Evaluation*, 10: 173–178.

Costello, R. and Thomson, R. (2008) 'Election pledges and their enactment in coalition governments: a comparative analysis of Ireland', *Journal of Elections, Public Opinion & Parties*, 18 (3): 239–256.

Coultrap, J. (1999) 'From parliamentarism to pluralism: models of democracy and the European Union's democratic deficit', *Journal of Theoretical Politics*, 11 (1): 107–135.

Cox, G. (1990) 'Centripetal and centrifugal incentives in electoral systems', *American Journal of Political Science*, 34: 905–935.

—   (1997) *Making Votes Count: Strategic Coordination in the World's Electoral Systems,* Cambridge: Cambridge University Press.

Crisp, B., Jensen, K. and Shomer, Y. (2007) 'Magnitude and vote seeking', *Electoral Studies*, 26 (4): 727–734.

Crisp, B., Olivella, S. *et al.* (2013) 'Vote-earning strategies in flexible list systems: seats at the price of unity', *Electoral Studies* (forthcoming), available at http://dx.doi.org/10.1016/j.electstud.2013.02.007.

Curini, L. (2010) 'Experts' political preferences and their impact on ideological bias: an unfolding analysis based on a Benoit-Laver expert survey', *Party Politics*, 16: 299–321.

Curini, L. and Hino, A. (2012) 'Missing links in party-system polarization: how institutions and voters matter', *The Journal of Politics*, 74: 460–473.

Cutler, F. (2002) 'The simplest shortcut of all: sociodemographic characteristics and electoral choice', *The Journal of Politics*, 64 (2): 466–490.

Daalder, H. (1984) 'In search of the centre of European party systems', *American Political Science Review*, 78 (1–2): 92–109.

Dalkey, N. C. and Helmer, O. (1963) 'An experimental application of the Delphi method to the use of experts', *Management Science*, 9: 458–467.

Dalton, R. J. (2000) 'The Decline of Party Identifications', in R. J. Dalton and M. P. Wattenberg (eds) *Parties Without Partisans: Political Change in Advanced Industrial Democracies*, Oxford: Oxford University Press, pp. 19–37.

Dalton, R. J. and Wattenberg, M. P. (eds) (2000) *Parties without Partisans: Political Change in Advanced Industrial Democracies*, Oxford: Oxford University Press.

De Graaf, J. (2010) 'The Irresistible Rise of Stemwijzer', in L. Cedroni and D. Garzia (eds) *Voting Advice Applications in Europe: The State of the Art*, Napoli: Civis, pp. 35–60.

De Groot, L. F. M. (2002) 'Een kritische evaluatie evaluatie van de StemWijzer 2002', *Tijdschrift voor beleid, Politiek en Maatschappij*, 30 (1): 20–30.

—   (2003) 'Verassingseffect StemWijzer is niet verrassend', *Tijdschrift voor beleid, Politiek en Maatschappij*, 30 (2): 201–203.

—   (2004) 'De voorspelkracht van stemprogramma's', *Tijdschrift voor Politieke Economie*, 25 (3): 88–115.

Delli Carpini, M. X. and Keeter, S. (1996) *What Americans Know about Politics and Why It Matters*, Yale University Press, New Haven and London.

De Rosa, R. (2010) 'cabina-elettorale.it: (Provides advice to Italian voters since 2009)', in L. Cedroni and D. Garzia (eds) *Voting Advice Applications in Europe: The State of the Art*, Napoli: Civis, pp. 187–212.

Deschouwer, K., Hooghe, M. *et al.* (2007) *Doe de Stemtest 2007: hoe, wat en waarom?* Information note for Flemish political parties.

De Vreese, C. H. (2003) *Framing Europe: Television News and European Integration,* Aksant Academic Pub.

De Vreese, C. H., Banducci, S. A. *et al.* (2006) 'The news coverage of the 2004 European Parliamentary election campaign in 25 countries', *European Union Politics*, 7 (4): 477–504.

De Vries, C. E. D. and Marks, G. (2012) 'The struggle over dimensionality: a note on theory and empirics', *European Union Politics*, 13 (2): 185–193.

Dillman, D. A. (2007) *Mail and Internet Surveys: The Tailored Design,* 2nd edn, New York, NY: John Wiley and Sons, Inc.

Dinas, E. and Gemenis, K. (2010) 'Measuring parties' ideological positions with manifesto data: a critical evaluation of the competing methods', *Party Politics*, 16: 427–450.

Dinas, E., Trechsel, A. H. and Vassil, K. (2014) 'A Look into the Mirror – Preferences, Representation and Electoral Participation', *Electoral Studies*, (forthcoming).

Disch, L. (2011) 'Toward a mobilization conception of democratic representation', *American Political Science Review*, 105 (1): 100–114.

Döring, H. (1995) 'Time as a Scarce Resource: Government Control of the Agenda', in H. Döring (ed.) *Parliaments and Majority Rule in Western Europe*, Frankfurt: Campus Verlag, pp. 223–246.

Dovi, S. (2011) 'Political Representation', in E. N. Zalta (ed.) *The Stanford Encyclopedia of Philosophy*, available at: http://plato.stanford.edu/archives/win2011/entries/political-representation/ (accessed 25 February 2013).

Dow, J. K. (2001) 'A comparative spatial analysis of majoritarian and proportional elections', *Electoral Studies*, 20 (1): 109–125.

—— (2010) 'Party system extremism in majoritarian and proportional electoral systems', *British Journal of Political Science*, 41: 341–361.

Downs, A. (1957) *An Economic Theory of Democracy*, New York: Harper and Brothers.

Dumont, P., Kies, R., Fehlen, F. and Poirier, P. (2006) *Les élections législatives et européennes de 2004 au Grand-Duché du Luxembourg: Rapport élaboré pour la Chambre des Députés*, Luxembourg: Service Central des Imprimés de l'Etat.

Dumont, P. and Kies, R. (2012) '*smartvote*.lu: usage and impact of the first VAA in Luxembourg', *International Journal of Electronic Governance* (Special Issue: Voting Advice Applications and the State of the Art: Theory, Practice and Comparative Insights), 5 (3/4): 388–410.

Duverger, M. (1954) *Political Parties*, New York: Wiley.

—— (1972) 'Factors in a Two-Party and Multiparty System', in *Party Politics and Pressure Groups,* New York: Thomas Y. Crowell, pp. 23–32.

Dziewulska, A. (2010) 'The Use of Voter Advice Application in Poland – Glosuje.com.pl', in L. Cedroni and D. Garzia (eds) *Voting Advice Application in Europe: The State of the Art*, Napoli: Civis, pp. 217–246.

Edwards, A. R. (1998) 'Towards an Informed Citizenry? Information and Communication Technologies and Electoral Choice', in I. Th. M. Snellenm and W. van de Donk (eds) *Public Administration in an Information Age: A Handbook*, Amsterdam: IOS Press, pp. 191–206.

Enyedi, Z. (2008) 'The social and attitudinal basis of political parties: cleavage politics revisited', *European Review*, 16: 287–304.

Erikson, R. S. (1989) 'Economic conditions and the presidential vote', *American Political Science Review*, 83: 567–573.

Erikson, R. S. and Tedin, K. L. (2007) *American Public Opinion: Its Origins, Content, and Impact*, 7th edn, New York: Pearson.

Estlund, D. (2008) *Democratic Authority: A Philosophical Framework*, Princeton: Princeton University Press.

Evans, G. and Chzhen, K. (2013) 'Explaining voters' defection from Labour over the 2005–10 electoral cycle: leadership, economics and the rising importance of immigration', *Political Studies*, 61 (1): 138–157.

Evans, G., Heath, A. F. and Lalljee, M. (1996) 'Measuring left–right and authoritarian–libertarian values in the British electorate', *British Journal of Sociology*, 47: 93–112.

Ezrow, L. (2008) 'Parties' policy programmes and the dog that didn't bark: no evidence that proportional systems promote extreme party positioning', *British Journal of Political Science*, 38: 479–497.

Fan, W. and Yan, Z. (2010) 'Factors affecting response rates of the web survey: A systematic review', *Computers in Human Behavior*, 26 (2): 132–139, DOI: http://dx.doi.org/10.1016/j.chb.2009.10.015.

Farrell, D. M. and Schmitt-Beck, R. (eds) (2002) *Do Political Campaigns Matter? Campaign Effects in Elections and Referendums*, London/New York: Routledge.

— (eds) (2008) *Non-Party Actors in Electoral Politics: The Role of Interest Groups and Independent Citizens in Contemporary Election Campaigns*, Baden-Baden: Nomos.

Ferrell, W. R. (1985) 'Combining Individual Judgments', in G. Wright (ed.) *Behavioural Decision-Making*, New York: Plenum, pp. 111–145.

Fiechter, J. and Leuenberger, R. (2009) 'L'offre de smartvote en termes de candidats est-elle représentative de l'ensemble des candidats à une élection donnée? Le cas des élections fédérales de 2007', *Working paper de l'IDHEAP*, no. 2/2009.

Fivaz, J. and Nadig, G. (2010) 'Impact of Voting Advice Applications (VAAs) on Voter Turnout and Their Potential Use for Civic Education', *Policy & Internet*, 2 (4): 167–200.

Fossen, T. (2008) 'Agonistic critiques of liberalism: perfection and emancipation', *Contemporary Political Theory*, 7 (4): 376–394.

Fossen, T. and Anderson, J. (2011) (2014) 'What's the point of Voting Advice Applications? Competing perspectives on democracy and citizenship', *Electoral Studies*.

Fossen, T. and van den Brink, B. (2014) *Electoral Dioramas: On the Problem of Representation in Voting Advice Applications*, unpublished manuscript.

Franklin, C. H. and Jackson, J. E. (1983) 'The dynamics of party identification', *The American Political Science Review*, 77 (4): 957–973.

Franklin, M. N. and Hobolt, S. B. (2011) 'The legacy of lethargy: how elections to the European Parliament depress turnout', *Electoral Studies*, 30 (1): 67–76.

Franklin, M. N., Mackie, T. and Valen, H. (eds) (1992) *Electoral Change: Responses to Evolving Social and Attitudinal Structures in Western countries*, Cambridge: Cambridge University Press.

Friedman, J. (2006) 'Taking Ignorance Seriously: Rejoinder to Critics', *Critical Review*, 19 (1): 1–22.

Fry, E. B. (1963) *Teaching Faster Reading: A Manual*. Cambridge: Cambridge University Press.

Garzia, D. (2010) 'The Effects of VAAs on Users' Voting Behavior: An Overview', in L. Cedroni and D. Garzia (eds) *Voting Advice Applications in Europe: The State of the Art*, Napoli: Civis, pp. 13–33.

— (2012) 'Understanding Cross-National Patterns of VAA-Usage: Integrating Macro- and Micro-Level Explanations', in A. Dziewulska and A. Ostrowska (eds) *Europeanisation of political rights: Voter Advice Application and migrant mobilisation in 2011 UK elections*, Warsaw: Centre for Europe, University of Warsaw.

— (2014) *Personalization of Politics and Electoral Change,* Basignstoke: Palgrave Macmillan.

Garzia, D. and Marschall, S. (2012) 'Voting Advice Applications under review – the state of the research', *International Journal of Electronic Governance* (Special Issue: *Voting Advice Applications and the State of the Art: Theory, Practice and Comparative Insights*), 5 (3/4): 203–222.

Garzia, D., Trechsel, *et al.* (2014) 'Indirect Campaigning: Past, Present and Future of Voting Advice Applications', in B. Grofman. M. Franklin and A. H. Trechsel (eds), *The Internet and Democracy in Global Perspective*, Cham: Springer.

Gemenis, K. (2012)'Proxy documents as a source of measurement error in the Comparative Manifestos Project', *Electoral Studies*, 31: 594–604.

— (2013) 'Estimating parties' positions through voting advice applications: some methodological considerations', *Acta Politica*, 48 (3): 268–295.

George, A. L. (2008) 'Quantitative and Qualitative Approaches to Content Analysis', in R. P. Franzosi (ed.) *Content Analysis: What is Content Analysis? Defining the Methodological Playing Field*, London: Sage Benchmarks in Social Research Methods, pp. 222–244.

Gibson, R. and Ward, S. (2009) 'Parties in the digital age: a review article', *Representation*, 45 (1): 87–100.

Golder, M. and Stramski, J. (2010) 'Ideological congruence and electoral institutions', *American Journal of Political Science*, 54 (1): 90–106.

Goodin, R. E. (2008) *Innovating Democracy: Democratic Theory and Practice After the Deliberative Turn*, Oxford: Oxford University Press.

Goren, P. (2012) *On Voter Competence*, Oxford: Oxford University Press.

Green-Pedersen, C. (2004) 'Centre parties, party competition, and the implosion of party systems: a study of centripetal tendencies in multiparty systems', *Political Studies*, 52: 324–341.

Greene, W. H. (2002) *Econometric Analysis*, Upper Saddle River, NJ: Prentice Hall.

Greene, W. H. and Hensher, D. A. (2010) *Modeling Ordered Choices: A Primer and Recent Developments*, Cambridge: Cambridge University Press.

Gulati, J. and Williams, B. (2007) 'Closing the gap, raising the bar: candidate web site communication in the 2006 campaigns for Congress', *Social Science Computer Review*, 25 (4): 443–465.

Guo, S. and Fraser, M. W. (2010) *Propensity Score Analysis: Statistical Methods and Applications*, Thousand Oaks, CA: Sage Publications.

Gutmann, A. and Thompson, D. F. (1996) *Democracy and Disagreement*, Cambridge (MA): Harvard University Press.

Habermas, J. (1996) *Between Facts and Norms: Contributions to a Discourse Theory of Law and Democracy*, Cambridge (MA): MIT Press.

Hansen, M. E. and Rasmussen, N. E. K. (2013) 'Does running for the same party imply similar policy preferences? Evidence from voting advice applications', *Representation*, 49 (2): 189–205, DOI: 10.1080/00344893.2013. 805161.

Heerwegh, D. (2003) 'Explaining response latencies and changing answers using client-side paradata from a web survey', *Social Science Computer Review*, 21 (3): 360–373.

Heerwegh, D. and Loosveldt, G. (2008) 'Face-to-face versus web surveying in a high-internet-coverage population: differences in response quality', *Public Opinion Quarterly*, 72 (5): 836–846.

Hellström, J. (2008) 'Who leads, who follows? Re-examining the part-electorate linkages on European Integration', *Journal of European Public Policy*, 15 (8): 1127–1144.

Herrnson, P. S. and Curry, J. M. (2011) 'Issue voting and partisan defections in congressional elections', *Legislative Studies Quarterly*, 36 (2): 281–307.

Hirzalla, F., van Zoonen, L. and de Ridder, J. (2011) 'Internet use and political participation: reflections on the mobilization/normalization controversy', *The Information Society*, 27 (1): 1–15.

Hix, S. and Crombez, C. (2005) 'Extracting ideal point estimates from actors' preferences in the EU constitutional negotiations', *European Union Politics*, 6 (3): 353–376.

Holzhacker, R. (2002) 'National parliamentary scrutiny over EU Issues: comparing the goals and methods of governing and opposition parties', *European Union Politics*, 3 (4): 459–479.

Honig, B. (2007) 'Between decision and deliberation: political paradox in democratic theory', *American Political Science Review*, 101 (1): 1–17.

Hooghe, L., Bakker, R. *et al.* (2010) 'Reliability and validity of the 2002 and 2006 Chapel Hill expert surveys on party positioning', *European Journal of Political Research*, 49 (5): 687–703.

Hooghe, L., Marks, G., and Wilson, C. J. (2002) 'Does left/right structure party positions on European integration?', *Comparative Political Studies*, 35 (8): 965–989.

Hooghe, M. and Teepe, W. (2007) 'Party profiles on the web: an analysis of the logfiles of nonpartisan interactive political internet sites in the 2003 and 2004 election campaigns in Belgium', *New Media & Society*, 9 (6): 965–985.

Hopmann, D.N., Elmelund-Praestekaer, C. *et al.* (2012) 'Party media agenda setting: How parties influence election news coverage', *Party Politics*, 18(2): 173–191.

Imai, K., Keele, L. *et al.* (2011) 'Unpacking the black box of causality: learning about causal mechanisms from experimental and observational studies', *American Political Science Review*, 105 (4): 765–789.

Jankowski, N., Foot, K. and Kluver, R. (2005) 'The Web and the 2004 EP election: comparing political actor websites in 11 EU member states', *Information Policy*, 10 (3): 165–176.

Jegher, A. (1999) *Bundesversammlung und Gesetzgebung: Der Einfluss von institutionellen, politischen und inhaltlichen Faktoren auf die Gesetzgebungstätigkeit der Eidgenössischen Räte*, Bern: Haupt.

Kahneman, D. (2011) *Thinking, Fast and Slow*, New York: Farrar Straus & Giroux.

Kalogeropoulou, E. (1989) 'Election promises and government performance in Greece: PASOK's fulfilment of its 1981 election pledges', *European Journal of Political Research*, 17 (3): 289–311.

Karp, J. A., Banducci, S. A. and Bowler, S. (2003) 'To know it is to love it? Satisfaction with democracy in the European Union', *Comparative Political Studies*, 36 (3): 271–292.

Katakis, I., Tsapatsoulis, *et al.* (2013) 'Social Voting Advice Applications: definitions, challenges, datasets and evaluation', *IEEE Transactions on Cybernetics.*, DOI: 10.1109/TCYB.2013.2279019.

Kelly, J. T. (2012) *Framing Democracy: A Behavioral Approach to Democratic Theory*, Princeton: Princeton University Press.

Key, V. O. (1964) *Politics, Parties, and Pressure Groups*, 5th edn, New York: Crowell.

Kies, R., Mendez, F. *et al.* (2004) 'Evaluation of the use of new technologies in order to facilitate democracy in Europe', public report for the *Scientific and Technological Option Assessment (STOA)*, European Parliament Directorate-General for Research, European Parliament.

King, G., Keohane, R. O. and Verba, S. (1994) *Designing Social Inquiry: Scientific Inference in Qualitative Research*, Princeton: Princeton University Press.

Kirchheimer, O. (1965) 'Der Wandel des westeuropäischen Parteiensystems', *Politische Vierteljahresschrift*, 6 (1): 20–41.

Kitschelt, H. (1994) *The Transformation of European Social Democracy*, Cambridge: Cambridge University Press.

Klingemann, H.-D., Hofferbert, R. and Budge, I. (1994) *Parties, Policies and Democracy*, Boulder: Westview Press.

Kluver, R., Jankowski, N. and Foot, K. (eds) (2007) *The Internet and National Elections: A Comparative Study of Web Campaigning*, London: Routledge, pp. 105–113.

Kriesi, H. (1998) 'The transformation of cleavage politics: the 1997 Stein Rokkan lecture', *European Journal of Political Research*, 33: 165–185.

— (2001) 'The federal parliament: the limits of institutional reform', *West European Politics*, 24 (2): 59–76.

Kriesi, H., Grande, E. *et al.* (2006) 'Globalization and the transformation of the national political space: Six European countries compared', *European Journal of Political Research*, 45 (6): 921–956.

Krippendorff, K. (2004) *Content Analysis: An Introduction to its Methodology*, 2nd edn, Thousand Oaks, CA: Sage.

Krosnick, J. A. (1991) 'Response strategies for coping with the demands of attitude measures in surveys', *Applied Cognitive Psychology*, 5: 214–236.

Krosnick, J. A. and Alwin, D. F. (1987) 'An evaluation of a cognitive theory of response-order effects in survey measurement', *Public Opinion Quarterly*, 51 (2): 201–219.

Krouwel, A. (2012) *Party Transformations in European democracies*, Albany: State University of New York Press.

Krouwel, A. and van Elfrinkhof, A. (2013) 'Combining strengths of methods of party positioning to counter their weaknesses: The development of a new methodology to calibrate parties on issues and ideological dimensions', *Quality and Quantity*, DOI: 10.1007/s11135-013-9846-0.

Krouwel, A., Vitiello, T. and Wall, M. (2012) 'The practicalities of issuing vote advice: A new methodology for profiling and matching', *International Journal of Electronic Governance* (Special Issue: *Voting Advice Applications and the State of the Art: Theory, Practice and Comparative Insights*), 5 (3/4): 223–243.

Kumar, R. (2011) *Research Methodology: A Step-by-Step Guide for Beginners*, London: Sage.

Lachat, R. and Selb, P. (2010) 'Strategic overshooting in National Council Elections', *Swiss Political Science Review*, 16 (3): 481–498.

Lacy, D. and Paolino, P. (2010) 'Testing proximity versus directional voting using experiments', *Electoral Studies*, 29: 460–471.

Ladner, A. (2012) 'Voting Advice Applications werden im Wahlkampf immer wichtiger. Es ist Zeit, dass wir uns darüber Gedanken machen', in B. Ziegler and N. Wälti (eds) *Wahl-Probleme der Demokratie: Schriften zur Demokratieforschung* (edited by Zentrum für Demokratie Aarau), Zürich: Schulthess, pp. 91–110.

Ladner, A., Felder, G. and Fivaz, J. (2010) 'More than Toys? A First Assessment of Voting Advice Applications in Switzerland', in L. Cedroni and D. Garzia (eds) *Voting Advice Applications in Europe: The State of the Art*, Napoli: Civis, pp. 91–123.

— (2012) 'Voting advice applications and party choice: Evidence from *smartvote* users in Switzerland', *International Journal of Electronic Governance* (Special Issue: Voting Advice Applications and the State of the Art: Theory, Practice and Comparative Insights), 5 (3/4): 367–387.

Ladner, A. and Fivaz, J. (2012) 'Voting Advice Applications', in N. Kersting (ed.) *Electronic Democracy. The World of Political Science – The development of the Discipline Book Series*, Opladen: Barbara Budrich Publischer pp. 177–198.

Ladner, A. and Pianzola, J. (2010) 'Do Voting Advice Applications Have an Effect on Electoral Participation and Voter Turnout? Evidence from the 2007 Swiss Federal Elections', in E. Tambouris, A. Macintosh and O. Glassey (eds) *Electoral Participation*, Berlin: Springer, pp. 211–224.

Laver, M. (ed.) (2001) *Estimating the Policy Position of Political Actors*, London: Routledge.

Leimgruber, P., Hangartner, D. and Leemann, L. (2010) 'Comparing candidates and citizens in the ideological space', *Swiss Political Science Review*, 16 (3): 499–531.

Lijphart, A. (2012) *Patterns of Democracy: Government Forms and Performance in 36 Countries*, New Haven and London: Yale University Press.

Lipset, S. M. and Rokkan, S. (eds) (1967) *Party Systems and Voter Alignments: Cross-National Perspectives*, New York: Free Press.

Lobo, M. C., Vink, M. and Lisi, M. (2010) 'Mapping the Political Landscape: A Vote Advice Application in Portugal', in L. Cedroni and D. Garzia (eds) *Voting Advice Applications in Europe: The State of the Art*, Napoli: Civis, pp. 143–158.

Louwerse, T. (2011a) *Political Parties and the Democratic Mandate: Comparing Collective Mandate Fulfilment in the United Kingdom and the Netherlands*, LEI, Universiteit Leiden.

— (2011b) 'The spatial approach to the party mandate', *Parliamentary Affairs*, 64 (3): 425–447.

— (2012) 'Mechanisms of issue congruence: the democratic party mandate', *West European Politics*, 35 (6): 1249–1271.

Louwerse, T. and Otjes, S. (2012) 'Design challenges in cross-national VAAs: the case of the EU profiler', *International Journal of Electronic Governance* (Special Issue: *Voting Advice Applications and the State of the Art: Theory, Practice and Comparative Insights*), 5 (3/4): 279–297.

Louwerse, T. and Rosema, M. (2013) 'The design effects of voting advice applications: comparing methods of calculating matches', *Acta Politica*, article in press.

Lupia, A. (2006) 'How elitism undermines the study of voter competence', *Critical Review*, 18 (1): 217–232.

McAllister, I. (2007) 'The Personalization of Politics', in R. Dalton and H. Klingemann (eds) *Oxford Handbook of Political Behavior*, Oxford: Oxford University Press.

McCombs, M. and Shaw, D. (1972) 'The agenda-setting function of mass media', *Public Opinion Quarterly*, 36 (2): 176–187.

McDermott, M. L. (1997) 'Voting cues in low-information elections: candidate gender as a social information variable in contemporary United States elections', *American Journal of Political Science*, 41: 270–283.

McDonald, M. D. and Budge, I. (2005) *Elections, Parties, Democracy: Conferring the Median Mandate*, Oxford/New York: Oxford University Press.

Macdonald, S. E. and Rabinowitz, G. (1998) 'Solving the paradox of nonconvergence: valence, position, and direction in democratic politics', *Electoral Studies*, 17: 281–300.

Maddala, G. S. (1983) *Limited-Dependent and Qualitative Variables in Econometrics*, Cambridge: Cambridge University Press.

Manin, B. (1997) *The Principles of Representative Government*, Cambridge: Cambridge University Press.

Mansergh, L. and Thomson, R. (2007) 'Election pledges, party competition, and policymaking', *Comparative Politics*, 39 (3): 311–329.

Mansbridge, J. (1999) 'Should blacks represent blacks and women represent women? A contingent "yes"', *The Journal of Politics*, 61 (3): 628–657.

— (2003) 'Rethinking representation', *American Political Science Review*, 97 (4): 515–528.

Margolis, M. and Resnick, D. (2000) *Politics as Usual: The Cyberspace Revolution*, Thousand Oaks, CA: Sage.

Mariani, M. D. and Hewitt, G. J. (2008) 'Indoctrination U.? Faculty ideology and changes in student political orientation', *PS: Political Science and Politics*, 41: 773–783.

Marks, G., Hooghe, L. *et al.* (2006) 'Party competition and European Integration in the East and West: different structure, same causality', *Comparative Political Studies*, 39 (2): 155–175.

Marks, G., Hooghe, L. *et. al.* (2007) 'Crossvalidating data on party positioning on European integration', *Electoral Studies*, 26: 23–38.

Marschall, S. (2005) 'Idee und Wirkung des Wahl-O-Mat', *Aus Politik und Zeitgeschichte*, 55 (51–52): 41–46.

— (2008) 'The Online Making of Citizens: Wahl-O-Mat', in V. B. Georgi (ed.) *The Making of Citizens in Europe: New Perspectives on Citizenship Education*, Bonn: Bundeszentrale für politische Bildung, pp. 137–141.

Marschall, S. and Schmidt, C. K. (2008) 'Preaching to the converted or making a difference? Mobilizing effects of an internet application at the German general election 2005', in D. Farrell and R. Schmitt-Beck (eds) *Non-Party Actors in Electoral Politics*, Baden-Baden: Nomos pp. 259–278.

— (2010) 'The Impact of Voting Indicators: The Case of the German Wahl-O-Mat', in L. Cedroni and D. Garzia (eds), *Voting Advice Applications in Europe: The State of the Art*, Napoli: Civis pp. 65–104.

Marschall, S. and Schultze, M. (2012a) 'Voting Advice Applications and their effect on voter turnout: the case of the German Wahl-O-Mat', *International Journal of Electronic Governance (Special Issue: Voting Advice Applications and the State of the Art: Theory, Practice and Comparative Insights)*, 5 (3/4): 349–366.

— (2012b) 'The Emergence of the "Voter 2.0"? VVA Users in a Changing Political Communication Sphere', paper presented at the *XXXVI Convegno SISP*, Rome, Italy, 13–15 September.

Marsh, M. (1998) 'Testing the second-order election model after four European elections', *British Journal of Political Science*, 28 (4): 591–607.

— (2009) 'Vote switching in European Parliament elections: evidence from June 2004', *Journal of European Integration*, 31 (5): 627–644.

Marsh, M. and Norris, P. (1997) 'Political representation in the European Parliament', *European Journal of Political Research*, 32 (2): 153–164.

Mayer, C. and Wassermair, M. (2010) 'wahlkabine.at: Promoting an Enlightened Understanding of Politics', n L. Cedroni and D. Garzia (eds) *Voting Advice Applications in Europe: The State of the Art*, Napoli: Civis, pp. 173–200.

Mendez, F. (2012) 'Matching voters with political parties and candidates: an empirical test of four algorithms', *International Journal of Electronic Governance* (Special Issue: *Voting Advice Applications and the State of the Art: Theory, Practice and Comparative Insights*), 5 (3/4): 264–278.

Merrill III, S. and Adams, J. (2002) 'Centrifugal Incentives in Multi-Candidate Elections', *Journal of Theoretical Politics*, 14: 275–300.

Miller, G. and Schofield, N. (2003) 'Activists and Partisan Realignment in the United States', *American Political Science Review*, 97: 245–260.

Morgan, D. L. and Krueger, R. A. (1993) 'When to Use Focus Groups and Why', in D. L. Morgan (ed.) *Successful Focus Groups: Advancing the State of the Art*, Newbury Park, CA: Sage Publications, pp. 3–19.

Morton, R. B. and Williams, K. C. (2010) *Experimental Political Science and the Study of Causality: From Nature to the Lab*, Cambridge/New York: Cambridge University Press.

Moscovici, S. (1961) *La psychoanalyse, son image et son public*, Paris: Presses Universitaires de France.

— (1976, 2nd edn) *La Psychanalyse, son image et son public*, Paris: Presses Universitaires de France.

— (1984) 'The myth of the lonely paradigm: a rejoinder', *Social Research*, 51: 939–968.

Mouffe, C. (2000) *The Democratic Paradox*, London: Verso.

Müller, W. C. (2000) 'Political parties in parliamentary democracies: making delegation and accountability work', *European Journal of Political Research*, 37: 309–333.

Müller, W. C. and Ström, K. (1999) *Policy, Office, or Votes? How Political Parties in Western Europe Make Hard Decisions*, Cambridge: Cambridge University Press.

Murphy, J., Hofacker, C. and Mizerski, R. (2006) 'Primacy and recency effects on clicking behaviour', *Journal of Computer Mediated Communication*, 11 (2): 522–535.

Murphy, A. (2007) 'Score tests of normality in bivariate probit models', *Economics Letters*, 95 (3): 374–379.

Mykkänen, J. and Moring, T. (2007) 'Dealigned Politics Comes of Age? The Effects of Online Candidate Selectors on Finnish Voters', unpublished manuscript.

Näsström, S. (2006) 'Representative Democracy as Tautology', *European Journal of Political Theory* 5 (3): 321–342.

Norris, P. (2000) *A Virtuous Circle: Political communications in post-industrial societies*, New York: Cambridge University Press.

Norris, P. and Curtice, J. (2008) 'Getting the Message Out: A Two-Step Model of the Role of the Internet in Campaign Communication Flows During the 2005 British General Election', *Journal of Information Technology & Politics*, 4 (4): 3–13.

Nuytemans, M., Walgrave, S. and Deschouwer, K. (2010) '"Do the Vote Test": The Belgian Voting Aid Application', in L. Cedroni and D. Garzia (eds) *Voting Advice Applications in Europe: The State of the Art*, Napoli: Civis, pp. 125–156.

Otjes, S. (2011) 'The Fortuyn Effect revisited: how did the LPF affect the Dutch parliamentary party system?', *Acta Politica*, 46 (4): 400–424.

Page, B. I. and Shapiro, R. Y. (1992) *The Rational Public: Fifty Years of Trends in Americans' Policy Preferences*, Chicago: Chicago University Press.

Panebianco, A. (1988) *Political Parties: Organization and Power*, Cambridge/New York: Cambridge University Press.

Parenté, F. J. and Anderson-Parenté, J. K. (1987) 'Delphi Inquiry Systems', in G. Wright and P. Ayton (eds) *Judgemental Forecasting*, Chichester: Wiley, pp. 129–156.

ParlGov (2012) *A new infrastructure for political science. ParlGov database.* Online. http://parlgov.org Version: 12/10, 15 October (accessed 15 April 2013).

Pateman, C. (1970) *Participation and Democratic Theory*, Cambridge: Cambridge University Press.

— (2012) 'Participatory democracy revisited', *Perspectives on Politics*, 10 (1): 7–19.

Petry, F. and Collette, B. (2009) 'Measuring How Political Parties Keep Their Promises', in L. M. Imbeau (ed.) *Do They Walk Like They Talk?*, New York: Springer, pp. 65–80.

Pianzola, J. (2013) *Mirror Me: The Effect of the Voting Advice Application smartvote on Voting Preferences and Behavior of Swiss Voters*, Lausanne: IDHEAP PhD.

Pianzola, J. and Ladner A. (2011) 'Tackling Self-Selection into Treatment and Self-Selection into the Sample Biases in VAA Research', paper presented at the *6th ECPR General Conference*, Reykjavik, Iceland, 25–27 August.

Pianzola, J., Trechsel, A. H. *et al.* (2012) 'The Effect of Voting Advice Applications (VAAs) on Political Preferences – Evidence from a Randomized Field Experiment', paper presented at *Annual Meeting of the American Political Science Association*, New Orleans, LA, USA, 30 August–2 September.

Pitkin, H. F. (1967) *The Concept of Representation*, Berkeley: University of California Press.

Popkin, S. (1994) *The Reasoning Voter: Communication and Persuasion in Presidential Campaign*, Chicago: University of Chicago Press.

Powell, G. B. Jr. (2000) *Elections as Instruments of Democracy: Majoritarian and Proportional Visions*, New Haven: Yale University Press.

—   (2004) 'Political representation in comparative politics', *Annual Review of Political Science*, 7 (1): 273–296.

Presser, S. and Krosnick, J. A. (2010) *Questionnaire Design: Handbook of Survey Research*, Oxford: Oxford University Press.

Rabinowitz, G. and Macdonald, S. E. (1989) 'A directional theory of issue voting', *American Political Science Review*, 83 (1): 93–121.

Rae, D. (1967) *The Political Consequences of Electoral Laws*, New Haven, CT: Yale University Press.

Ragin, C. C. and Sonnett, J. (2005) 'Between Complexity and Parsimony: Limited Diversity, Counterfactual Cases, and Comparative Analysis', in S. Kropp and M. Minkenberg (eds) *Vergleichen in der Politikwissenschaft*, Wiesbaden: VS Verlag für Sozialwissenschaften, pp. 180–197.

Rallings, C. (1987) 'The Influence of Election Programmes: Britain and Canada 1956–1979', in I. Budge, D. Robertson and D. Hearl (eds) *Ideology, Strategy and Party Change: Spatial Analyses of Post-War Election Programmes in 19 Democracies*, Cambridge: Cambridge University Press, pp. 1–14.

Ramonaitė, A. (2010) 'Voting advice applications in Lithuania: promoting programmatic competition or breeding populism?', *Policy & Internet*, 2 (1): 117–147.

Rehfeld, A. (2006) 'Towards a general theory of political representation', *Journal of Politics*, 68 (1): 1–21.

—   (2009) 'Representation rethought: on trustees, delegates, and gyroscopes in the study of political representation and democracy', *American Political Science Review*, 103 (2): 214–230.

Reif, K. and Schmitt, H. (1980) 'Nine second-order national elections: a conceptual framework for the analysis of European election results', *European Journal of Political Research*, 8 (1): 3–44.

Renwick, A. (2011) 'Electoral reform in Europe since 1945', *West European Politics*, 34 (3): 456–477.

Riker, W. H. (1982) 'The two-party system and Duverger's Law: an essay on the history of political science', *American Political Science Review*, 76: 753–66.

Rose, R. (1980) *Do Parties Make a Difference?*, Chatham, NJ: Chatham House Publishers.

—   (2013) Representing Europeans. A Pragmatic Approach, Oxford: Oxford University Press.

Rosenberg, S. W. (ed.) (2007) *Deliberation, Participation and Democracy: Can the People Govern?*, New York: Palgrave Macmillan.

Rowe, G. and Wright, G. (1999) 'The Delphi technique as a forecasting tool: issues and analysis', *International Journal of Forecasting*, 15: 353–375.

Rowe, G., Wright, G. and McColl, A. (2005) 'Judgment change during Delphi-like procedures: the role of majority influence, expertise, and confidence', *Technological Forecasting and Social Change*, 72: 377–399.

Royed, T. J. (1996) 'Testing the mandate model in Britain and the United States: evidence from the Reagan and Thatcher eras', *British Journal of Political Science*, 26 (1): 45–80.

Ruusuvirta, O. (2010) 'Much Ado About Nothing? Online Voting Advice Applications in Finland', in L. Cedroni and D. Garzia (eds) *Voting Advice Applications in Europe: The State of the Art*, Napoli: Civis, pp. 47–77.

Ruusuvirta, O. and Rosema, M. (2009) 'Do Online Vote Selectors Influence Electoral Participation and the Direction of Vote?', paper presented at *The European Consortium for Political Research (ECPR) General Conference*, Potsdam, Germany, 10–12 September.

Sani, G. and Sartori, G. (1983) 'Polarization, Fragmentation and Competition in Western Democracies', in H. Daalder and P. Mair (eds) *Western European Party Systems: Continuity & Change*, London/Beverly Hills: Sage, pp. 307–340.

Sartori, G. (1976) *Parties and Party Systems: A Framework for Analysis*, London/New York/Melbourne: Cambridge University Press.

Saward, M. (2010) *The Representative Claim*, Oxford: Oxford University Press.

Schädel, L. (2011) *Ist vor der Wahl auch nach der Wahl? Wahlversprechen und tatsächliches Stimmverhalten von Schweizer Parlamentsmitgliedern*, Saarbrücken: VDM Verlag Dr. Müller.

Schädel, L., Schwarz, D. and Ladner, A. (forthcoming) 'Promises and Lies: An Empirical Comparison of Swiss MPs' Pre- and Post-Electoral Positions', in M. Bühlmann and J. Fivaz (eds) *Political Representation: New Insights into Old Questions*, Basingstoke: Palgrave Macmillan.

Scharpf, F. W. (1999) *Governing in Europe: Effective and Democratic?*, Oxford: Oxford University Press.

Schattschneider, E. E. (1942) *Party Government*, New York: Holt, Rinehart and Winston.

Scheufele, D. and Tewksbury, D. (2007) 'Framing, agenda setting and priming: the evolution of three media effects models', *Journal of Communication*, 57 (1): 9–20.

Schlesinger, P. (1999) 'Changing spaces of political communication: the case of the European Union', *Political Communication*, 16 (3): 263–279.

Schofield, N. and Sened, I. (2005) 'Modeling the interaction of parties, activists and voters: why is the political centre so empty?', *European Journal of Political Research*, 44: 355–390.

Schofield, N., Martin, A., Quinn, K. and Nixon, D. (1999) 'Multiparty electoral competition in the Netherlands and Germany: a model based on multinomial probit', *Public Choice*, 97: 257–293.

Schuck, A. R. T., Xezonakis, G. *et al.* (2011) 'Party contestation and Europe on the news agenda: the 2009 European parliamentary elections', *Electoral Studies*, 30 (1): 41–52.

Schumpeter, J. A. (1942) *Capitalism, Socialism, and Democracy*, New York: Harper & Brothers.

Schuszler, P., de Graaf, J. and Lucardie, P. (2003) 'Zin en onzin over de StemWijzer 2002: een reactie', *Beleid en Maatschappij*, 30 (3): 194–200.

Schwarz, D., Schädel, L. and Ladner, A. (2010) 'Pre-election positions and voting behaviour in parliament: consistency among Swiss MPs', *Swiss Political Science Review*, 16 (3): 533–564.

Schwarz, D., Bächtiger, A. and Lutz, G. (2011) 'Switzerland: Agenda-Setting Power of the Government in a Separation-of-Powers Framework', in B. E. Rasch and G. Tsebelis (eds) *The Role of Governments in Legislative Agenda Setting*, Oxon/New York: Routledge, pp. 127–143.

Shugart, M., Valdini, M. and Suominen, K. (2005) 'Looking for locals: voter information demands and personal vote-earning attributes of legislators under proportional representation', *American Journal of Political Science*, 49 (2): 437–449.

Sijtsma, K. and Verweij, A. C. (1992) 'Mokken Scale analysis: theoretical considerations and an application to transitivity tasks', *Applied Measurement in Education*, 5 (4): 355–373.

Simon, H. A. (1956) 'Rational choice and the structure of the environment', *Psychological Review*, 63 (2): 129–138.

Singh, S. P. (2010) 'Contextual influences on the decision calculus: a cross-national examination of proximity voting', *Electoral Studies*, 29: 425–434.

Skop, M. (2010) 'Are Voting Advice Applications (VAAs) Telling the Truth? Measuring VAAs' Quality. Case Study from the Czech Republic', in L. Cedroni and D. Garzia (eds) *Voting Advice Applications in Europe: The State of the Art*, Napoli: Civis, pp. 199–230.

Smets, K. and van Ham, C. (2013) 'The embarrassment of riches? A meta-analysis of individual-level research on voter turnout', *Electoral Studies*, 32 (2): 344–359.

Smith, J. A. (1995) 'Semi-Structured Interviewing and Qualitative Analysis', in J. A. Smith, R. Harré and L. van Langehove (eds) *Rethinking Methods in Psychology*, London: Sage Publications, pp. 9–26.

Somin, I. (2006) 'Knowledge about ignorance: new directions in the study of political information', *Critical Review*, 18 (1–3): 255–278.

Steenbergen, M. and Marks, G. (2007) 'Evaluating expert judgements', *European Journal of Political Research*, 46: 347–366.

Stern, M. J. (2008) 'The use of client-side paradata in analyzing the effects of visual layout on changing responses in web surveys', *Field Methods*, 20 (4): 377–398.

Stimson, J. A. (2004) *Tides of Consent: How Opinion Movements Shape American Politics*, Cambridge: Cambridge University Press.

Stokes, D. (1963) 'Spatial models of party competition', *American Political Science Review*, 57: 368–377.

Taagepera, R. and Shugart, M. (1989) *Seats and Votes: The Effects and Determinants of Electoral Systems*, New Haven, CT: Yale University Press.

Tavits, M. (2009) 'The making of mavericks: local loyalties and party defection', *Comparative Political Studies*, 42 (6): 793–815.

Thomassen, J. J. A. (1994) 'Empirical Research into Political Representation: Failing Democracy or Failing Models?', in M. K. Jennings and T. E. Mann (eds) *Elections at Home and Abroad*, Ann Arbor: University of Michigan Press, pp. 237–265.

Thomson, R. (2001) 'The programme to policy linkage: the fulfilment of election pledges on socio-economic policy in the Netherlands, 1986–1998', *European Journal of Political Research*, 40 (2): 171–197.

Tilley, J. and Wlezien, C. (2008) 'Does political information matter? An experimental test relating to party positions on Europe', *Political Studies*, 56: 192–214.

Tomz, M. and Houweling, V. (2008) 'Candidate positioning and voter choice', *American Political Science Review*, 102 (3): 303–318.

Tourangeau, R., Rips, L. J. and Rasinski, K. (2000) *The Psychology of Survey Response*, New York: Cambridge University Press.

Trechsel, A. (2007) 'Inclusiveness of old and new forms of citizens' electoral participation', *Representation*, 43 (2): 111–121.

Trechsel, A. H. and Mair, P. (2011) 'When parties (also) position themselves: an introduction to the EU Profiler', *Journal of Information Technology and Politics*, 8 (1): 1–20.

Triga, V., Serdult, U. and Chadjipadelis, T. (2012) 'Introduction: Special issue on Voting Advice Applications and state of the art: theory, practice and comparative insights', *International Journal of Electronic Governance* (Special Issue: *Voting Advice Applications and the State of the Art: Theory, Practice and Comparative Insights*), 5 (3/4): 194–202.

Tsebelis, G. and Garrett, G. (2000) 'Legislative politics in the European Union', *European Union Politics*, 1 (1): 9–36.

Tully, J. (2008) *Public Philosophy in a New Key*, Cambridge: Cambridge University Press.

Urbinati, N. and Warren, M. E. (2008) 'The concept of representation in contemporary democratic theory', *Annual Review of Political Science*, 11 (1): 387–412.

Van der Ark, L. A., Croon, M. A. and Sijtsma, K. (2007) 'Possibilities and Challenges in Mokken Scale Analysis Using Marginal Models', in K. Shigemasu, A. Okada, T. Imaizumi and T. Hoshino (eds) *New Trends in Psychometrics*, Tokyo: Universal Academy Press, pp. 525–534.

Van der Brug, W. and van Spanje, J. (2009) 'Immigration, Europe and the 'new' cultural dimension', *European Journal of Political Research*, 48 (3): 309–334.

Van der Eijk, C. (2001) 'Measuring agreement in ordered rating scales', *Quality and Quantity*, 35: 325–341.

Van Holsteyn, J. J. M. and Andeweg, R. B. (2010) 'Demoted leaders and exiled candidates: disentangling party and person in the voters' minds', *Electoral Studies*, 29 (4): 628–635.

Van Praag, P. (2007) *De stemwijzer: hulpmiddel voor de kiezers of instrument van manipulatie?*, Amsterdam: Lezing Amsterdamse Academische Club 24-05-2007.

Vassil, K. (2012) *Voting Smater. The Impact of Advice Applications on Political Behavior*. Doctoral Dissertation. Florence: European University Institute.

Vergeer, M., Hermans, L. and Sams, S. (2013) 'Online social networks and micro-blogging in political campaigning: the exploration of a new campaign tool and a new campaign style', *Party Politics*, 19 (3): 477–501.

Vicente, P. and Reis, E. (2012) 'The "frequency divide": implications for internet-based surveys', *Quality & Quantity*, 46 (4): 1–14.

Volkens, A. (2007) 'Strengths and weaknesses of approaches to measuring policy positions of parties', *Electoral Studies*, 26 (1): 108–120.

Wagner, M. and Ruusuvirta, O. (2012) 'Matching voters to parties: voting advice applications and models of party choice', *Acta Politica*, 47: 400–422.

Walgrave, S. and van Aelst, P. (2006) 'The contingency of the mass media's political agenda setting power: towards a preliminary theory', *Journal of Communication*, 56 (1): 88–109.

Walgrave, S., van Aelst, P. and Nuytemans, M. (2008) '"Do the vote test": electoral effects of a vote advice application at the 2004 Belgian elections', *Acta Politica*, 43 (1): 50–70.

Walgrave, S., Nuytemans, M. and Pepermans, K. (2009) 'Voting Aid Applications and the effect of statement selection', *West European Politics*, 32 (6): 1161–1180.

Wall, M., Krouwel, A. and Vitiello, T. (2012) 'Do voters follow the recommendations of voter advice application websites? A study of the effects of kieskompas.nl on its users' vote choices in the 2010 Dutch legislative elections', *Party Politics*, published online, available http://ppq.sagepub.com/content/early/2012/03/05/1354068811436054 (accessed 11 September 2013), DOI: 10.1177/1354068811436054.

Wall, M., Sudulich, M. L., Costello, R. and Leon, E. (2009) 'Picking your party online: an investigation of Ireland's first online voting advice application', *Information Polity*, 14 (3): 203–218.

Westholm, A. (1997) 'Distance versus direction: the illusory defeat of the proximity theory of electoral choice', *American Political Science Review*, 91 (4): 865–883.

Wheatley, J. (2012) 'Using VAAs to explore the dimensionality of the policy space: Experiments from Brazil, Peru, Scotland and Cyprus', International Journal of Electronic Governance (Special Issue: Voting Advice Applications and the State of the Art: Theory, Practice and Comparative Insights), 5 (3/4): 318–348.

Wheatley, J., Carman, C., Mendez, F., Mitchell, J. (2012) 'The dimensionality of the Scottish political space: results from an experiment on the 2011 Holyrood elections', *Party Politics*, published online, available http://ppq.sagepub.com/content/early/2012/09/26/1354068812458614 (accessed 18 June 2013), DOI: 10.1177/1354068812458614.

Williams, M. S. (1998) *Voice, Trust, and Memory: Marginalized Groups and the Failings of Liberal Representations*, Princeton: Princeton University Press.

Wlezien, C. (1995) 'The public as thermostat: dynamics of preferences for spending', *American Journal of Political Science*, 39 (4): 981–1000.

Wooldridge, J. M. (2002) *Introductory Econometrics: A Modern Approach*, Australia, Cincinnati, Ohio: South-Western College Pub.

Wright, S. (1921) 'Correlation and causation', *Journal of Agricultural Research*, 20: 557–585.

Yan, T. and Tourangeau, R. (2008) 'Fast times and easy questions: the effects of age, experience and question complexity on web survey response times', *Applied Cognitive Psychology*, 22 (1): 51–68.

Yannakoudakis, E. J., Tsomokos, I. and Hutton P. J. (1990) 'n-Grams and their implication to natural language understanding', *Pattern Recognition*, 23 (5): 509–528.

Zaller, J. (1992) *The Nature and Origins of Mass Opinion*, Cambridge: Cambridge University Press.

Zelle, C. (1995) 'Social dealignment versus political frustration: contrasting explanations of the floating vote in Germany', *European Journal of Political Research*, 27: 319–345.

Zittel, T. (2009) 'Lost in technology? Political parties and the online campaigns of constituency candidates in Germany's mixed member electoral system', *Journal of Information Technology and Politics*, 6: 298–311.

Zittel, T. and Fuchs, D. (eds) (2007) *Participatory Democracy and Political Participation: Can Participatory Engineering Bring Citizens Back In?*, New York: Routledge.

Index

numbers in *italics* refer to material in figures and tables

www.ingramcontent.com/pod-product-compliance
Lightning Source LLC
Chambersburg PA
CBHW072058020426
42334CB00017B/1560